B
TUAOLO          Tuaolo, Esera,
                1968-

                Alone in the
                trenches.

$24.95

| DATE | | | |
|---|---|---|---|
| | | | |
| | | | |
| | | | |
| | | | |
| | | | |
| | | | |
| | | | |
| | | | |
| | | | |
| | | | |
| | | | |
| | | | |
| | | | |

# ALONE IN THE
# TRENCHES

MY LIFE AS A GAY MAN IN THE NFL

ESERA TUAOLO

with John Rosengren

SOURCEBOOKS, INC.®
NAPERVILLE, ILLINOIS

Published by Sourcebooks, Inc.
P.O. Box 4410, Naperville, Illinois 60567-4410
(630) 961-3900
Fax: (630) 961-2168
www.sourcebooks.com

Library of Congress Cataloging-in-Publication Data

Tuaolo, Esera.
  Alone in the trenches / Esera Tuaolo, with John Rosengren.
     p. cm.
  ISBN-13: 978-1-4022-0505-7
  ISBN-10: 1-4022-0505-8
  1.  Tuaolo, Esera. 2.  Football players--United
States--Biography. 3.  Gay athletes--United States--Biography.  I.
Rosengren, John. II. Title.

GV939.T78A3 2006
796.332'092--dc22

2005025014


            Printed and bound in the United States of America.
                 LB 10 9 8 7 6 5 4 3 2 1

To my husband, Mitchell
I can only thank God above for sending me you.

*Your love saved me,*
*Your smile embraced me*
*Your hugs comforted me,*
*Your tears awoke me*

Ote Alofa ia te oe
I Love You


To Mitchell Jr. and Michele
I just wanted you both to know that I did this book so someday when you read it, you will truly know who your father was (or is). Also, this is my two cents for creating a world of tolerance, praying that when people read it they will realize that there is hope and that hate in any form is wrong.

# CONTENTS

# CHAPTER ONE

## The Torments of Success

I SETTLED INTO MY STANCE for the last play of Super Bowl XXXIII. The field glowed under the lights. Flashbulbs popped around the stadium. We, the Atlanta Falcons, faced the Denver Broncos led by their superstar quarterback John Elway. Denver had the ball with a 34–19 lead. I lined up at my usual position, nose guard, across from the Denver center, who was poised to snap the ball to Elway. My knuckles gripped the turf.

The Broncos quarterback took the snap and dropped to his knee to let the clock run out. I touched him first. When the ball carrier is on the ground, someone on the defense must at least touch him so he's ruled down. Since I touched Elway, I was credited with the tackle.

A routine play, but it terrified me. And that was not the first time. That game and that play were televised to one billion people around the globe. Someone could have recognized me and blown my cover. In the past, whenever my image appeared on the screen—when I made a big play, sang the national anthem—I lived with the fear that I might be outed. This was January 31, 1999, and at that point I had been playing for eight years in the NFL. Before that, I had played four years of college football. In all that time, not one teammate, coach, or sportswriter knew I was gay.

The National Football League is the number one entertainment in the world, and the Super Bowl is its showcase event. Media from all over—places like Japan and Lebanon, where they don't even play football—report on the spectacle. The Super Bowl is the biggest event that happens every year in the United States.

What if one of those billion people watching recognized me as the stranger he had picked up in a gay bar? All he had to do was out me to the press and the story would be all over the headlines: "Gay Man Makes Final Tackle in Super Bowl." My football career would be finished.

No more Super Bowls, no more Sundays playing ball. No more paychecks, no more financial security. No more locker-room banter, no more camaraderie with the guys. I would be banished from the NFL fraternity.

During my nine years in the NFL, I lived that close to the edge of destruction. My success tormented me. The better I did, the more exposure I received. The more exposure, the greater the chance of someone discovering my secret. A secret that a man who plays the most macho of team sports is not supposed to have. The stress nearly killed me.

I am a Samoan who grew up in Hawaii. My family lived in a hut with a dirt floor. I'd gone from that poverty to the fortunes of the NFL. Football gave me a college scholarship, the chance to buy a house for my mother, the opportunity to travel, and much more.

My NFL career lasted nine years with five teams—the Green Bay Packers, Minnesota Vikings, Jacksonville Jaguars, Atlanta Falcons, and Carolina Panthers. I'll go down in history as the first player to sing the national anthem and then start an NFL game, the first rookie nose guard to start all sixteen games, and the last guy to "tackle" John Elway in his storied Hall of Fame career.

The dream to succeed in the NFL and achieve all that football had to offer was a nightmare at times. I struggled to survive the combative, macho world dominated by a culture that despised who I really am. Had opponents and teammates known I was gay, they would have mocked me the way I heard them ridicule others with sexual slurs. More than likely—as several former teammates admitted—they would have tried to injure me so that they would not have been viewed as guilty by association. In other words, they would have taken me out so that their own masculinity would not be questioned for playing alongside a sissy. It's rough down in the trenches, where linemen weighing more than three-hundred pounds hurl themselves at one another in brutal hand-to-hand combat, but it is nothing compared to the pain I kept buried inside so I could play out my dream.

This is the story of how I dared to dream, not only of surviving professional football, but of living openly for who I am, a gay man.

# CHAPTER TWO

## God Bless My Daddy

**F**IRST THING I REMEMBER, I'm running naked on the beach. Racing across the strip of sand that separates land from sea. Four years old, racing naked, free. The ocean breeze bathes my skin. I'm happy as far as you can see the water.

That sand, Makaha Beach, was my home away from home. My family traveled there every summer to fish. We camped on the beach in a hut my father and mother fashioned from coconut leaves woven over two-by-fours. To my playful imagination, the hut looked like a fort.

My parents fished with my older brothers. I watched them lay out their nets, and they told me to stay out of the way. They packed their catch in the coconut-leaf baskets my mother made and drove to the market in Daddy's green Thunderbird. I played games with the ocean, pretending I could control the waves like Aquaman. I would summon each wave to the shore, and the ocean obeyed my command. I commanded tsunamis to smash against the mountain. It was a magical time.

The smell of *opakapaka* fish cooking over an open fire filtered through the evening air. Stars cluttered the sky at night, tons and tons of them. So big and bright that it looked like you could reach right up and grab one. I would lie inside our fort on the *fala* mats—made out of *lahala* leaves—snuggled under a blanket beside my mother. She rubbed my back in a hypnotizing rhythm. I would fall asleep wrapped in her arms.

I was born July 11, 1968, on the island of Oahu, Hawaii, to Laki Tavai Tuaolo and Maiuu Mike Tuaolo, the youngest of eight children in an immigrant Samoan family. Our summers on the beach ended when I was five years old and we moved to Waimanalo, directly opposite Honolulu. My father, Maiuu, leased a small piece of land—about twenty acres—on the windward side of the island with plans to transform it into a banana plantation like those back home. This was part of his plan to give his family a better life when he left Samoa.

Daddy was an enterprising man. He never went to school—he couldn't read or write—but he was savvy. I don't know how he did it, but he leased that land. He used to tell me, "If you don't know what you're talking about, make like you do." People didn't question him.

He charmed people into doing things for him. Because he couldn't read or write, he couldn't take the written test required for his driver's license. He flirted with the woman behind the counter, and she took the test for him. Leonardo DiCaprio's character in *Catch Me If You Can* reminds me of Daddy and the way he was able to get people to do things for him. He was always a good talker.

Makes sense, since he was the first son of a high-talking chief, the one who speaks for a village. His mother Tusipasi was the talking chief for the village of Pago Pago. Once Daddy started his family, he did not want to carry the responsibilities of chief that he would inherit from his father. He wanted more for his family. He was a dreamer, an explorer. I think that's where I get my ambitions. He instilled in me the sense that there's something more for me out there to explore and try. That's the way I felt on Oahu growing up. I felt there was a lot more to the world and life than the island. That must have been the way my father felt when he went searching for something better. His parents weren't married when he was born, so he gave up his father's name, Deveaux, and took his mother's name, Tuaolo, and moved his young family to Hawaii before I was born.

Like his father before him, Daddy was a ladies' man. He was very handsome and well manicured. He dressed sharply in clothes given to him by admiring women. My job as a small boy was to shine my father's shoes, to make sure they were bright black or white. He used to tell me, "If you go into a bank dressed as a hobo, you won't get a loan. But go in looking put together and you will."

That served him in business and other ways. He would tell Mama he was taking me out for ice cream. Instead of going to the ice cream parlor, he would take me to the house of one of his lady friends. I watched television in the living room while Daddy worked his charms in the bedroom.

My mother, Laki Tavai Tuaolo, came from a respectable family as well. The Tavai family was also one of the monarchies of American Samoa. Her father was a high chief of his village. She met Daddy when he was working as a chauffeur for the governor of Samoa.

One day, when she was still a teenager, my mother tagged along with her two cousins to the governor's house. The cousins went round the back to collect slop for their pigs. Mama waited out front and decided to climb the mango trees to pick some of the sweet fruit. My father confronted her.

"These aren't your mangos," Mama shot back.

He must've been taken by her spunk and, of course, her beauty.

When her cousins returned, they asked her, "How are we going to carry those mangos with these buckets?"

Mama hesitated.

"Put them in my Jeep, and I'll drive you home," Daddy offered.

On the way, he stopped to buy them ice cream. That ice cream was a big treat to someone as poor as Mama. She couldn't help but notice how handsome he was.

Nine months later, my oldest brother, Fale, was born.

When Daddy leased the land, my three oldest siblings had already left home. The remaining four older siblings cleared the land by hand alongside my parents. Trees and thick growth covered those acres. When I got older, I did the same. That work—swinging a machete and carrying fifty-pound bunches of bananas down the hillside—was probably how I developed my strength. But when we first moved to Waimanalo, I was too young to use a machete, pick, or shovel. My job was to stay out of the way. I fetched water and listened for the phone.

As far as I know, Daddy was the first Samoan to lease land in Hawaii. That was something unheard of in those days. There were those who didn't want us there, including the neighbors who lived next door. The prejudice against Samoans in Hawaii at that time, the early seventies, ran high. After they had been drinking a while, the neighbors would yell into the night, "Fuckin' Samoans, go back home!" It was a territorial fear, exactly like what a successful black family faced moving into a white neighborhood in American suburbs. That resentment would eventually kill my aunt.

Our little banana farm was outside Waimanalo, one of those blinks along the two-lane highway that ran around the eastern side of the island. A small cluster of shops without even a stoplight to make you notice. Its glory, to my child's mind, was the Jack in the Box—a fast-food hamburger joint—that was my favorite place to go.

We lived at the end of Kakaina Street, three miles off the main highway. The mountains rose from our backyard. Mama had a green thumb. We had every flower imaginable growing in our yard. It was a lush setting, typical of Hawaii's tropical beauty.

The school bus didn't come up the road, so I had to walk down to the highway to meet it. Worse, I had to walk back up that hill, which terrified me at night. If I stopped at a friend's house after school, it would be dark by the time I headed home for dinner.

I had to walk past this huge banyan tree. Have you ever seen a banyan tree? It's the most wicked-looking thing. From a distance, it looks like a giant mushroom. Once you get up close, you can see the trunk twisted around the base, like veins and muscles in a leg with the skin removed. My brothers told me that a kid had hanged himself from its branches. I dreaded walking by that tree. My imagination would go crazy the closer I got to it. I'd start running and race by it.

Most of our friends and neighbors lived down near the highway. The ones who hated us lived about twenty yards away, our houses separated by bushes and trees. They resented foreigners coming in and doing well for themselves. We planted banana trees, sugar cane, papaya, mountain apples, coconuts, and passion fruits that we sold at the weekly swap meet set up in a drive-in theater parking lot. Daddy built a Samoan hut, where we lived. About fifteen tree-trunk poles supported an oval-shaped roof of coconut leaves. The sides were open. At first, we slept on *fala* mats laid out on the smooth river pebbles, but eventually he built a plywood platform floor. The neighbors' place was run-down. Junked cars littered their overgrown yard while Mama's flowers decorated ours. I think they were jealous and didn't want to see us make it.

It seemed as if every time we tried to do something to better our situation, they tried to pull us down. For instance, we used to shower down at the beach, about a ten-minute drive away. When we would come back, we would find that they had cut down our bananas and pushed over our hut.

Daddy argued frequently with the neighbors' father. Sometimes they put their fists into their words. It got ugly. My older sister Sina fought with one of their girls. The neighbors threw rocks or fired pellets at us when they saw us inside our hut. We built a plywood barricade on that side for protection. When it got violent, somebody would call the police. The cops would come, but they didn't do much. They were Hawaiian and didn't seem to care what happened to a Samoan family.

I remember being so scared during that time. I was afraid somebody was going to get hurt badly. I didn't know someone I loved would be killed.

This feud had been going on for about two years, ever since we first moved there. One Sunday afternoon when I was six, some of my family, including my father's sister, came over for a meal after church. When we had finished eating, the grownups sat around the open hut talking and laughing. I was playing on the floor. The phone rang, and I pushed it toward Daddy. He reached back for it. Suddenly, a gunshot popped. Aunt Sina collapsed.

Chaos erupted. My aunts and uncles screamed. I started crying. The neighbor jumped in a car and took off down the road. My uncles and brothers went crazy and attacked his house, shattered all the windows. My older sister Tusi grabbed me, and we ran into the banana fields to hide, but I could still see everything that was happening.

We came out when the ambulance arrived. I can still see them placing my aunt on that stretcher, tucking her in the back, and closing the doors.

The police arrived and asked a lot of questions. Daddy got angry. He wanted them to catch the guy. "Why are you talking to me? Go grab him!" This time they had to do something.

The cops caught Aunt Sina's killer that week. Daddy and Mama testified at his trial, but he got off. The murder couldn't be pinned on him. Even though everybody knew he did it, nobody saw him actually pull the trigger.

A couple years after that, the same neighbor and his cousins beat my dad's cousin Fafawia to death. They pummeled him with a tire iron so savagely that Daddy and Mama could not recognize him in the morgue. They identified him by his name tattooed on his forearm. That time, the neighbor landed in jail. His cousins turned on him and said he'd been the one who swung the tire iron. I heard later that one of my cousins killed him in jail for his crimes against our family.

My aunt's funeral was at the Samoan church. The organ played. The choir sang. My aunts cried. I heard that Auntie was in heaven, but no one explained it to me. Dead? What do you mean *dead?* My six-year-old mind couldn't make sense of the chaos, screaming, fear, crying, and sadness. I couldn't make sense of the murder and grief I'd seen. Death equaled fear and confusion.

I didn't know what to do about that. I tried to hide from it. At a young age, I learned to stuff pain in the closet. I thought that way I wouldn't have to deal with it. That was my way of containing the evil I started to see in the world.

I was a cartoon junkie as a kid. I watched *Superfriends* whenever I could. I tried to do whatever I saw them do on TV. I tried to fly by holding an umbrella and jumping off a huge rock. I climbed trees, and in my mind I was climbing like a superhero, jumping from vine to vine and doing flips. Imagination is so vivid for children.

I preferred make-believe to the pain in my life. I turned myself into Wonder Woman and deflected negative feelings with my bracelets.

When I was five years old, I heard a friend call another friend *mahu*. I asked him what that meant. "Faggot," he told me in Samoan. *Oooh, he likes boys,* I thought, *that's bad.*

Then I thought, *Uh-oh.*

I never liked playing with stuff other boys wanted to play with. I played with Ken and Barbie dolls. I wanted an Easy-Bake oven. I was fascinated by the way my sisters dressed. I tried on their jewelry when they weren't looking. I remember watching GI Joe on TV and thinking he was cute. I had a crush on a buddy at a young age.

*Oh shit,* I thought. *Mahu. That might be me.* I started playing with things other boys played with. I asked for a cowboy gun. I started being tougher. I ended up calling other kids *mahu*. I feared I'd be teased the way they teased that other boy. I didn't want to get labeled and teased. I didn't want that to be me. I imagined it wasn't.

I started to live a double life. A superhero is a lot like a gay person—both hide their true identity. No one can know who you are or else you'll lose your powers. A gay person must've made up superheroes.

One day during first grade, I was playing outside near the monkey bars. Another kid started calling me *Sarah*. (In Samoan, my name is pronounced A-sarah.) He wouldn't stop. I thought, *Either I'm going to take this, or I'm going to do something about it.* I was already a big kid. I was afraid of *Sarah* turning to *sissy*, to *mahu*. So, I picked up my tormentor and threw him to the ground.

The school sent a note home to my parents. Mama spanked me. Daddy spanked me again when he found out. They were upset that I'd done something to get into trouble. I knew they would be angry, but I figured if I let that kid call me names, then others would, too. I wanted to make others think I was tough. It worked. That kid never made fun of me again.

Before the missionaries came to Samoa, we used to know what it meant to smell the roses, to appreciate the mountains, the sky, the water. We knew our connectedness to nature and to life. We ran naked and free on the beach like children. The Christian missionaries brought the negatives. They told us what we shouldn't do, for example, that women shouldn't walk around topless, natural. The missionaries brought the fear of God.

My parents raised me in an Assembly of God, a Pentecostal church. It seemed like we were in church every day, not just Sunday. There was always some type of meeting to go to. As a kid, I didn't mind. I loved going to church. I liked seeing my friends and learning about God's goodness.

I took what I heard literally. The preacher told us that Jesus was in our heart. I asked Mama, "Won't he stick out?" I listened to him with the trust of a young child.

But there was a dark side to church that I didn't like. The preacher was a fire-and-brimstone type. He blasted women who wore makeup, men who cheated on their wives, and homosexuals.

The preacher called homosexuals a "curse." He cast them in the same lot as adulterers and murderers. He said they were going to burn in the lake of fire for eternity. I sat in the pew and held on to Mama. I knew I was attracted to boys before I heard it was a sin.

Every time I heard a sermon on homosexuality, I did something to try to change my feelings. I would run into the banana patch, drop to my knees, and ask God to take away this curse that I'd just heard the preacher preach about. The way he talked, it was as easy as that. All I had to do was ask God and the sickness would go away. But it didn't.

I prayed harder. I made sacrifices. I gave up soda pop so God would take away my curse. I made offerings to God, throwing away favorite toys. But God didn't change me.

I thought that maybe if I could like a girl I wouldn't have feelings for boys anymore. So in fourth grade, I made up a crush on Rosemary, a popular girl in my class. I walked her home from school. I bought her trinkets at the swap meets—necklaces, broaches, candy. I hoped something would click, that I would fall in love with Rosemary, but I never felt that special tingle.

Eventually, I would figure out that God loved me the way I am. I was born gay. God made me that way. God doesn't make mistakes, so I'm not a mistake. But as a child I had not yet come to that understanding. At night, I would lie awake, terrified that God was going to cast me into the lake of fire.

I didn't fall in love immediately with football. I wasn't that interested in playing at first, but I went out for the team because my friends did. Football was a way to hang out together. I was part of something bigger, this extended family of athletes. That was important to me as a Samoan. We count even the most distant relatives as family.

That first year of peewee football, when I was nine, I wasn't a starter, but I was in the mix. I was still about the same size as the other guys. I didn't finish that first season. We each were given a box of chocolate to sell as a fundraiser, but I ate all of the chocolate bars I brought home. Daddy pulled me from the team because I owed all that money. I had embarrassed him and the family. Daddy paid back the money and gave me the whipping of my life—he broke a broom over my back.

We practiced at Waimanalo Park, down by the beach. I dreaded the bull ring drill. Everyone stood in a circle, with one guy in the middle. The coach called someone's number, and that guy charged out to hit the guy in the middle. You had to be on guard. I did pretty well at that drill, but I was always afraid I wouldn't. I feared failing. I feared looking bad. I didn't want somebody to put me on my ass and all the other kids to tease me. That anxiety fueled my fire.

In sixth grade, we played a game at Eva Beach against a team with a girl on it. My friends thought it was stupid to play against a girl. I thought it was cool. Somehow, it gave me a little more confidence. Our coaches used to berate us, "You played like girls, like sissies!" and "You hit like a girl!" Seeing a girl out there playing on the line—and playing better than the guys at that level—seemed to wipe out all the negative stuff I heard from the coaches. I was cheering her on, and at the same time, I was cheering myself on. At the end of the game, I shook her hand and said, "Good game." Maybe now the coaches would want us to play like girls.

Let me tell you about my best friend. My daddy and I had something special. Despite his flaws, I loved him with the intensity and innocence of the child that I was. The youngest of his eight children, I was the favorite. He was not shy about showing this, and I could feel the affection he had for me. Even if he did not tell me often, I knew I was special to him. My older brothers teased me and called me names, but they knew better than to do that in front of Daddy. He was there to protect me, keep me safe. I thought it would always be that way.

Mama told me when I got older that Daddy was a heavy drinker. During Prohibition he could not buy alcohol, so he squeezed lemons and limes into bleach and drank that. I didn't measure how much he drank when I was a kid. I just knew Daddy drank. I remember that whenever we went to a party he never ate. We made a plate of food for him to bring home. He ate then. At the party, he drank. There are people who can drink and people who can't. My daddy was one of those who could. When he had some liquor in him, others wanted to be around him. He was always smooth and charming, but when he drank, he became even more so. Daddy was the life of the party. Everybody gathered around him, and he made them all feel good.

That drinking finally caught up with him. At fifty-two, he wound up in the hospital with liver problems and circulation trouble. I was ten and didn't understand all of this at the time. I only understood that Daddy was sick and needed an operation.

It was strange to see my daddy laid up in a hospital bed. With all of his schemes, Daddy had been a busy man. For the longest time I watched while he worked on projects with my older brothers. They cleared the fields, planted the crops, and harvested the fruit while I watched. I wanted a job that was important, more important than fetching water and listening for the phone. I wanted to be working alongside of him, but I was too young, too small.

Finally, when I was ten, Daddy decided that I was ready to work on a project. He wanted to build a flagpole and picked me to do it with him. I was so excited to be working on our first project together, just Daddy and I. We put that flagpole right outside the house where we would see it every day.

It's funny, we did everything opposite of the way it should've been done. We put up the pole, but we hadn't placed the ball on top. I had to climb up the pole like a monkey to put the ball up there. I had to climb up again to loop the rope through the guide. And I had to climb up again to paint the pole. My daddy was a visionary—he didn't always think through those sorts of details. But I didn't mind. I would've climbed that pole every day to keep him happy.

Once we finished the pole, it became my job to raise the American and Samoan flags on holidays or special occasions, like when we had a party. That was the most exciting job I had as a kid. I always felt so proud raising the flags. Every time was like flying my daddy's affection for me.

After his surgery, we went to visit Daddy in the hospital. I stood by his bedside and worried about him looking so sick. The day my aunt was killed, the bullet had been meant for him. By a simple twist of fate, I had saved his life when I pushed the telephone toward him and he leaned for it. This time, I worried that he wouldn't be able to lean out of harm's way. He pulled me close. "I'm coming home tomorrow," he told me. "Go home and raise the flag."

That day, I strung up the flag with great excitement. I wanted to let everyone know, *Daddy's coming home!*

But that night, screams woke me. Mama wailed from deep within her soul. I'd never heard her crying like that. I knew something awful had happened. My older brothers and sisters tried to explain to me, "Daddy died." I immediately thought of Aunt Sina and knew that "died" meant Daddy wasn't coming home. Right away, I went into denial. "It can't be," I said, "because I raised the flag. I raised the flag!"

My family rushed to the hospital. I ran into his room and started crying. "I raised the flag, Daddy. I raised the flag." But he didn't come home.

That hit me at his funeral, which was at the same church where we had Aunt Sina's funeral. At her funeral, I had been scared and confused. At my daddy's, I was hurt and angry. At my aunt's funeral, I learned that death meant someone went away. At Daddy's, I learned it meant he was never coming back. Death meant gone forever.

Ever since I was a small boy, I've loved to sing. Mama and Daddy always wanted me to dance and sing at parties. The first song I learned was "God Bless My Daddy." I remember belting out as a five-year-old in front of family and friends:

God bless my daddy, who's over there
said a little tiny boy in his little tiny prayer . . .
Wait for me, Mama, I'll be home real soon.
I never knew how much you meant to me,
now that I'm so many miles across the sea . . .

I never knew that would become the song of my life.

When I was in eighth grade, Mama sent me to Henderson, Nevada, to live with my brother Fale and his family. In the United States, your immediate family is your family. In Samoan culture, your family includes all of your aunts and uncles and cousins. The idea that it takes a village to raise a child describes our culture. We look out for one another. For instance, if my mother had an aunt who was elderly, Mama would send one of my sisters to care for her. We call that "Samoan adoption."

I think one of the reasons Mama screamed at the walls when Daddy died was because she did not know how she could care for all of her children by herself. She asked Fale to raise me to take some of the pressure off herself. In Polynesia, the oldest is always right. I did not argue with her decision.

Henderson is in the middle of the desert, dry and barren—a long way from the lush, tropical beaches of Hawaii. At first I was excited to be in a new place, even if it was the desert, but Henderson soon turned horrible.

As my older brother, Fale became my father figure. I was not supposed to question him. Fale drank. He used drugs. He hit his wife, his kids, and me. He would come home drunk and hit me. I lived in fear. I couldn't deflect his blows with my superhero fantasies.

At first I didn't know why he wanted me to live with him. Then one day, I found the stubs of my social security checks in the glove compartment of his car. He had been cashing the three-hundred-dollar monthly payments I received after my father's death. I confronted Fale. He hit me.

That was the worst time of my life. I was so afraid of him. I also felt bad for his kids—my nieces and nephews. They feared him, too. I couldn't say anything to Mama back in Hawaii because if she said something to him, he would hit me. She couldn't protect me. I learned to keep my mouth shut. Instead, I cried myself to sleep at night. I tried to shove all of that fear and pain into the closet.

Football saved me. I arrived after the season in eighth grade but played linebacker and tight end my freshman year at Baseline High. I liked away games best because Fale didn't go to those. I could escape. At home games, I heard him screaming at me from the stands. I was afraid that he would hit me if I played poorly. I was so afraid of him hitting me that his screaming motivated me.

Football gave me something much more than an escape from my brother. It gave me affirmation. I needed that. The coaches praised me for doing well. I didn't get that at home, not since my daddy died. I strived for that. I wanted to hear those praises. I worked harder and played better just to hear them say, "Great job, Esera." That's when I learned that football was my way out. Football was a way to feel good. Even though there was all the homophobic stuff, football gave me a way to escape the pain.

That was an important discovery. Ever since I was little, I knew there was something better for me, much like my father wanting to leave Samoa for a better place. I was always willing to try something new to see if that was it. I never knew what I was going to be good at, until I discovered what football had to offer me.

# CHAPTER THREE

~

# Baby Fridge

I INHERITED MY FATHER'S EXPLORING HEART. Growing up on the island, I sensed my destiny lay somewhere beyond the water. I returned to Oahu with my brother when he moved back to run the family farm. I didn't want to repeat the awful times with Fale back in Hawaii. All I wanted was to get away from him, to explore my visions as a kid on Makaha Beach. My mother's sister visited us that summer and sensed that things were tough for me. She invited me to live with her family in Chino, California. I jumped at the chance.

California. That was an exciting foreign country. At the same time I was nervous, not knowing what was in store for me. Chino is a rugged, farming town of about 65,000 in San Bernardino County, fifty miles east of Los Angeles. Don Antonio Lugo High, where I arrived in tenth grade, was a huge block building—completely opposite of the open campuses of Hawaii, spread out over beautiful tropical grounds. Don Lugo High looked like a prison.

I worried it was one of those rough schools I'd seen on TV. They had lock-downs—something I'd never heard of—where they locked all of the doors except the front one after the morning bell. If you came late, you had to go in through the office to get a pass. Don Lugo frightened me.

The big, Samoan kid in the hallway—I got noticed right away. The principal told me, "You need a 2.0 GPA." I had to ask a friend what he was talking about. "Football," the friend said. "You need at least a 2.0 to be eligible to play." They automatically tagged me as a football player.

Despite the escape football had provided in Henderson, Nevada, I hadn't moved to California to play football. I simply wanted to get away from Fale, who had such control over my life. The game still wasn't that important to me. I did like the attention and praise it won me, though, so I decided to go out for the team my junior year.

The first day of practice scared the hell out of me. There must have been a hundred kids out there. Not all of us would make it. I'd played before, but this was California football, much bigger than anything I'd seen in Hawaii or Nevada. This was the big time. Trying out for the varsity seemed like trying out for a college team. I was a decent size, six foot one and one hundred eighty pounds, but not the biggest guy out there. The starters from last year's team really intimidated me.

I didn't know if I would make it until one starter began talking trash to me. "This is my house," he taunted. "I own this team." He kept pushing it. That pissed me off. I chose him to go up against in a one-on-one drill. I hit him really hard. I mean, I destroyed him. That got the adrenaline flowing and the coaches' attention. I felt like the superhero Colossus from the X-men.

I became one of the few guys playing both ways, a linebacker and tight end. I was able to leave all of my frustrations on the field. I would just go out there and forget it all and play a great game. I earned all-conference honors. I don't remember a specific performance that year. I just remember hearing the praises from the fans, players, coaches, and parents, telling me I played great. It was almost like I blacked out during the game. I played for those compliments afterward. The better you did for the team, I figured, the better they would love you. I ended up one of the stars on that team.

We played a game that year against Claremont High, which had won the state title for several years. They had a six-foot-four quarterback named Dan McGwire, the brother of baseball's slugging superstar Mark McGwire. Dan would go on to play quarterback for the Seattle Seahawks and Miami Dolphins. Claremont came to our field undefeated but left with a loss. They won another championship that season, but their team T-shirt the next year read 13–1. We knew that one was Don Lugo, our claim to glory for the season.

The 2.0 minimum GPA turned out not to be a problem, though it could've been. Teachers in Hawaii had pegged me as a special ed kid. I thought I was smarter but wasn't given the chance to prove it. In California, I retook the tests and scored in the average range. They put me in normal classes. I had thought I would be stuck in basic math the whole way through school, but I made it through algebra. I pulled Bs and Cs at Don Lugo. That boosted my self-esteem.

I probably couldn't have done that without the help of some special teachers. I spoke Pidgin English when I came to California. I'd heard that the workers in Hawaii's sugarcane fields had created Pidgin English so the owners wouldn't understand them. But it didn't serve me well in California. My English teacher would correct me in front of the entire class. That embarrassed me. Other kids teased me. I became discouraged. One day, I asked the teacher after class why she was so hard on me. "I see potential in you," she told me. "A lot of people would let you slip by, but I'm not going to." That opened my eyes and motivated me. Once I understood, I tried harder. Now, I look back and am grateful to her.

Without warning, I almost lost it all. After my junior year, my aunt and her husband decided to move their family back to the island. I had to tell my football coach, Mr. Monger, that I was leaving. I started to cry. I didn't want to go back to Hawaii. When I'd gone there in the summer and told my friends I'd been all-conference, they laughed at me. You're not a football player, they said. But in California, they knew I could play football. They cheered for me, and my teachers believed in me. I didn't want to leave that; I didn't want to go back to the bullshit in Hawaii.

A lot of coaches might have said, "Sorry, bye." Not Coach Monger. He found a place for me to stay. Sharon and Larry Bjur, whose sons Kevin and Doug played on the team, took me in and became my California family. I was grateful to them for opening their home to me. Coach Monger also appointed me one of the team captains.

That was the first time in my life that I felt I was The Man, that I was wanted and needed, not just as a football player but as a person. That made me feel special. Because of my hard work and dedication, I felt wanted. I didn't want to lose all of that. My coach worked things out so I didn't have to.

Because of all the success and support I was getting in California, being gay didn't seem like such a big deal. Football was a pleasure that boosted my self-esteem. I was one of the popular kids in school along with the other players. I never acted on my sexual feelings in Chino. I found other guys attractive, but I was too scared to ever have a crush on any of my teammates. My biggest fear was getting an erection in the shower. I waited until the other guys had finished, or sometimes I showered at home. I was paranoid. I feared that all the compliments and praises would stop if someone found out I was gay.

The coaches would call us *sissies* when we didn't play well. Teammates teased kids and called them *faggots* and *queer bait.* People ask, "Why did you stay with football and put up with that crap?" I focused on the positives. When you're young and find something you're good at, you want to pursue it. I was getting all this praise from coaches and teammates that I didn't get from my family. I lettered twice in track and field as a discus and shot put thrower and once in wrestling, where I won the conference championship at my weight, but football won me the most attention. I grooved on that.

At a young age, it's all about being accepted. Football gave me that acceptance. Even though I was gay and heard so many of those negative comments, I thought because I was the star no one would know the truth about Esera.

My football success made me think maybe I wasn't gay. I started to question and doubt myself. Maybe I'd just been going through a phase. My other gay friends now tell me they've gone through this, too. *If I'm a football player,* I reasoned, *I can't be gay.* At the time, I didn't know of any football players who were out and proud. I bought into the stereotype: football players aren't gay.

Senior year was a lot of fun. That was the year William "The Refrigerator" Perry, the Chicago Bears' three-hundred-pound defensive tackle started running the ball. Everybody was getting these huge fullbacks. By then, I'd grown to almost two hundred ten pounds. Coach Monger said, "Hey, Esera, you want to run the ball?" I thought, *What, me?* But the idea of carrying the ball excited me.

We had two plays, dive right and dive left, both between the center and the guard. I did well enough to become the starting fullback. We added more plays. They called me *Baby Fridge.*

I still played linebacker, too. Senior year, I moved from the outside to the more important inside linebacker slot. That's where I really made my mark.

Our Pomona Valley Conference rival Pomona High had a running back named J. J. Flanagan who ended up playing at the University of Colorado. We all knew about him. We had read about him in the papers. He averaged about two hundred yards a game, though it seemed more like eight hundred. Our game plan the week before we faced Pomona focused on stopping one player, J. J. Flanagan. After one of our team meetings that week, Coach Monger pulled me aside and said, "You know how big the game is this week. I'm going to put you on J. J."

The coach's assignment made me feel invincible. A feeling of being accepted washed through me. Being put on their best player made me feel like our best player. Coach Monger had chosen me as special, this knight in shining armor.

I was pumped. It seemed everybody was watching the match up, Esera Tuaolo versus J. J. Flanagan. We were already on the field when Pomona came out of the locker room. They lined up on their side of the field holding hands and walked the entire length of the field—our field—that way. I was a quiet player, one who never talked trash. I let my play talk for me. But when we got back into the locker room after warm-ups, I screamed at my teammates, "Who the hell do they think they are, coming in and doing this to us?"

J. J. didn't get a hundred yards rushing that game. We shut him down. I stuck to him like chewing gum, and I knew the flavor. We won. The party after that game was sweet.

Games like that got me noticed. I had started hearing from colleges my junior year. Coach Monger passed on the letters they sent. I'm embarrassed to say this, but I had to ask him what a scholarship was. He said, "That's where you play football and others pay for your college." A light went on. If I wanted to give back to my mom and family, this was a wonderful opportunity. No one in my family had gone to college. It was never in my thought process that I might. I figured after high school I would be caught in the life cycle, that I would go back to Hawaii, work on the banana farm, and be pressured to marry and have a bunch of kids. The possibility of going to college and breaking the life cycle excited me. I started playing even better. I was trying to accomplish something no one else in my family had ever done.

Senior year, my name was in the papers. Other coaches talked about me. I met players from other teams who said, "I had to be you for the whole week on the dummy team." I was all-conference again and voted best defensive player of the conference. College coaches came to visit me in Chino. I was like, *Wow, I can't believe I'm getting all of this attention.* The scholarship offers flooded in.

There were plenty of invitations from schools out East, but I narrowed down my choice to schools on the West Coast. I didn't want to go farther from home than I had to. I never followed college football, so the powerhouse programs' reputations didn't tug at me. I made my five official visits allotted by the NCAA to the University of Nevada at Las Vegas, the University of California, San Diego State University, the University of Arizona, and Oregon State University.

I was a blue-chip prospect; those schools wooed me eagerly. They had pretty coeds show me around campus. They brought the recruits to clubs. I was underage—still naive—and impressed that we were able to get in. They brought us to parties. The alcohol flowed freely, and I had a good time. Some of those visits, I was so drunk that I don't even remember getting back to my hotel room. I'm sure some of the coeds made themselves available to the other recruits, but I wasn't looking for that. I was hoping instead, in my own private fantasy, that a football player would come on to me. Of course, that didn't happen.

The players would pick us up in luxury cars they said alumni bought for them. They wore designer clothes, expensive watches, and other big jewelry—all gifts from alumni. The stories came out when we drank. They bragged about the perks of playing college football. There were money incentives like those in a pro contract, say one hundred dollars for every touchdown they scored, an extra bonus if they made All-America, and so on. I wasn't sure if it was fact or if they were trying to impress us. Either way, their talk turned me off. Mama had raised us to be honest.

The coaches wined and dined us at nice restaurants, told us to order whatever we wanted on the menu. Having someone buy me—a kid from a banana plantation with a dirt floor hut—steak and lobster made me feel like a million bucks.

Looking back on it, I see they were doing what they did not for me but for them, so I would choose their school. It was like everybody was in on the joke except me. It's like *The Truman Show*, where Jim Carrey's character's life is a movie. He's being exploited by all those around him playing their parts, but he has no clue. Once you've signed a letter of intent to play at their school, the special treatment all stops. They've got you.

Oregon State University, my last visit, made a good first impression. Oregon State, in the college town of Corvallis, faced a tough recruiting challenge with the University of Oregon, forty minutes down the road, where Nike founder Phil Knight has been generous with his alma mater. The University of Oregon had facilities that looked like an NFL team's. Oregon State had probably the worst facilities in the Pacific-10 Conference. The locker room was located under the basketball court—you had to walk across the hall to the showers. The weight room was a dungeon. Our high school stadium looked nicer than theirs. But something about OSU's ivy-covered brick buildings appealed to me as soon as I drove onto campus. Right off, I loved the architecture. I think I knew as soon as I saw the place that was where I would go. I called my mom afterward and told her that I was leaning toward Oregon State.

Oregon State was not a football powerhouse, but I fell in love with the place. The coach, Dave Kragthorpe, didn't bullshit me like some of the others. He told me I had the chance to come in and play. It wasn't a sales pitch. He just said in a straightforward way that he thought I could make a difference on the team. There was also nothing shady about OSU, like I'd seen elsewhere. I respected that. Coach Kragthorpe and his program seemed trustworthy.

Oregon State also offered something the other schools didn't: anonymity. Because it was a smaller school—only about twelve thousand students in 1986—and its football program was modest—awful, really—everybody ignored the Beavers. Corvallis, a sleepy college town in an overlooked corner of Oregon, was the perfect place for me to hide out. I wasn't thinking about football as a profession. I just wanted a college education—without being found out. Little did I know that I would bring the spotlight to the school.

# CHAPTER FOUR

~

# Who's Esera Tuaolo?

MY COLLEGE FOOTBALL CAREER began with humiliation. My first year at OSU, I was a Prop 48—I hadn't scored high enough on my SATs to be eligible. The NCAA had just passed a rule, Proposition 48, that let players keep their scholarships but required them to sit out a season and lose a year of eligibility. I couldn't play, couldn't practice—I couldn't do anything with the team. I couldn't even lift weights or eat with the players. I was self-conscious and embarrassed about that.

I remember being anxious the first time I took the SAT. The room was filled with these young Japanese kids that intimidated me. I knew when I finished that I hadn't passed. Since then, I think I've proven that tests are just tests. How you do on them doesn't mean you're not going to be successful or happy; they're simply an obstacle you have to get through. But I didn't know that then. I just felt stupid, thinking I hadn't been able to pass the test.

Toward the end of my freshman year, Coach Kragthorpe called me into his office and told me someone had made a mistake. The testing board had sent the school the wrong scores—I'd actually passed the SAT on my second try. I hadn't been a Prop 48 after all. Coach Kragthorpe said, "We got a year back for you." The first year would be a redshirt season; I was still eligible to play four years. That didn't take away the embarrassment I had felt, but it was good news.

I was glad to start working out with the team that spring. The Oregon State Beavers didn't exactly strike fear into the hearts of opponents. We'd finished three and eight overall the 1986 season—the year I sat out—last place in the lowly Pac-10 Conference. Still, I found the level of play tougher. In high school, I'd been The Man. But you get to college, and everybody else had been The Man, too. Coming off that lost season, I was afraid people would think they wasted a scholarship on me. I had something to prove.

I was a humble player who let my performance speak for me. That first season, I wanted to gain the respect of my teammates and coaches. In drills, I picked the best junior or senior to go up against. I figured if I could beat them, I would prove myself. It worked.

I played in all eleven games of 1987 as a defensive end and started the final three. The team had a tougher time earning respect. We didn't win a damn conference game and finished dead last in the Pac-10.

I wasn't just playing for myself. I was playing for my family and for my heritage. There are not a lot of us Polynesians out there. In my four years playing at OSU, there was only one other Samoan on our team, Joe Polumalu, among about forty black guys. We Polynesians take pride in ourselves.

More personally, I played for my mom, to give her a better life. I knew if I did well enough, I could go pro and make enough money to take care of her. I could still hear her screams from the night Daddy died.

———

Sai Poulivati was my closest buddy in college. I met him on the sidelines during a game my sophomore year. Coming off the field after warm-ups, I spotted this Tongan kid. Any time you see another Polynesian guy in Oregon—or anywhere outside the islands for that matter—you get excited, there are so few of us. I introduced myself. He was this wide-eyed high school player from Portland, Oregon, who wanted to attend OSU. We hit it off.

I invited him down a few weekends to watch games. He was a defensive lineman with great athletic ability but didn't get a scholarship. I told Coach Kragthorpe before Sai came to school that he had talent, he could play. Sai made the team as a walk-on. I took him under my wing. He became a little brother to me.

Sai made it into OSU under the equal opportunity program. Money was tight for his family, and he had trouble affording school. After his first season, he was thinking he might not return to OSU. I talked to Coach Kragthorpe and told him we might lose Sai. He gave Sai a scholarship. It's a good thing because Sai took over my defensive line spot after I left—and even broke some of my school records.

Sai is a quiet guy, but don't get him pissed off. In college, he would get into fights, and I would get questioned. The other guy would tell the police, "It was a big Polynesian guy." No one knew Sai by his name; they only knew Esera. The police would come talk to me. After this happened a few times, I told Sai, "You better cool it down, or I'm going to tell them your name." He did.

One day during my sophomore season, I went to a Polynesian gathering in Portland, where I met a Samoan professional wrestler. He looked just like my older brother Fale, so I figured we must be related. He asked, "Who was your father?"

"Maiuu Mike Tuaolo," I said.

He started crying. "I'm your father's brother."

We talked for a while, then he said, "I want you to come work for me this summer."

"What do you do?" I asked.

"Security." His wrestling career was winding down. "I'll pay you five hundred dollars a week."

That sounded good. I lined up Sai for a summer job, too.

Turned out "security" meant bodyguards for some Mexican guy. I never did learn his name. Everybody just called him *Boss*.

"What do we do?" I asked my uncle.

"Wherever he goes, you go," he said.

We ended up at a nightclub. *Cool,* I thought. I was still underage but had a job that got me into nightclubs.

Cool quickly wore off. The hours were ungodly. Boss wouldn't sleep because of the drugs he was doing. He would go forty-eight hours or more without going to bed. We had to stay with him.

Nobody would tell us what was going on. I finally figured out that I was working for a Mafia kingpin. My uncle was head of his security. He had recruited a bunch of Samoans like Sai and me to work for him.

About three weeks into our summer job, my uncle took us to the house of a guy who owed Boss money. We pulled up in a semi tractor-trailer and cleared out the guy's place. Sai and I hauled out the refrigerator, the oven—everything—while the guy's mom begged us to stop.

Afterward, Sai told me, "This is messed up. I can't do this." He left. I told my uncle that Sai had a family emergency in California.

I tried to quit myself, but my uncle wouldn't let me. "You can't leave the family," he said.

About that time, my uncle had an ugly split with the Boss. He decided, screw the Boss, he would use his connections to start his own business. One day, my uncle's friend Joe left to do a deal but didn't come back to the house. I went outside to check on him and saw police down the street. I hopped into my uncle's car, drove around the block and spotted Joe in cuffs. They had nabbed him in a sting. I called my uncle.

"You've got to do me a favor," he said. "Bring me the stuff."

He told me he had two kilos of cocaine packed in the storage compartment of his Harley-Davidson motorcycle parked in the garage. I did what he asked. I grabbed the two bundles and dropped them off in the next town. I asked myself, *What am I doing? What if I get busted? This is life, not a game. I could be in deep shit. I could lose football and a whole lot more.*

I called Sai. He said, "You've got to get out of there."

I was still trying to figure out how a couple of nights later when we went to this Chinese restaurant in Portland, a place we called *The Office.* There were six of us—my uncle and his Polynesian security squad—when the Boss walked in with five big, black guys and sat down at a table. The Boss was seething. Nobody screwed him. Everybody perked up. "Get ready," my uncle said in Samoan. He started pairing us up. "Es, you take that guy," he pointed to the biggest black guy at the table. I was thinking, *Shit, I don't want to get shot.*

One of the Boss' guys walked over to our table and told my uncle, "The Boss wants to talk to you."

"You tell your boss, 'go fuck yourself,'" he said in his broken English.

"What did you say?" The black guy leaned over like he was going into his jacket, reaching for a gun.

My uncle took the glass in his hand and smashed it into the guy's face.

The place erupted in a barroom brawl, just like you see in a Western. Glasses and bottles started flying. I was so scared I blacked out. I was sure someone was going to pull out a gun and start spraying everyone. But I don't think they had time because we were on them right away. I started throwing tables, smashed one over a guy.

They grabbed the Boss and hustled him out. We were too big for them.

We got out of there fast, too. I could hear the cops coming. "Where can we go?" we asked my uncle. The glass he'd smashed into the guy's face had cut up his palm and wrist pretty bad. His thumb dangled like it was about to fall off. We couldn't take him to the hospital.

"Take me home," he said. He told his wife to get him a needle and thread. He stitched himself up.

The next day, we went back to the restaurant and my uncle paid thousands of dollars for the damages.

I told him, "I can't do this."

"Nobody leaves the family," he said.

"Then I've got to tell my mom what I'm doing," I said.

"No, no, no," he said.

I headed back to Corvallis to wait for summer practice to start. Sai and I couldn't believe what had happened.

Not long after that, we were watching *Cops* on TV and saw that they busted a drug ring in Portland. They started showing pictures of everybody in the gang. We were scared shitless, but our pictures didn't come up. My uncle wound up in prison on drug charges.

I took tamer summer jobs after that. I went back to work at a lumber mill in Roseburg, Oregon, where I had worked after my first summer. Several other players and I pulled the wood chains or worked the stacker. The work was never anything difficult, and the OSU alumnus who ran the mill paid us more than the other workers for doing the same thing. Oregon State wasn't a storied powerhouse, but its alumni looked out for its athletes.

I heard about other players receiving "gifts"—cash, stereos, televisions, other stuff—from alumni. When I started having more success in my junior and senior year, alumni would shake my hand with twenty- or fifty-dollar bills. I'd always say, "No, thank you." I was scared of getting caught, but it also went against the way I was brought up. My mom raised me to respect other people and to do what was right. Not to sound like a Goody Two-shoes, but their offers simply turned me off. I didn't want to be part of that.

It's important to find an edge in college. In high school, you don't really pay attention to the little things, like the guy you're going up against—you just know what team you're playing that week. You might watch a little film of that team, but you don't study it. Even at first in college—when I didn't think football would take me anywhere—I didn't take the preparations that seriously. Eventually, when I realized the game's possibilities for me and my family, I started paying attention to the little things like mechanics and mental strength that really make all the difference in college and the pros.

That didn't sink in until my junior year when Brady Hoke arrived to coach the defensive line before the 1989 season. He was an awesome coach. All of the players liked and respected him. Coach Hoke was able to instill confidence in a player and teach useful techniques. He's the one who taught me how to use my mental strength to conserve energy.

In high school you're more reckless. You go all out, all the time. But in college everybody's good. If you don't conserve energy, you're going to blow it all and not make it through the game. Brady taught me how to turn the intensity on and off. He likened it to a light switch. When you flip it on, the power surges to the bulb; flip it off, the power rests. Every time the ball was snapped, he told me, my power had to surge until the play stopped. The whistle turned it off. By learning how to relax, I discovered how to push myself to reach my limits so I could be on 110 percent during the play.

Brady didn't win me over right away. He switched us from a four-three defense (with four men up front on the line and three linebackers behind them in the gaps) to a three-four (three men up front, four linebackers behind them) with me at nose guard. Until then, I'd been playing mostly tackle and sometimes end. I'd gotten used to that. I didn't want to switch. He was my third new line coach in three years. I thought, *Here's another new guy coming in, trying to be top dog and wanting us to learn a new technique.* He pissed me off. Even though we were coming off a 4–6–1 season and needed to make changes, I fought it.

Brady wanted me to play a tilted nose guard, where I lined up to the power side of the center and pointed my butt toward the tight end. The only time I'd seen something like that was when I watched the Pittsburgh Steelers on TV and thought, *What are they doing?* The first time I tried it Brady's way in the opening game of the season against Stanford, the offense was like, "What the hell?" They had seen no film of us doing that. They had no idea who to block. The guard didn't know if he should crack down on me or go after the linebacker. That gave me an edge on my opponent. It completely threw them off. We beat the Cardinal 20–16 at home. I had a great game—including two quarterback sacks and another two tackles for yardage losses—and was voted the Pac-10 Conference defensive Player of the Week. I loved it. *Wow,* I thought, *I can deal with this.* That smoothed the transition.

Saturdays, we played. Sundays, we watched film.

Players hurt in the game reported early, around 11 a.m., to the training room so the doctor could meet with them. Everybody else came in for a light weightlifting session around 1 p.m. Then we had a team meeting where Coach Kragthorpe addressed the team. He either complimented us or yelled at us, depending on whether we won or lost. Mostly, he yelled.

After the team meeting, we split into offense and defense meetings to rehash the game and watch the film. If we played extra horribly the day before and the head coach was really pissed off, we watched the film as a whole team. No one liked that. The coaches started pointing things out and embarrassing players. As a player, you suck it up, but you think, *Oh, shit. I hope I didn't do something bad enough to get singled out.*

Other guys are like me that way. None of the players ever liked watching game film. No one likes getting humiliated in front of his teammates.

If we won, the coach sometimes didn't make us watch the film but dismissed us early. It was awesome, to have a break, but it didn't happen that often at OSU. We didn't win enough games.

Usually, the defense met an hour or two longer than the offense because we spent so much more time on the field. It would piss me off when I saw the offense leaving and we weren't halfway through our film.

After the movies we headed out to the field for a light workout without pads. We ran sprints and worked on plays.

Monday, we took a break.

Tuesdays, we had our team meeting first, like we did every practice day. Coach Kragthorpe told us about our opponent the coming Saturday, showed us some key flicks, and pointed out who we needed to watch. During our defense meetings, we watched film of the opponent, noting their weapons, play selection, and formations. The defensive coordinator added new plays that might thwart the offense, usually various blitzes. Then, the defensive line met and the defensive line coach told us what plays we would use and whether or not we would play an eagle defense, where I shaded toward the tight end, or a basic D, where I shaded away. We spent more time watching the opponent, studying the formations, the quarterback, the offensive line, and the blocking schemes. Then we practiced in full pads for two hours.

Tuesdays were the hardest day of the week—we hit at full speed. Part of the practice the offense ran plays against a dummy defense made up of second- and third-string players. I watched on the sideline. Then, the defense ran plays against a dummy offense.

After practice, we showered and ate together in one of the dorm cafeterias.

Wednesday and Thursday were more of the same: film and a "pads" practice—only shoulder pads and helmets. The coaches discarded what they thought wouldn't work. Friday, we did our final walk-through in shorts and T-shirts, fine-tuning the plays for the next day. I sometimes brought home film to do some extra studying of opponents' offensive lines to prepare for that Saturday's game. I also got together with the rest of the defensive line and even the linebackers during lunch or after practice to study film.

I know if I had spent as much time on my classroom studies I probably would have graduated with honors. As it was, I got by with Cs. Kragthorpe was always on us to stay above the minimum GPA of 2.0. I had to drop some classes because I got too far behind to catch up, but I stayed eligible. You hear about academic scandals like the one with the University of Minnesota men's basketball team (where the coach paid a university employee to write papers for players), but that wasn't going on at OSU. We weren't the big time, where the money was. We were the doormats—they didn't have to worry about OSU breaking rules.

I wish somebody had been writing my papers and taking my tests. Some of the guys slept with girls in their classes so they could cheat from them. I didn't have that luxury. That's one of the reasons why my grades weren't so good.

I started out as a business major. That didn't last too long. I just wasn't interested in the classes. I ended up a speech communications major. Not all of the players stayed in school once the season ended, but I'm proud I finished out my classes spring semester of my senior year even though I was still a semester of credits short of earning my bachelor's degree. Football gave me the education I did get.

The week culminated on Saturday. All of the film, all of the hitting, all of the talk came to fruition on game day. For me, everything hinged on the snap of the ball. I had a mental checklist to review before each play. First, I checked the backfield. An I-formation (the fullback and tailback directly behind the quarterback) probably meant run. Ninety percent of the time, teams run out of that formation. The fullback goes into the hole first to clear space for the tailback carrying the ball. I noted where the tight end lined up because most of the time the offense runs to the side where he can provide an extra block.

If the offense split the backs, they were more likely to pass. Sometimes they did that to bluff, though, so I couldn't be sure. A team with a good running back might run the ball most often out of a single-back formation. No backs in the backfield meant pass.

I also had to consider the down and yards to go for the first down. There are certain obvious passing situations—say, second-and-eight or -nine yards, third-and-six or more—and obvious running situations—second or third and short yardage. Others are gray areas. Third-and-four or five could go either way. Second-and-five, they figure, *We ran for five on first down, we can get another five with a run.* But they might catch you thinking that way and surprise you with a pass. We studied the offense's tendencies that week in practice and broke them down into their statistical likelihood to pass or run in each situation.

I checked the linemen's knuckles. If they were white, the linemen had all their weight on their hand, ready to drive block—which meant run. You wouldn't be able to tell on an ordinary person, but when a guy's three hundred eighty pounds, you can see it—you can tell when a mountain's going to fall. If the knuckles weren't white, they had little weight on them, meaning they were ready to stand upright to pass block.

I also checked the linemen's eyes. For each play, everybody on the line has an assignment to block a specific opponent. I watched the linemen break from the huddle and approach the line. Sometimes, I could catch them picking out their blocking target, and I knew where the play was headed. In my stance across from the center, I glanced left and right at the guards. If I saw one of them looking at me, I figured they were getting ready to double-team me instead of going after a linebacker.

I studied the center, too. I could often tell by the way he grabbed the ball whether it was going to be a pass or run. He gripped the ball harder on the run—he had to get it back to the quarterback extra fast to be able to block his man. On a pass, he only had to hold his ground. Some centers squeezed the ball harder the split-second before they hiked it. When I saw that, I knew I'd explode the next split-second. We worked a lot in practice at getting off the ball quickly. The offensive linemen all knew when the ball was going to be snapped, but if I could be quicker than my opponent, I gained an edge.

All this took place the instant the offense lined up. Then I settled into my stance, ass slanted toward the tight end's side.

That's when the battle began. It's hand-to-hand combat there in the trenches, the closest thing these days to the gladiators. You're going against another human being with no weapon. It's just brute strength and skill. You get a tremendous rush from it.

Everything happens so fast. On a running play, you have to be able to feel the other guy's weight on you and shift yours to shrug him off. He's trying to reach you—get to your outside shoulder to block you in. All your energy and power resist that. Defense is all about gap control. Everybody has his assigned gap. Mine was the A gap between the center and guard—sometimes both of the A gaps. You can't let yourself get reached. But at nose guard, they

43

come at you from all sides. My defensive line coach, Brady Hoke, told me when I felt myself double- or triple-teamed, I should dive for legs and start taking people out to plug the gaps with a pileup. There are times when you are so off-balance that it's either get knocked aside and be embarrassed or take a dive and try to take others with you.

There are some basic moves I used on the pass rush. The butt and jerk: you explode into the offensive lineman, knock him back and off-balance, then jerk him aside when he comes back at you. The bull rush: you put your helmet into his chest and push him back to the quarterback—this works best against bigger guys you can get off-balance. It's basically a sumo wrestling move. The swim move: you grab the corner of his shoulder pads on the near side and swing—or swim—your other arm over his shoulder so your body's past him. It doesn't work so well on taller guys because it's harder to reach up to them. The club: you get the guy off-balance and club him aside with your forearm. The spin was one of my favorite moves. You attack a shoulder, have him commit, then spin across his body to wind up on the opposite side. It worked especially well with linemen who liked to lunge at you, something you could pick up on film.

People like to think you just line up and go for it, but they don't realize there are a lot of things to think about. I always had a move in mind on the pass rush. You can't try one and switch if it doesn't work—there isn't time. You have to commit to one. I tried to set them up. For instance, if I was going to use the swim move, I lined up straight on, so he would think I was going to bull rush. Thing is, the opponent has also been studying you and knows your favorite moves. Sometimes they work; sometimes they don't. It's not as easy as people might think, especially at nose guard where you get hit from everywhere.

Others might not agree, but I think nose guard is the key position for the defense. You have to be a different breed to play nose guard. You have to be able to fight off two or three guys. If you don't, you'll get blown out and leave a huge hole. The defensive end may get double-teamed if the tight end lines up on his side, but the nose guard doesn't know if he'll get double- or even triple-teamed. You take on the center but don't know which guard is coming to get you, maybe chopping you at the knees. There's a play where all three will get me. Both guards rub off me on their way to the linebackers. That's over a thousand pounds coming at you, and you have to be able to hold your ground.

The philosophy of a nose guard has to be that he can't be blocked by just one person. You make the offense double-team you. If you can do that, it frees up the linebacker, and he's your best friend. If one person can block you, you're not doing your job. You've got to be the pillar. You've done your job when you make the team run outside, where there's more support. If teams can run up the middle at will, it's a long day for the defense.

I had thought I would be able to hide out at OSU. Nobody paid attention to the doormats of the Pac-10. I figured I would be happy simply playing college football, earning my degree, and moving on. That all changed one Saturday afternoon in Lincoln, Nebraska, the place that put me on the map.

We traveled there to play the Cornhuskers on September 30, 1989. It was a huge mismatch, like a peewee team playing a pro team. I was amazed when I first saw these guys in the weight room. They were humongous—six foot six, six foot seven. They had state-of-the-art equipment with computerized controls—

nothing like our run-down dungeon tools. Looking at them you think, *They must be on steroids.* Some of them probably were. One thing I like to do is look in the eyes of other athletes. That Saturday, I saw fear in my teammates' eyes.

I was going up against Jake Young, their All-America center. I had heard he was very difficult to play against. Nebraska ran the ball 80 percent of the time. I expected the worst: a long, hard day of getting beaten up.

We walked into their stadium and into a sea of red. Everybody was shouting and cheering—but not for us. When the Cornhuskers ran onto the field, they didn't seem like giants to me anymore, maybe because I was so pumped up.

On the first play, I took on Jake Young. He came driving at my feet, and I remember thinking, *Is that it?* Not in an arrogant way, but more matter-of-factly. I breathed a sigh of relief and enjoyed the rest of the game. I made a ton of tackles.

At halftime, we led 7–3. Friends back in Corvallis told me the radio announcers were saying, "This could be the biggest upset of the century."

Going into the locker room at the half, red fans lined the railings above the runway and cheered for us, but I think they were saying, "Enjoy it while you can. It's not going to last." It didn't.

Once inside the locker room, we started shouting and going crazy. I checked my teammates' eyes. They held a look of wonder. *Oh, my gosh, we're beating a top-ten team!* We ran back out there and got our asses kicked. The Cornhuskers outscored us 32–0 and won 35–7.

After that game, though, the national media knew my name. I made a team-high thirteen tackles, including three for losses. People started asking, "Who's Esera Tuaolo?" It seemed every game after that I went up against an All-America player. The media billed the games as Esera versus Whoever.

My play created a buzz that to beat OSU you had to beat Esera Tuaolo. One of UCLA's coaches said I was "the best defensive lineman we saw play against us." A guy who played on the University of Washington's offensive line told me after I retired that when he was a freshman, the coach put up a picture of our defense in a team meeting and circled me. "If we're going to beat OSU, we've got to beat this guy."

My own coach, Dave Kragthorpe, said about me, "Esera's strongest attribute is that he goes hard all the time, every day in practice and in everything he does, and I think that puts him in a class by himself."

Before we played UCLA, Frank Cornish, the Bruins' All-America center, told a reporter, "I bench four hundred pounds. I think I should be able to take Esera Tuaolo." I was so pissed. Right then and there, he gave me the edge. If he had kept his mouth shut, I wouldn't have had that extra fire in my belly to try to kill him. I remember one play I tossed Cornish like Raggedy Ann and sacked the quarterback. I usually didn't talk trash, but if another guy started, I would finish it. I walked back and said, "You bench four hundred pounds, huh?"

We upset UCLA in our house, Parker Stadium, 18–17. I made five solo tackles, assisted on two more, sacked the quarterback twice, and caused a fumble, which set up our first touchdown of the game. Frank Cornish didn't have much to say about that afterward.

My play peaked junior year. I finished third on the team in defensive points, a figure that takes into account tackles, sacks, fumbles caused, and tackles for a loss. That's an unusually high finish for a nose guard. I had four and a half sacks for minus twenty-eight yards and made a school-record thirteen tackles for losses in 1989. I was named first team all-conference, Outstanding

Defensive Lineman in the Pac-10, and the team's Outstanding Defensive Player and Most Inspirational Player. The team finished 1989 4–7–1 overall, 3–4–1 in the Pac-10, good for sixth place, which was actually the highest we finished in my years at OSU.

We played Nebraska in Lincoln again my senior year. Before the game, I was walking on the field with my buddy Sai. One of the groundskeepers said, "Hey, aren't you Esera Tuwawallaoh?" Of course, he pronounced it wrong.

Sai said, "Yeah, that's him."

The worker said, "You had an incredible game against Jake Young last year."

Sai started teasing me, but I thought it was cool to have a guy like that notice and remember me.

The National Football League noticed me, too, in that forgotten corner of Oregon. My plays against Young, Cornish, and other high-profile players that year inspired NFL scouts to rate me the best interior lineman in the nation. You have to realize, I was coming from a school that went 11–32–2 during my four years. We hadn't had a winning season in a long time. Getting that recognition was quite an accomplishment. Football promised a new world of possibilities.

The last game of my junior season, we headed to Honolulu to play the University of Hawaii. I was about to board the plane when Coach Kragthorpe pulled me aside. "Congratulations, Esera," he said. "You just won the Morris Trophy."

"What's the Morris Trophy?" I asked. I was never big into awards. I was more of a team player, maybe because of the humble way my mom brought me up. She taught me that everything in life is a team effort. My teammates were my extended family. I played for them, not for individual glory.

When Coach explained the Morris Trophy was given to the Pac-10's best defensive lineman—as voted by the conference's starting offensive linemen—the award tasted bittersweet. I felt proud that I'd won this prestigious award, but it reminded me that I was living a lie in order to be accepted—and rewarded—by society. My success hinged on the ability to protect my secret.

# CHAPTER FIVE

# Killer Beavers

**B**OARDING THE PLANE FOR HAWAII, I was excited to be headed back to my homeland to play in front of family and friends who had never seen me play. It meant a lot to have them see a part of my life that I had worked so hard to develop. I wanted them to understand what it was that my exploring heart pursued when I left the island. We Polynesians celebrate everything. My family took pride in my success and wanted to celebrate it.

My family threw a huge, traditional Samoan luau for the team that the guys are still talking about today. My family honored the head coach with gifts, roasted a pig, and served a lavish spread of traditional food that included *poki*, a raw fish marinated in soy sauce and seaweed; *palusami,* coconut milk with tarot leaves; and teriyaki beef. There was live music with drums. We sang songs and danced. My mom made me dance in front of my teammates in full costume—shirtless and in a *lava lava,* a wraparound cloth like a skirt. My teammates loved that. I think they appreciated gaining a sense of my culture. Looking around that night, seeing my teammates and family at home on the banana plantation, I felt like I was in paradise.

---

Brady Hoke moved to inside linebacker coach, and I had another new defensive line coach senior year, my fifth in four seasons. I was playing volleyball in the gym one day when he walked in. The athletic director introduced us—Mike Wauffle. He started in right away on his militant philosophy. The eyes almost popped out of his head when he talked. *Oh no, here we go again,* I thought. I just wanted to get back to my volleyball game. *I've dealt with three coaches so far. I can deal with another one.*

Wauffle was a discipline freak, quite a change from Hoke's laid-back style, but after I got to know Wauffle, I came to respect him. As a player in high school and college—and even later in the pros—I thought, *There's always somebody better than you out there.* Wauffle confirmed this philosophy. He told me, "There's somebody else out there working out when you're sleeping. For you to get the edge, you have to do something extra." The month before summer workouts began, he woke me up at 3 a.m. three days a week to run at the stadium. He went down there with me, whistle in one hand, stopwatch in the other. In the glare of his car headlights angled across the field, I ran fifteen hundred-yard sprints under time.

Wauffle didn't have anyone else doing that, just me. I think he saw potential he wanted to develop. He wanted to teach me more about mental toughness. "It's about creating your own zone, the Esera zone," he would say. "When you're tired and feeling sorry for yourself on the field, I want you to remember these 3 a.m. workouts."

At first I thought he was crazy, but it worked. He taught me to push myself to the limit in order to gain an edge on my opponent.

Some guys would do anything to get an edge. My first year playing in college, I stumbled upon some offensive linemen shooting themselves up at a teammate's house. I pissed them off, because I said, "Those steroids are supposed to enhance your performance, but you guys still suck." We were a shitty team at that point, not like OSU today.

I never saw anybody taking steroids in college other than that one incident, but I would guess maybe 10 to 20 percent of the team used them. You see a teammate's back in the shower covered with acne or a guy who weighs two hundred pounds one year coming back the next weighing two hundred sixty pounds and solid muscle and you sense he's shooting up.

Everybody swore I was on steroids. I was like, *Yeah, right.* I never felt pressure to take them. Even if I had, I don't think I would've shot up. For starters, you have to spend too much time in the weight room. I never liked lifting. I would do what I had to do there and get out. Mine was more country strength from my days working on the banana farm. We Polynesians take pride in our natural strength.

We had an annual weight-lifting contest at the end of the spring drills called the "Night of Champions." The tradition pitted the offense against the defense in various weight-lifting categories. Not being a big lifter, I wasn't scheduled to be in the contest the spring of my junior year. Those in it did not have to lift the day before, but the rest of us were supposed to max out—lift the most we could—that day. I was doing power cleans—where you raise the barbell straight from the floor to your chest. The coach kept adding weights, and I kept raising them. Finally, he told me to stop. "I want you to be in the competition tomorrow night," he said.

That night, I hefted three hundred fifty pounds to break the school power-clean record. After that, people knew that I was sandbagging it in the weight room, going through the motions easily. They saw, too, that I didn't need drugs to add strength.

I also knew that steroids were wrong. Everything could be taken away from me if I got busted, just like somebody finding out I was gay. Even more importantly, I didn't want to bring embarrassment to my family.

One afternoon during my first year at Oregon State, I returned to the dorm from a late class and saw a bunch of guys huddled outside the room next to mine, Pellom McDaniels' room. Pellom was a defensive lineman who went on to play for the Kansas City Chiefs. He was crazy. I walked up to the group and looked inside. Pellom was full on doing it with a girl in his room, the door wide open. I don't know if they were both drunk or what, but the guys bunched in the hallway delighted in the performance of the football stud.

College was a time of sexual experimenting for me, like it is for a lot of college kids. I slept with a few women, not that I wanted to. It was mostly for appearances. A football player is supposed to have a cheerleader at his side. I wanted to make sure that my teammates and friends didn't think I was gay. The first year and a half at college, I hung a picture of a girl from back home in my room and told people she was my girlfriend. That was my excuse for not dating women, but I wore it out. I had to hang out with women and do the one-night stands. That was the football player thing to do, even if done late in the afternoon with the door open. People expected it.

Laura was a beautiful girl from an Oregon town so small she was one of only eight students in her senior class. She lived in the dorm room next to mine my first year at OSU. We used to hang out together. One afternoon when I was going through a phase of thinking I might not be gay because I was a football player, we were studying in her room. I looked at her, she looked at me, and we kissed. No sparks. I wasn't even sure I was going to get an erection. We went further and further, undressing each other until we faced each other naked. I wasn't feeling anything, so I started fantasizing about men I had seen in porn tapes. I managed an erection, and we made love.

I must say, my first time with a woman felt great physically, but emotionally there was nothing. I knew after that experience that I truly was gay because if a beautiful girl like Laura couldn't change me, then no other woman would.

There were times I slept with a woman to see if all those things the preacher said when I was young were true. I wanted to see if sex could break the curse like the fairy tale where the frog turns into a prince. Never happened. I think that was just denial on my part.

I always felt bad after a night with a woman. I had deceived her. I wanted to treat people with respect. I didn't want to use them.

Laura was the first woman I chose to have sex with, but not the first woman. When I was thirteen, my older brother Fale's girlfriend came into my bedroom one night. Before I could think or say anything, she was on top of me. She was ten years older, which was a lot at that time. I couldn't believe what was happening. She was smiling down at me, grinding away. For most thirteen-year-old boys, that might be a fantasy come true. It hurt me. I wanted to push her off, but I was frozen in the moment, not knowing what to do. There certainly wasn't anything romantic to it. She simply climbed on top of me and took what she wanted.

The next morning she was there, smiling at me. Fear kicked in. My brother would beat the crap out of me if he found out. If she told him, even though she had approached me, it would come out as my fault. She was older, and in the Polynesian culture the oldest is always right. Growing up, every time I got a spanking, even if it was for something my brother or cousin had done, I would still be wrong because as the youngest I must've done something to instigate it. She molested me, but I thought it was my fault because it aroused me. Being molested screws up your whole brain and sense of reality. I was robbed of sexual experience as a way to feel loved. It took me a long time to learn it wasn't my fault and that sex could be an expression of love that felt good.

I lived out a lot of sexual fantasies with men in my head, all stuff I knew I could never act out because of the sport I played. I heard stories about wild things that happened—like two fraternity guys getting busted making love down in the boiler room. I wanted the sex to happen to me, but feared the getting caught. I had crushes on other guys, but never other football players. We were more like a tight-knit family, especially as I got older and felt like their big brother. But my fraternity brothers senior year . . . there was some wishful thinking on my part. The fantasies kept me satisfied but safe. My wrists got a real workout.

One afternoon during my junior year, I went over to a teammate's apartment to pick up a class assignment. I'll call him Anthony because now he is married with children. I remember red, yellow, and brown leaves on the trees and the air brisk on my face. I was down, having one of my bad days. Anthony asked, "Something wrong?"

I responded the way a depressed person often does, "No, nothing."

He put his hand around my shoulder and pulled me close to give me a brotherly hug. Our eyes connected. Suddenly, we kissed. And kissed and kissed. It was wonderful, but as fast as we embraced, we separated and stared at each other. My heart pounded. I started losing my breath. *Stay in control,* I thought. *What just happened could ruin the great season I'm having.*

We stood there, and Anthony said, "I'm not that way."

"Fuck you," I said. "You think I'm that way?!"

But, of course, I knew I was. I returned to my room and cried. I ached for the affection and affirmation he had denied.

Somehow, with Anthony, I wasn't worried because I knew he would never tell anyone. The next morning, we saw each other and pretended nothing had happened. My fantastic season continued, and I didn't think about it again. I shoved that event in the closet the way I had shoved other painful things I wanted to block out when I was younger. I still had the denial powers of a superhero.

One night during my senior year, a group of us football players were out partying on the town. Another teammate and I wanted to keep partying, even though we were already drunk, so the two of us headed back to his place. After more drinks, we wound up naked in his bed. He reached over to touch me, but I turned away. Here I was, lying naked next to this handsome man who wanted to have sex with me. I could have responded to his touch and later blamed it on alcohol like a lot of people do, but I couldn't bring myself to do that. Even given the opportunity, I didn't dare. I was the team captain, one of the top defensive linemen in the country. The thought of losing all of that made me paranoid. I turned away and pretended to be asleep.

When you come from a background like mine—when you come from nothing—and then are given opportunities like those football gave me, you don't want to lose them. If football failed me, I would have to go back to the banana plantation. I would be stuck in the hand-to-mouth cycle of life that had caught my brothers and friends back home. That scared me. It might have been different for my teammates from wealthier families. If they lost their scholarship, their families could still afford school. Not mine. I had nothing to fall back on.

I was too terrified to act out my gay fantasies in Corvallis, but back in Hawaii I could venture out and be myself. I went home at Christmas or during the summer—my family couldn't afford both trips in one year. I would end up at Hula's Bar & Lei Stand, a gay nightclub in Honolulu. I'd been sneaking in there since I was thirteen. (As a big kid, I always looked older than I was—I had a mustache at twelve). In the locker room at Oregon State, I was always afraid somebody would find out I was gay. Not at Hula's. It was freeing to go to Hula's. I wasn't afraid of people there finding out I was gay because everybody there was, too. I felt comfortable, at home among my kind. I didn't have to play the charade I did at college.

I sometimes had one-night stands with tourists I met at Hula's. I was always careful that they wouldn't find out who I was. I never gave them my real name. Although I went to gay clubs, I continued to hide in the closet because I wasn't telling the truth. I still wasn't completely free to be myself.

I suffered a shock my senior year when I returned from summer vacation. I walked into the locker room and spotted the promotional poster with the team's schedule that would hang all over town—and elsewhere. It said, "Killer Beavers," but instead of the usual team photo, there was a picture of just me with my name. My breath came up short. I felt an instant ache in my gut. Other players would have been happy to see their faces on a poster, but being a gay man, I felt paranoia.

That poster would go back to Hawaii. What if one of the one-night stands from Hula's recognized the man they met and realized his name wasn't Kavika? I didn't sleep with a lot of men when I went home because I wouldn't always know where they were from. I tried to be careful, discreet, but I spent the next couple of weeks looking over my shoulder. I was nervous every time I walked into the coaches' room or elsewhere. I feared my coach summoning me in a menacing tone, "Esera, I need to talk to you."

Football could end for me, just like that. I had worked so hard to go to college. I had played well enough to have a shot at the NFL. I'd brought honor to my family. It hurt to know that it could all be taken away from me just by someone telling the truth about who I really was. No one should have to live in that fear. No one should lose everything simply for telling the truth about who they are. You grow up with your family, spend your life making friendships—and to think it could be taken away just because of the truth. I hear from people in the gay, lesbian, bisexual, and transgender (GLBT) community who lose their families, friends, homes—everything. That could be me.

During two-a-day practices in August, Coach Kragthorpe announced the team captains. My teammates selected me defensive captain my senior year. When I heard my name, I thought, *Wow*, and *Oh, shit.* Honor comes with a price. I knew my teammates liked me because of my laid-back, friendly personality and my performance. They nicknamed me "Mr. Aloha." On the field, I was always the leader by the way I played. Being given that role officially as a team captain meant more stress, more sleepless nights. There was the pressure to go out every Saturday and perform, to be a role model. I didn't want to let my teammates down. I couldn't get into trouble; I had to guard my secret more carefully.

My biggest fear in college was that somebody would find out I was gay. That dominated my life, colored everything. The bigger my role and the more attention I got, the more I had to lose. I was building a reputation as an outstanding football player. College players trade upon that reputation, but I knew my stock could go bust at any moment.

Drinking became a way to take the edge off the stress. I found alcohol eased the pain of anxiety and depression. I saw other players happy with their girlfriends while I was struggling to accept myself. I would wake up alone and depressed. Alcohol became a good substitute. I drank in high school, even wrapped a car around a tree the summer after graduation. Fortunately, no one in the car was hurt beyond needing stitches. In college, I started to tank it down.

In my room, I mixed up jungle juice, blending a bunch of fruit with Everclear, which is 95 percent pure grain alcohol. I wanted the cheapest, strongest booze I could find. The pubs in town served us free pitchers of beer. None of us were of age, but the better I played, the more they wanted me drinking in their bars. I was considered a good drunk. Instead of getting rowdy and wild, I became happy and approachable. Guess I was like my daddy that way. Alcohol drew out our charming and charismatic qualities.

Occasionally, I showed up at practice hungover, but drinking never hurt my play. The coaches weren't stupid. I'm sure they assumed we drank. They gave speeches to the team, pretending they were talking to the few guys over twenty-one who were legally old enough to drink but really talking to all of us. "Don't get into trouble," they told us. In other words, don't do anything that could get you suspended. I didn't.

Oregon State was approximately 65 percent Greek, so Sai and I pledged Pi Kappa Alpha my senior year. The frat house was also a good place to party. The older brothers didn't harass us during the initiation because they knew we could beat them all up.

At that time, hazing wasn't much of an issue at our school, even on the team. I think the coaches had that locked down. A freshman who smarted off to the older guys would wind up duct-taped to the goal post, but that sort of thing was always to teach somebody a lesson, not to pick on him.

---

I used to sing all the time in the locker room. One day, our trainer, who was also the trainer for the basketball team, asked, "If I could get you the chance, would you sing the national anthem before the basketball game?"

"Sure," I said. I thought he was joking. It was always celebrities—or someone from the music department—who did that.

The next day he said, "You're on Friday."

I was so nervous that I practiced in the shower, the car, everywhere.

That Friday night, I was fine—just a few butterflies—until they announced my name. I stood alone in the middle of the court. It was so quiet. Sometimes, before the national anthem, you can hear people still talking. Not this time. You could hear a pin drop. All eyes were on me. It was like a horror movie. My legs started wobbling. I had to walk so I didn't fall on my ass.

Once I came out with the first note, my nerves settled. I brought down the house. I enjoyed it. After that first time, people started to notice my singing. The Portland Trailblazers asked me to perform at one of their games. I sang the national anthem at the 1990 NCAA women's gymnastics championship finals held at OSU. Perhaps the most special time occurred at my last game at Oregon State. We played the University of Oregon at Parker Stadium. My mom was there for that one.

Mama had heard me sing for friends at parties but never before thousands of people in a football stadium. From where I stood in my pads and Beavers jersey on the fifty-yard line, I could see her in the stands with my sisters Tusi and Gene, Gene's husband Pete, and my brothers Afa and Tua. Except for my sister Gene, this was their first time at Oregon State. They had watched me play that game in Hawaii, but never heard the whole stadium cheering for me the way they would that day. I grasped the microphone and poured my heart into the words.

By the time I reached "home of the brave," the crowd, already on its feet, screamed and started chanting, "ES-E-RA, ES-E-RA." I could see the emotions playing out in my mom's face. She had heard that people loved me as an athlete; now she witnessed that love. I almost broke into tears watching the pride and happiness wash over Mama. My family had never really understood the extent of my success as a football player in college because I was always away. To have them experience that moment, to have them hear the love from the fans—that was priceless.

My second biggest fear in college was getting hurt. It happened my senior year before the season even started.

Until then, I had been an ironman. I had a streak of twenty-six straight starts, going back to my freshman year. Sophomore and junior years, I was part of the team's Tough 20 club, those who hadn't missed a spring practice. The Beavers' media guide proclaimed, "It almost takes an act of Congress to get Esera off the field when the defensive unit is out there." But I couldn't will away injury.

It happened innocently. We planned to try something new: have me carry the ball in short yardage situations the way I had as Baby Fridge in high school. Someone hit my left knee during a drill. It twisted and partially tore the medial collateral ligament. That ended my running career before it started. Worse, it almost cost me my NFL career.

I should have at least had arthroscopic surgery on my knee. The team doctors discouraged me from doing that. They told me I should let my knee heal naturally so that I could come back sooner. If I had surgery, they said, I might miss the entire season and the chance to be drafted. It crossed my mind that I might be getting screwed with some bad advice. The sports world is all about winning. Losing one of your best players wasn't the best thing for the team. Other players lose morale. The level of play goes down. That was their thinking. But as a young athlete, you don't really understand what's at stake. You make decisions based on emotions. I just wanted the chance to play my senior season.

I was up for the Vince Lombardi/Rotary Award, given annually to the college lineman who, in addition to outstanding performance and ability, best exemplifies the discipline of Vince Lombardi, as determined by coaches and media. I was also up for the Outland Trophy, given by the Football Writers Association of America to the nation's best interior lineman. My knee kept me out of the first three games of the season, the most crucial part of the awards campaign. The voting is based on statistics from the first five games. We played some easy teams those three games. I would've put up good numbers. But all I could do was limp around the sidelines and hope my knee would heal soon.

I finished the season in pain. There was a lot of loose cartilage floating around that would lock in the wrong place and cause excruciating pain. I'd have to come out for a couple of plays and work it out before I could go back into the game. The knee sometimes swelled during the week, and I had to have it drained before games. I finished the season with forty-two tackles, matching my total from the '89 season, and notched four QB sacks to set an OSU record for most career sacks—fourteen—all on a bum leg. That injury not only knocked me out of contention for the Lombardi and Outland awards, it tagged me as damaged goods before the NFL draft.

I should have declared myself early for the draft after junior year. That was the year Junior Seau came out early from UCLA. But I didn't have anyone giving me that advice. I couldn't ask my OSU coaches because I knew they wanted me to play another season for them. They tried to convince me that I should complete my education. They told me there was no guarantee that I would play if I went pro early. I wasn't injured at the time. I thought maybe next year I would be able to go even higher in the draft if I had an even better season. I had a chance to win the Outland Trophy, after all. It seemed like a good idea at the time. As it turned out, I almost junked my football career to play another year for a sorry program.

I had chosen OSU as a place to hide out. I hadn't chosen Oregon State to showcase myself. The attention I received in college educated me about football's possibilities. Leaving OSU, I didn't want to lose that.

# CHAPTER SIX

Road to the Draft

I THOUGHT FOOTBALL WOULD END after my senior season. My knee injury erased my NFL hopes. I had a decent, though not outstanding season: All Pac-10 but not All-America. Going to a small college hurt me there. The NFL scouts ranked me either the number one or number two nose guard in the country my last two years, but the All-America selections came from the top schools. Oregon State was too small for the members of the American Football Coaches Association to consider me legitimate. I didn't expect any pro teams would want to take a chance on me.

Coming out of high school, I hadn't realized the economic implications of playing at a Pac-10 bottom feeder. At the time, I wasn't thinking about a career in professional football. I was just enjoying the attention and educational opportunity football gave me. If I had chosen to play at one of the bigger schools that recruited me, say UCLA or USC, I might have had an All-America linebacker title behind me. Other teams could not have afforded to put two blockers on me. I would have stood out more and most likely would have been named All-America. There weren't any All-America linebackers at OSU; it was extremely rare that I didn't get double-teamed. Winning All-America honors would have placed me higher in the NFL draft and put more money in my pocket—the higher you go, the higher the signing bonus.

That's where the decision to play my senior year instead of declaring early for the draft really hurt me. After my junior year, I most likely would've been a first round pick, which would have meant a signing bonus in the neighborhood of $1 million. I don't mean to badmouth OSU, nor do I regret playing there. It's just in hindsight, I'm wiser.

Scouts from several teams—the Packers, Raiders, 49ers, and Cowboys, among others—came to Corvallis, sometimes in groups, sometimes alone. They timed me in the forty-yard dash. They worked me out at linebacker to test my agility and quickness. They told me what to do but not how I did. It was hard to know what they thought. They wouldn't have a conversation with me. I knew they wanted to check my knee. It hurt, but I didn't let on.

After the season ended, I had my knee scoped to clean out the loose cartilage. That gave me a few weeks to rest before the all-star bowl games. But the knee remained a question mark until I proved it sound on the NFL field.

The NCAA allows players to hire an agent once their team's season is over. I hadn't realized you needed an agent to get to the NFL. Brady Hoke set me up with Ken Kramer, from IMG (International Management Group). The two had played football together at Ball State, where Ken had been an offensive lineman. You hear horror stories about agents taking advantage of players, but Ken was trustworthy and knowledgeable. I was blessed to meet him.

I received offers to play in several all-star bowls. I really wanted to play in the Aloha Bowl in Hawaii, but Ken advised me that I should play in the Senior Bowl instead. NFL coaches ran the Senior Bowl. The game would give me a better chance to show the people who mattered how I measured up against the country's top talent.

The week before the game, the players showed up in Mobile, Alabama, to get ready. Practices were intense. We were all there for the same thing—to shine. I was nervous, sizing up the other top defensive linemen who wanted to get drafted before me. Some of the guys talked crap. Everybody hit hard. This was our NFL audition.

I'm a happy-go-lucky guy, "Mr. Aloha." I warmed up to the other guys off the field. We went out to clubs together. Drinking helped us cut the tension.

Somebody had heard about my singing and invited me to sing "The Star-Spangled Banner." This was January 1991. Right before I sang, they announced that Operation Desert Storm had just begun—American troops had taken action in the Persian Gulf—and asked for a moment of silence. I stood at the fifty-yard line in my full pads, facing the crowd. I remember looking up and seeing men and women crying. I almost broke down myself, but somehow, after the silence, I squeezed out the words.

From Mobile, it was on to Palo Alto, California, for the East-West Shrine Bowl. The atmosphere there wasn't as intense. I hit it off with a defensive lineman from Oklahoma University, an offensive lineman from the University of Texas, and Eric Bieniemy, a running back from the University of Colorado. We became quick buddies, but I still kept my distance. I didn't want them to get too close and find out who I was. I worried they might catch me looking at another guy or a guy might flirt with me. Basically, I was by myself.

I never knew who might want to out me for their own advantage. As a result, I can't remember two of these guys' names now.

We drove up to San Francisco to party and missed the team introduction meeting. The coach was calling our names, but we weren't there. Meet—nobody! No one had told us the meeting was mandatory. The problem was that they gave us rental cars. We had wheels.

We missed the West team photo, too. Same thing, we'd driven to the city. I had thought San Francisco would be a chance to meet some other gay men and have a wild time, but I simply ended up down on the pier, eating crab and drinking beer with teammates.

Mark McGwire's brother Dan, who had played against me in high school, had gone on to play quarterback at San Diego State. I thought it was cool that the Shrine Bowl brought us together on the same team.

I started both all-star games and turned in decent performances. I loved the challenge of going up against the nation's best. I wanted a shot at the NFL as bad as any of them did. The coaches didn't want anyone to get hurt doing stunts, so it was all straight-on play—no stunts, no blitzes. That limited me, but I did well enough to get invited to the Combine.

The NFL Scouting Combine, as football fans know, gathers the nation's top college football prospects in Indianapolis during February to be inspected by coaches, scouts, and administrators from all of the league's teams. (Back then, it was three days, Thursday through Saturday; now it's a full week.) They conduct medical, strength, and agility tests. It's their chance to poke, prod, weigh, measure, and observe the merchandise. The Combine is a total meat market.

Only three hundred prospects are invited. That's like making the first cut for the draft. A lot of guys don't get that far. For somebody like me, coming out of OSU, to get invited was a big deal. I felt out of place alongside marquee players that I'd read about and watched on TV. These guys played for schools that went to national championship bowl games. I watched in awe as the media fussed over them in the hotel lobby.

They showed us an educational film on domestic violence and diversity. I was hoping maybe there would be something in the movie about gay men, but there wasn't. With racial issues—preparing guys to play alongside people of different colors—the NFL is far ahead of society; but when it comes to sexuality, the league is in the Dark Ages. It would've made a world of difference if they had shown something about sexuality at the Combine. I wouldn't have felt so restricted later.

They gave us a psychological test, the Wonderlic. Teams want to minimize their risks. They don't want to draft a serial killer, but even that would probably be better in their minds than drafting a gay player. I feared that somehow my answers would reveal that I was gay. I filled out the test quickly and turned in my sheet.

Ever Mr. Aloha, I quickly struck up a friendship with my main competition, Chris Zorich and Russell Maryland. Zorich, a nose guard out of Notre Dame, had won the Vince Lombardi/Rotary Award. He was the one with whom I had traded the number one nose guard spot on the NFL scouts' list. Russell Maryland was a defensive tackle out of the University of Miami who had won the Outland Trophy.

We didn't go out drinking together. There's no partying at the Combine. It's all business. We knew that weekend could make or break our NFL careers. We joked and laughed during the sessions to lighten the tension. We became the three amigos.

Every prospect endured thorough physicals. The doctors had me bend over to check my back. They tested the flexibility of my elbows, shoulders, everything. If you sprained an ankle in high school, they x-rayed it. The physicians spent extra time examining my knee. They twisted and tugged it in all directions. My knee was so sore that I had to ice it back at the hotel after each physical.

Every team interested in drafting a defensive lineman gave me its own physical, same thing every time. After about the tenth physician twisting and tugging at my knee, I said to him, "My god, can't you just get the file from the Vikings?" Maybe that's why that team didn't draft me. But there's no sharing among hawks. They all wanted to be thorough and sure about every-thing. They didn't want to take any chances. It's understandable, considering the size of their investment.

We lined up like cattle in a large room at the Indianapolis Colts' facility to be weighed and measured. Russell Maryland asked Chris Zorich, "How tall are you?"

"Six foot," he said.

We started ragging on Chris because he was shorter. He might've been six foot in the Fighting Irish program, but you couldn't hide from the truth of the tape measure. They would call out our names and measurements across the room.

Russell was six foot two, 275 pounds. I was six foot two, 270 pounds myself. That was big back then. Today, there are more than three hundred fifty guys in the NFL weighing over three hundred pounds, but back in 1990, there were only thirty-five three-hundred-pounders.

Chris took his turn, and the guy called out, "Chris Zorich, five foot, eleven inches."

Russell and I laughed our asses off. "Six foot, my ass!"

Chris soon had his chance to show us up.

We gathered in the Colts' weight room for the strength test, which was to bench two hundred twenty-five pounds as many times as you could. A guy showed us how we had to bring the bar down to touch our chest then all the way up—that was one repetition. I was nervous about how I was going to do in this test. The size of the guys in that room intimidated me. I looked around and saw these chiseled monsters. They were obviously serious lifters, some probably on steroids. I, of course, had done little lifting myself. I tried to remind myself that one's appearance didn't dictate one's performance. I had gone up against some of these guys in the Senior Bowl. They may have looked like Tarzan, but they played like Jane.

One of the first guys was a chiseled white guy from the University of Mississippi. He raised the bar slowly—one. He struggled on the second rep. The third time, he couldn't budge the bar off of his chest. And this guy was bigger than a house! We went alphabetically by last name. I was sweating by my turn. Ole Miss could only do two. Nobody had told me there was a weightlifting test. I didn't have the chance to practice. Others were ticking off ten, fifteen reps. I giggled with Chris and Russell, "I'm not a lifter. I hope I can get at least ten."

When they finally got to "T" I ripped off seventeen. Russell did about the same. I was feeling pretty good. Then Chris got up there and did thirty-eight, thirty-nine—they had to stop him. We teased him that his arms were so short and his grip so wide that he was only raising the bar six inches each rep. "Yeah, if we had alligator arms like you, we could've done more, too." But he blew us out of the water, and we knew it.

Next, they ran us through a series of agility and speed drills. They had us sprinting and shuffling among cones spread out on the field. They timed us all in the forty-yard dash and the linemen in the twenty-yard dash. Running backs or wide receivers have to go faster longer; linemen need to be able to explode quickly in short bursts. They wanted to see how fast. All of the scouts in the stands timed us on their own stopwatches.

After the physicals, my knee was killing me. Usually offensive and defensive linemen run the forty in five-plus seconds. I ran it in 4.8.

That was my strength—the ability to put mind over matter. I looked at the drill we were about to do, and my mind was able to get my body to perform. I paid afterward with the pain. But I managed to hide my injury. I walked around without a limp and pretended my knee didn't hurt.

The NFL draft is a crapshoot where teams gamble the future and players trade on their hopes. Of course, no one can tell the future, but the draft pretends to decide it on both sides. Each team is assigned a pick for each of the twelve rounds. With twenty-seven teams in 1991, that meant 334 players would be drafted. Teams jockey for position with trades so they can be in line to select the top prospects that match their needs. The better they do, the brighter their future. The lower a player goes, the lower his hopes. It's cutthroat and tense.

The guys who would be the top picks, the top ten or so, knew where they were going. Russell Maryland, for instance, was projected to go to the Dallas Cowboys as the first selection overall. Word was that I was one of the top defensive picks because the NFL scouts had ranked me one of the top nose guards in the country and I had a good Combine. I still didn't know what teams were serious about me. My agent, Ken Kramer, couldn't tell me where I would go nor when. I still feared nobody would take me.

The 1991 draft was April 21. I wasn't going to watch. I was cleaning the house I rented at OSU with Sai, tight end Phil Hammit, and Dean Bartolome, a friend from Hawaii, when some teammates came over with champagne, ready to celebrate. "You'll be taken," they said. "Don't worry." We flipped on ESPN.

Russell Maryland was the top pick. The Chicago Bears would take Chris Zorich in the second round, the forty-ninth pick overall. Nothing happened for me the first round. Bye-bye million dollar signing bonus.

After a commercial break midway through the second round, a woman announcer came back and said, "We have the first difficult name of the draft. Esera Tuolowalo from Oregon State University goes to the Green Bay Packers, the thirty-fifth pick overall."

That made me the highest defensive player draft pick in the history of OSU. It surprised a lot of people, including me. Sai popped the champagne. I called my mom. She cried happy and excited tears. Ken Kramer called. He told me to get off the phone. "The Packers are going to be calling you," he said.

Sure enough, Lindy Infante, the Packers head coach, called. He welcomed me to the Packers. "Know where Green Bay is?" he asked.

"Yes," I lied.

I didn't even know Green Bay was in Wisconsin. My world ended at Vegas. I'd never spent time past there other than quick trips for games. I had no idea about the Packers' history and tradition. That's how big a football fan I was—or wasn't.

The emotions started to flow in my celebration with my friends. My dream to play in the NFL—which had started to take shape when I won the Morris Trophy but then seemed lost after my injury—was coming true. I'd been drafted. My friends told me, "Second round is high. You're going to make a lot of money." They said, "You're going to be playing for a great team, the Packers." The excitement intensified.

My brothers in Hawaii and friends in California called, "Your name and picture just flashed across the TV screen." I realized my name was going to be in the papers and that the Hawaiian media especially was going to be all over me.

That night, I had an anxiety attack in bed. I couldn't catch my breath. I'd never told the guys I met at Hula's my real name, but now they would see it on TV and in the papers with my picture. The draft publicity blew my cover. I knew all somebody had to do was make one phone call, "Congratulations, Green Bay, you just drafted a gay guy."

That's what I expected to be in the papers the next day. I lay there remembering guys I slept with, wondering which one was going to tell. Who would've been pissed off at me? Which one would want bragging rights for breaking the story?

In the morning, I rushed to grab the paper before anyone else could. I saw myself, but it was only news of the draft. Nobody had outed me.

The whole week after the draft was like that. I thought, *Oh, shit, I could lose all of this, it could all just go away in a flash.* That paranoia never left me.

# CHAPTER SEVEN

⁓

# Lombardi's House

**A** **FEW DAYS AFTER THE DRAFT,** the Packers flew me to Green Bay for a press conference along with their first- and third-round draft picks. I had done my homework and learned about Vince Lombardi, the Packers' championships, the fabled "Ice Bowl," the litany of Hall of Fame players who'd worn the green and gold, and the world-famous Packer fans. The more I learned, the more impressed I was that Green Bay had drafted me and the more excited I became to be part of the great Packer tradition.

One of the Do Boys (as in Do this, Do that for the players) picked us up from the airport and brought us to the Packers' facility at Lambeau Field. Like we were celebrities, we were introduced to everybody from Head Coach Lindy Infante to the trainer. In the locker room, the green and gold walls and green carpet oozed Packer pride. I gazed at the stalls with the equipment neatly arranged and the rows of clean, shiny, yellow helmets. I spotted names I recognized: Sterling Sharpe, the All-Pro wide receiver; Brian Noble, linebacker and defensive captain; Don Majkowski, quarterback, nicknamed "Majik Man" for the last-second touchdown pass he threw to Sharpe that beat the Chicago Bears in 1989 once an instant replay review ruled Majkowski had not crossed the line of scrimmage as initially flagged.

They showed me to my stall, with my own nameplate, shiny yellow helmet, and green jersey—the number 98 and my name on the back.

I was never one of those guys with the attitude, *I'm better than you.* I had always downplayed myself. Maybe that was due to the insecurity of growing up gay. I had never been embraced by anyone other than my mom. I was overwhelmed to be welcomed onto this team. I stood there with the other top draft choices, and I couldn't believe this was happening to me.

The reporters asked questions, but I didn't know what to say. That was unusual for me. A lot of people think I'm really comfortable in crowds. I'm not. There's just something that pushes me forward in public situations. It's easier for me when I'm the center of attention, the one receiving praise. That day, though, I was nervous. *They're putting so much trust in me. Am I good enough to do this?*

When training camp started in July, my agent, Ken Kramer, still hadn't come to terms with the Packers. He wanted to wait until the other second rounders signed, so he could ask for a comparable amount. I waited out the negotiations in the Green Bay Holiday Inn, ready to report once Ken worked out the deal.

I wasn't sure how much money they were talking about for a signing bonus, whether it was hundreds or thousands. Every time

I talked to Ken, I was too timid to ask specifics. Coming from not having any money and going into uncharted territory, I figured it was best to let Ken take care of business. He was a professional. He worked for Tom Condon, the highly respected president of IMG's football division, and Brady Hoke endorsed him. I saw everyone older as someone I was to respect, including my agent, my financial manager—everyone. I was raised not to question their authority. I knew they worked for me, but I still saw them as my elders. Also, I didn't want to piss them off. If they left, how would I do this myself?

After I had missed the first week of training camp, Ken finally worked out a deal for me to receive a $300,000 signing bonus. That's not a lot compared to what guys sign for today, but at the time it was great, probably more than any other second rounder signed for. The amount blew me away. That was more money than I could imagine. Once I realized that the money would be there for me, it made me feel good to know that I would be able to help my mom. My dream was coming true.

I reported to Saint Norbert, the small Catholic college campus outside Green Bay where the Packers held training camp, at dinnertime. I signed the papers in the general manager's office, then headed to the cafeteria. I didn't know the tradition that all of the rookies had to sing a song before they ate until Don Davey, the third-round pick, told me, "They're going to make you sing."

"I'm not going to sing," I said. "Did you?"

"Yeah." He had sung his alma mater's fight song. "It was horrible."

No one there knew I could sing. I sat down with my tray.

The veterans started calling off the rookies' names. Vinnie Clark, the number one pick, sang. Then they called the next guy. "No," he protested. "Number Two just got here. Make him sing."

"No, I'm not going to." I was playing them.

Sterling Sharpe pointed his finger at me. "Get your ass up there, or you're not going to eat."

The other players started pounding the tables and chanting, "Second Round! Second Round!" They couldn't pronounce my name.

I stood up and admitted, "I don't know my fight song." We were so horrible at OSU that we heard every other team's fight song after they scored, but we rarely heard ours. I had memorized theirs but not my own.

"Sing anything!" the veterans shouted.

So I sang a Luther Vandross gospel version of "Mary Had a Little Lamb."

That busted up everybody. They were rolling on the floor. "That guy can *sing!*" they exclaimed.

Every night after that, the veterans made me sing. I had to go to McDonald's for dinner with the other rookies who didn't want to sing because I ran out of songs. When I walked past other players' rooms and they were talking to their wives or girlfriends, they called out, "Hey, Es, come in here. Sing my girl a song." I thought it was cool to be serenading their girls over the phone.

Other times, Don Majkowski invited me into his room. I sang while he played guitar. Music brought me acceptance.

The atmosphere was not so friendly on the field, where we competed for one another's jobs.

The Packers' systems weren't hard for me to learn. I never had trouble learning defenses. Maybe because of my street smarts, they came easy to me. I also paid attention during meetings and studied in my room. I knew this was a huge opportunity for me.

The practices, on the other hand, were intense. Twice a day, morning and afternoon, full pads in the Wisconsin heat and humidity. Guys tried to rip your head off. We woke early to be on the field by 7:30 or 8:00 a.m. We drilled, ran plays, and scrimmaged. We ate lunch after morning practice and headed back to our rooms for a nap, but it seemed like we only had ten minutes to fall asleep before we had to go back for the afternoon practice. My knee held up fine, but the rest of my body was exhausted.

Ken had warned me that the other players might not be helpful. It didn't help that I showed up late and had to play catch-up with the other rookies who had already been there a week. I tried asking Bob Nelson, the starting nose guard, questions. He grunted terse replies. He knew I had been drafted high, which meant management considered me the future.

First- and second-round choices are expected to make the team, but there is no guarantee. I felt the need to prove myself. This was higher ground, the National Football League. I was astonished that these guys were such amazing athletes. Not only was a guy six foot, seven inches, and three hundred fifty pounds—he could run as fast as I could. This was definitely a big step up from college.

I knew training camp was the time to prove that I belonged on the team. There would be no second chance after that. I tried my hardest in drills, gave 110 percent. The fire in my belly had gotten me drafted. I wanted to let the coaches see it.

My thing in college was to show up on film. When the coach showed the game film, I wanted to be in it. Even if I was not making the tackle, I wanted to run into the frame so the coach would note, *This guy hustles*. That's how I approached drills in training camp.

Some of the veterans gave me shit for going full speed on everything. They said, "Slow down. You've got the job."

I was caught between pleasing the coaches or the players. The coaches yelled at us to go hard. The veterans didn't want me to make them look bad. Some of them didn't want me to look good. They played head games. They would say, "Good job, you're amazing," or "You suck." I was never certain I could believe either. Not only do rookies get beaten up physically, they take an emotional beating, too.

In college, you can tell who's The Man. The starters are usually clearly defined. Not so in the pros. Except for the All-Pros, everybody's job is on the line at training camp. In drills and the preseason games, I was always behind Bob Nelson, last season's starting nose guard. That didn't surprise me. Back then, it was rare for a rookie to start at any position, especially one as critical as nose guard, the pillar of the defensive line. It's such a huge jump from college to the pros, teams worried that players wouldn't be able to adjust because they lacked professional experience or were not mentally ready. Teams took their time developing a player. Free agency changed all that.

When I broke into the league, free agency was just taking off. Teams carried more veterans. Now, teams are younger. Management puts its money on the big players. If a player leads the league in sacks, touchdowns, or yardage, all the money goes to him. With the salary caps, the team can't afford to pay too many others big money. Teams have to play guys with less experience.

Free agency has made things better for players. In the NFL, you have to go where the money is. You have to get what's yours while you can. A lot of people get angry with players for leaving teams, but they don't understand that this is our livelihood. For many guys, it's the only way they can make money. You can't blame a player for trying to get more for himself and his family.

My confidence soared one day during practice. I ran a stunt with the defensive end. He slanted in, and I came around him, right at offensive tackle Tony Mandarich. He had been the highly-publicized second overall draft pick in 1989. I had read about him in *Sports Illustrated* and watched him on ESPN. He was huge and muscular—intimidating. I came around on the stunt and caught Mandarich off balance. I bull rushed right over him. I couldn't believe that I had just taken down the mighty Tony Mandarich. It was a great feeling.

It's natural for the veterans to give rookies crap. That's part of pro football's pecking order. Robert Brown, one of the elder defensive linemen, shielded me from that. He was a big black man, the nicest guy. He would say, "Don't worry about them. You'll be taking their job."

One day, I didn't have a ride back to the dorm after practice, so I was walking there with another rookie. Robert pulled up, and we hopped in. The other rookie tried to break into Robert's conversation with the star outside linebacker in the front seat. Finally, Robert turned around and said, "Hey, shut up. Be more like Esera—he's just sittin' there chillin.'"

After that, Robert invited me to sit with the veteran defensive linemen for meals. I felt the heat of Nelson's dirty looks. I could get along with anybody, but this guy wouldn't give me a chance. I understood he resented me as a high-draft-pick rookie out to take his job. Once Robert took me under his wing, nobody talked bad to me. When the veterans barked at me to get them a drink, Robert yelled back, "Get your own fuckin' water. Esera, sit down."

—————

I've heard that in baseball, when you come in from practice and find a note in your locker telling you to go see the coach, you know that the team has let you go. Football isn't that delicate. My rookie year, one of the Packers' assistant coaches, a short, cocky guy, walked up behind you in the locker room and tapped you on the shoulder. Or, worse, he shouted from across the room, "Hey, So-and-so, can I talk to you?" He called the name out loud. Showed no respect. You don't do that. Everybody knows the guy's going to get cut. That coach was cold.

Sometimes, he showed more discretion with the older guys who had been with the team for a while. He caught them alone after the other players had cleared out. You would go into the team meeting and see the chair of the person who usually sat next to you empty. You looked around to see what happened, and somebody made a slashing motion across his throat. The guy had been cut.

It's sad because a player works so hard only to find himself suddenly without a job. Many of them have families to support but no way to earn a living outside football. You feel sorry for the guy. Maybe you've become friends. Suddenly, he's no longer part of the team. It's awkward. You say something like, "Hey, you'll get picked up."

I remember my first cut day. The day after our first preseason game, I walked into the locker room, and it was like a morgue. Everybody was quiet. The rookies and free agents felt the anxiety most acutely. We stood the most risk. You could taste the tension.

When the cocky assistant coach walked in, it was like we'd all seen the Grim Reaper. We tried to become invisible.

One of the vets—pretending to be the cutting coach—put his hand to his mouth and boomed, "Esera Tuaolo, may I see you in my office?"

Even though guys told me, "Don't worry, you're a second rounder, you're not going anywhere," I worried. What if I fucked up in a game? Would I be gone, like that? I played the numbers game in my head, *Okay, they'll keep six linemen.* I sized myself up against the others there. *Am I one of the top six?* I felt that tension every cut day.

Robert Brown tried to reassure me. "You think they'll give you $300,000, then let you go?" he said. "No, they want to get their money's worth."

I wasn't convinced. I had to prove that I was worth that money.

The head coach breaks training camp after the third preseason game. The week before the final preseason game, the team practices just once a day. Players leave the college campus. I returned to the Holiday Inn. I didn't want to rent an apartment yet. I'd heard about guys signing a lease, then getting cut and being stuck with six months of rent. At least with a hotel room, the organization picked up the tab.

During training camp, I hadn't worried about anybody discovering my secret. I thought, *I'm thousands of miles from Honolulu. No one is going to recognize me.* I obsessed about making the team.

By the time of the final cut, I was pretty sure I would be on the opening-day roster but not play. I had accepted my role as a backup Packer. I felt confident enough to rent a duplex.

The day after our last preseason game, Don Davey, the third-round draft pick from the University of Wisconsin, walked up in the locker room and congratulated me. "For what?" I asked.

"They let Nelson go ," he said.

"You're shittin' me."

They had just cut the first-string guy. That made me the starter. The torch had been passed to me. All the hard work and dedication—running sprints at 3:00 a.m., studying film, playing in pain—had paid off. I was grateful for all those who had helped me get there: Mr. Monger, my high school coach, Dave Kragthorpe, Brady Hoke, Mike Wauffle.

I walked into the defense room and felt everyone looking at me. I figured some of them were thinking, "Shit, we've got a rookie nose guard." The linebackers were probably thinking, "It's going to be a long year." I took a deep breath.

Predictably, as usually happened with me, the panic kicked in. Being a starter was a huge responsibility. The next game was the first of the season. It didn't take a week before, Greg Blache, the defensive line coach, lit into me. "Rookie, get your ass up," he yelled during drills. He wanted me to be ready. He cared about me and wanted me to do well. He had me watch extra film to get an edge. We faced the Philadelphia Eagles and their unsackable quarterback, Randall Cunningham, the Michael Vick of that era.

I couldn't sleep Saturday night. That's why coaches always tell players to get a good night's sleep on Friday (or Thursday, in college), because they know you won't sleep the night before a game. Sunday morning, I got up at 4:00 a.m., made coffee, and paced the house, going over plays in my head. It seemed like an eternity until it was time to go to the stadium.

I drove myself. It was weird. I heard voices, like Vince Lombardi had crawled inside my head. I heard him preaching, giving me a pep talk. I don't know if I was hallucinating because I was so nervous or what. At the same time, I also had my composure, coming from this great feeling. *Wow, I've made it, I'm going to play.* I hadn't thought I would because once the season starts, second-string players rarely see action. Coaches want their starters in the game.

I had walked into the Packer locker room many times, but that Sunday, game day, I walked in for the first time as a starter. I could see in the other guys' eyes, *This is important, everything counts now.* Everybody was getting dressed. Some guys screamed to get themselves up. I was part of that. I was going to play.

Along came Don Davey, who had made the team as a backup defensive end. "You nervous?"

"Fucking right, I'm nervous."

After I got my ankles taped, I walked outside in my yellow pants and a Packers T-shirt to test the turf. A lot of guys do that to make sure they're wearing the right shoes. I was amazed to see the stadium packed. Packer fans are the number one fans in the league. They show up three hours before the game. When they spotted us on the field, they began to cheer and ask for our autographs. By then the newspapers had reported that I was the starting nose guard. That made me a sudden celebrity. The fans knew who I was. Kids asked me to sign my rookie card. It was magical. I felt I could fly.

I flew out on the field with the starting defense. During the coin toss, the national anthem, the opening kickoff, my heart pounded. It took the first hit, contact with the opposing team, to relax me.

Whoever was playing center for the Eagles drove me nuts. After every play, he said something like, "Nice hit, man," or "Great spin move." I couldn't tell if he meant it. I suspected he was mocking me. But I finished the game with five tackles (three solo) and a quarterback sack.

Everything changed in the third quarter. We ran a stunt. I came around the end and saw him, Randall Cunningham. I thought, *I'm going to get my steak dinner.* Greg Blache promised his defensive line a steak dinner for every quarterback sack. I tackled Cunningham and was celebrating with my sack dance—I used to cross my forearms, X marks the spot—when the public address man announced the play. I heard my name echo through the stadium, and I freaked out. I knew all eyes were on me. *One pair of those eyes might be somebody I slept with.* It was stupid because I hadn't slept with anyone in Green Bay, but I wasn't thinking right. I couldn't breathe. I froze. I don't know how I even got back to the huddle.

We lost the game. I drove home and tanked down on a bottle of tequila to ease the anxiety. Later, I met the other players for drinks at McSwiggin's, the team's hangout. After drinking enough, I was able to calm myself with the thought that I was too far from Hawaii for anybody to recognize me. I told myself, *Nobody's going to know.* I wanted to believe that.

After that game, I understood the magnitude of the NFL. I had looked up from the sidelines and seen the names of former Packer greats emblazoned on the stadium walls. Bart Starr, Paul Hornung, Herb Adderly, Willie Davis, Henry Jordan, etc. This was their field. Lombardi's house. Now, I was part of that—a starter on opening day in the storied history of the Packers. Playing before the greatest fans on earth.

It hit me just how huge the NFL was. This was the number one form of entertainment in the world. I was in the National Football League—for better or worse.

# CHAPTER EIGHT

# A Samoan in Green Bay

I EXPERIENCED SEVERE CULTURE SHOCK in Green Bay. The NFL made me think of metropolises such as Los Angeles, Chicago, and New York. I flew to Green Bay on a propeller plane that landed in a tiny airport among cornfields for that first press conference and thought, *How can a pro team be in such a small town?*

In 1990, Green Bay had a population of fewer than one hundred thousand residents; over 90 percent of them were white. I thought Oregon State, where there were not a lot of Polynesians, was a culture shock, but going to Green Bay was like going to Siberia.

I came from a small island where everybody looked the same. The white people of Green Bay talked differently, they walked differently, they dressed differently. I missed home. I missed not being able to see Polynesian people, to speak Samoan, and to eat our food.

Since Green Bay was a small town, most people there had never seen a Samoan. They didn't know how to categorize me. They thought maybe I was a big Mexican.

The isolation of being a Samoan in Green Bay seemed mild, however, compared to the isolation of being a gay man in the NFL.

Don Davey, the third-round draft pick, was from Manitowoc, a small Wisconsin town about thirty-five miles southwest of Green Bay. He had always wanted to play for the Packers. When they drafted me second, he was pissed at me because he didn't think they would draft another defensive lineman in the next round. I was happy they did. We became good friends.

I made the mistake of teaching Don slang in Samoan. My nickname for him was "Fufu," which means jack-off. So, he called me that, too. If I made a good play, he would chant when I ran off the field, "Hey, Fufu! Hey, Fufu!" That proved embarrassing when Sai or other Polynesians visited.

Don, in turn, showed me the ropes of Wisconsin. He came from a close, happy-go-lucky family. They knew how to party. When they visited, they took us to the loser bars, where no one else went. Don and his family taught me the Wisconsin dances, such as the sprinkler, the lawn mower, and the supermarket. My favorite was the bobsled. We stood in a tight line on the dance floor and started running in place. Suddenly, we dropped to the floor on our buns and leaned left and right to the beat of the music, like we were in a bobsled hitting the curves. I thought that was hilarious.

My daddy, Mike Tuaolo.

Daddy building our family's Samoan hut outside of Waimanalo.

Me, age two and a half.

The Samoan hut where we lived before we built the house. This is where my Aunt Sina was shot.

# 1990 OREGON STATE FOOTBALL

THE YEAR OF THE
Killer BEAVS

| SEPTEMBER | |
|---|---|
| 1 MONTANA | 6 PM |
| 8 at Kansas | 11 AM |
| 15 UNLV | 6 PM |
| 22 at Stanford | 1 PM |
| 29 at Nebraska | 11:30 AM |

Killer Beavers—the promotional poster that freaked me out when I returned to OSU for my senior season.

Baby Fridge—me running the ba senior year at Don Lugo High.

Taking down the Stanford quarterback in our first game my junior season when Brady Hoke's new formation led me to being named Pac-10 Conference Defensive Player of the week. (Courtesy of Mike Shield)

Tackling Barry Sanders my rookie season.

Proud to be a Packer. (Rookie Season, 1991)

In the trenches versus the Miami Dolphins my rookie season.

Mama and me, at Joe's Stone Crab in
Miami Beach during Super Bowl week, 1999

My brother Tua hangin' loose.
Note the tattoo from his belly to
below his knees.

Praying with the team in the Vikings locker room after a game during the 1993 season. A Vikings executive whose name I've forgotten, me, head coach Denny Green, backup quarterback Brad Johnson (left to right).

Mitchell and me in my Jacksonville condo on our first Christmas together.

Singing the National Anthem before a game with the Atlanta Falcons during the 1998 season.

Hanging out with my buddy Brett Favre
at Makapu'u Lookout Point on the island of Oahu.

With my Tongan buddy, Sai Poulivati,
at the house of Mitchell's parents
during the party Shelley threw
for my Atlanta teammates.

With Billy Bean at the GLAAD awards
in Los Angeles.

Meeting David Kopay (center) at his house.
On the right is Howard Bragman, a friend of
David's and the greatest publicist in the world.

Mitchell eating his first birthday cupcake.

Michele and me, on her first birthday.

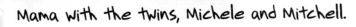

Mama with the twins, Michele and Mitchell.

Mitchell's parents, Shelly and Dan, with the twins on a New Year's Cruise, welcoming 2003.

The twins' first Halloween. Big Daddy as Tigger and Little Daddy as Pooh.

My Family, Christmas 2004

People kept telling me after the draft about Green Bay's cold weather. The average high temperature in January is twenty-three degrees Fahrenheit; the average low is five degrees. That's climate shock for someone like me from the Hawaiian tropics.

I remember being introduced to the freezing temperatures in Green Bay on December 15, when we played the Detroit Lions. I walked into the locker room and found a pair of panty hose hanging in my stall. I looked around and expected guys to break out laughing at the joke. Instead, I saw that Joe Namath wasn't the only football player to wear panty hose. All of my teammates were pulling them on. "What's going on?" I asked.

Brian Noble, our defensive captain, explained to me that players wear panty hose because they're as warm as lycra tights but not as restrictive. As a football player, you don't want to feel constricted. The guys joked about wearing nylons and laughed. I left mine hanging. I think as a gay man I was afraid of doing anything that resembled dressing in drag.

I may have felt out of place as a Polynesian in Green Bay, but it's a great place to play football. Packer fans stuck by their team even during bad years. The Packers had finished the 1990 season 6–10, losing the last five games, but the fans still filled Lambeau Field for the early games my rookie year. I figured the cold would test their loyalty.

It was cold, with a wind-chill of something like minus forty degrees Fahrenheit. "Think they'll show?" I asked Robert Brown.

"Just wait," he said.

Sure enough, we trotted out for our pregame drills, and the stadium was packed. Guys bared chests painted green and gold. They are loyal, dedicated fans in Green Bay.

Fans like that took care of their players. We basically ate and drank for free in town. You could also get a lot more for your money. For example, I was able to trade my allotted four tickets to the Bears game for a Nissan Pathfinder to use during the season.

On the field, I experienced an incredible feeling summoning the crowd's cheers. Like the child of my earliest memory summoning the waves, all I had to do was raise my arms and the sea of green in the stands roared. I was a superhero all over again.

It was so cold that everybody moved about one mile per hour on the field, but the Detroit Lions' great running back Barry Sanders ran on the ice without a problem. He was incredible. I did manage to take him down in that game. I've got a picture of it. That was a big moment: I tackled the great Barry Sanders.

———

The rookie in the NFL must adjust to a lot, including the hierarchy, which affects even the smallest things, like the taping of ankles before practices and games. The trainers each had a chalkboard with their name on top. Players wrote down their numbers under the name of the trainer they wanted to tape their ankles. Rookies couldn't use the top trainers. All the players wanted to have the head trainer tape their ankles because he did the best job. Rookies had to sign up with the interns and risk having their ankles taped too tightly. Sometimes, I tried putting my name on the second trainer's board, but then a veteran would come by and bump me off the table. Once I established myself as a starter, I qualified for the head trainer's table.

Other teams didn't show me that respect. They played rough with the rookie starter. One game, early on, the center set me up, and the guard chopped me down at the knees. I landed on my ass. "Welcome to the NFL," they said.

There's a code among players that you respect one another. Not everybody abides by that code all of the time. The league has cracked down on the rough play, but when I came into the game at the beginning of the nineties, there was a lot of dirty stuff going on. I played against dirty offensive linemen who spat, poked their fingers through my facemask, and punched me at the bottom of a pileup. Some guys in the league are just dirty players. They have reputations as cheap-shot artists. When somebody plays outside of the code, people get hurt.

Most of the time, the dirty stuff ends pretty quickly because a guy will tell his other defensive linemen and they'll gang up on the dirty guy. My rookie year, an opposing offensive lineman tried to take out the knees of one of our defensive linemen. When we came off the field, our coach was steaming. "I want that fucking guy out of the game!" he screamed. "I want you to take out his fucking knees."

*Whoa,* I thought. *That's serious.* That was the first time I realized how tight-knit we had to be as pros. We looked out for one another.

Then the coach said, "Esera, you hit him." Another guy was going to hold him up, and I was to take out his knees.

I was scared. I didn't want to hurt another guy's knees. That can end a career. I remember thinking, *Should I do this?*

The defense returned to the field. Back on the line, the offensive guy was talking trash. I thought, *Okay, if you're not going to stop, I'll do it.*

You might think that kind of play would be obvious to the officials, but it's not. There's a lot of acting that goes into taking out a guy. It's easy to fall on another guy or have one of your guys grab you and push you into an opponent to make it look like he did it.

My teammate stood him up, and I dived for the knees. I didn't hurt him, but he got the message, "You cheap-shot us, we'll go after you." Instantly, his dirty play stopped because he knew, easy as one-two-three, we would take him out.

There are always those guys that think they're tougher than the world, but a knee injury makes them realize they're just as vulnerable as anybody else.

Football is a man's sport. Walk into an NFL locker room, and you can feel the energy. Testosterone seethes from each player. The good old boys reign. These strong, young, virile men earn their living by smashing into and overpowering one another. The effects of this testosterone-crazed culture often play out sexually.

The locker room banter is prevalent and graphic. Guys brag about a girl they just "fucked." Married men boast about the girl they just "plowed." I couldn't believe the way these guys talked about women. Being a gay man, it wasn't my style. It was hard to hear that negativity toward women. When somebody degraded a woman, I'd think about my mom, or wonder, *Don't they realize they're talking about somebody's daughter?*

Homophobia peppered the banter. They called each other "fags," "fucking queers," "fudgepackers"—they took it to the crude and graphic limits. I laughed at the gay jokes to be part of the conversation. I hid behind my laughter. Inside, I cried.

No one hassled me as someone who might be gay. I wasn't a pretty boy quarterback or running back. I was one of the big guys in the trenches. I fit the image of the defensive lineman. No players came on to me or gave me suggestive looks, either. No one would expect me to be gay and approach me. Also, I never gave off signals that I was gay. And I never pursued sex with other men, except when I went back to Hawaii. At work, I managed to hide behind the macho image of the defensive lineman.

It's not like every single day I heard "faggot-this, queer-that," but every day, I walked into the fear. The fear that if I slipped up, said the wrong thing, looked at another naked player too long, got an erection in the shower, I'd get outed—and then they would hurt me. I feared somebody would take me out, go for my knees, simply because I was gay.

My Packer teammate Sterling Sharpe, an All-Pro receiver, confirmed this in an interview on HBO's *Real Sports with Bryant Gumbel* when I came out. He said if the guys found out another player was gay on a Monday, he wouldn't be able to play on Sunday. My teammates would take me out in practice. That would be the punishment for violating the NFL's macho code. A gay player would be "outcast for life," Sharpe said, because he would cast suspicion upon other players. "Question my heart, question my ability, but do not question my machoism," Sharpe said, summarizing the attitude that prevailed among the league's players. The tight-knit devotion to the macho code superseded their devotion to a teammate.

～

Sex was easy for the straight guys to find. Women threw themselves at the players wherever we went. In the hotels where we stayed on the road, women wearing cocktail dresses hung out in the lounges. The single and married guys took them up to their rooms. Not every married player cheated on his wife, but far more of them than I expected indulged in the macho world's infidelity. It seemed every guy wanted to prove he was a stud.

After our Monday meetings—the team met together the day after a game to watch film and rehash our play, the way we did in college—all of the players went to Red Lobster for dinner, drinks, and bullshit. After dinner, the married guys went home and the single guys moved on to McSwiggin's, where we drank more and danced.

One Monday night at McSwiggin's, a woman approached me, said she was from out of town—the oldest story in the book—and I fell for it. I figured I would take her home for show. If the other guys saw me with a woman, they wouldn't think I was gay. It would be safer with a woman from out of town. I took her home and slept with her. I didn't even remember her name.

The next day at practice, Clarence Weathers, one of the veteran receivers, said, "Hey, Esera, I saw you leave with Sasha (or whatever her name was)."

"How'd you know?" I asked.

"That woman has been with everybody," he said.

Here I thought I'd found this sweet, innocent girl who had come to visit her mom. Little did I know she had slept with half of the team. I was the innocent one. But the other players noticed, so it worked.

It must be hard for the straight guy. You don't know who you can trust. A lot of the women are looking for somebody to get them pregnant, or to be able to brag that they slept with an NFL player.

The FBI came in during training camp to brief players. The agents warned us about rape. They said some of these girls, all they are looking for is a quick ride. In a way, I can sympathize with Kobe Bryant. Having seen the way some women throw themselves at professional athletes, I can see how someone would see he was a star and go after his money. Rape is never a good thing, of course, if that's the way it happened. I'm just saying I can see how the woman would claim that even if it didn't happen.

The FBI agents also warned us about the Beauty Queen Bandit. He made the rounds of NFL teams claiming to represent beauty queens. The Bandit showed players pictures of beautiful women and offered to set the players up with them. He would go up to a guy's room with a woman, then slip a drug in the his drink so the player would pass out. The Bandit would then take photographs of the unconscious players with naked men. He blackmailed the players with those photos.

Hearing stuff about betrayal and blackmail fueled my fear. What if someone recognized me? How much money would he ask me for? The FBI agents said, "If this sort of thing ever happens to you, call this number." Right. I'm going to call and say, "Yeah, I slept with this guy, and he might have photos."

I was too scared to sleep with any men in Green Bay or the other cities where we played. I had hooked up with several gay friends who knew who I was, and I feared them too. I had trusted that they wouldn't say anything about me. But I never knew who might come out and say something. I lived in fear of someone finding out.

From the time I heard my name echo over Lambeau Field after my first sack, I had many nights I couldn't sleep. Tons of people watched us in Green Bay, even at practice. I had this fear of walking out to practice and seeing one of those guys waiting to ambush me. During practices and games, I looked out at the crowd and saw the faces of guys I slept with. They pointed at me. I would do a double take, and it wasn't them. The fear played tricks on my mind.

I didn't play professional football for love of the game. Sure, I enjoyed football. I also enjoyed playing in the NFL. It was fun.

Don't get me wrong, how can you not have fun being in the NFL? It's just that I battled with demons. I played for the money and the wonderful things I was able to do with that money, like fix up the old family house for my mom. I knew without football, I would go back to nothing. That's why I stuck with the NFL as long as I could.

It was weird to come from nothing and suddenly have a lot. I would look around my house at the stuff I'd bought—the furniture, the television, the stereo—and think, *This is all mine.* It didn't sink in. I kept thinking either I would wake up from a dream and all my stuff would be gone or someone would come to take it all away.

One of the best moments of my rookie year happened when my mom came to visit me. I took her shopping at an upscale department store. It was a great feeling to know that I could buy her anything in there that she wanted. I spotted the jewelry counter and offered to buy her a nice diamond. She was looking at prices, and I said, "No, Mama, get whatever you want." Before the NFL, maybe I would've gone to the Salvation Army to buy her something. I never could have afforded anything in an expensive jewelry department.

She picked out a beautiful ring. Not the most expensive one, but a very nice one. The clerk took it out. Mama slipped it on her finger. She started crying. I started crying. My father had never given her a wedding ring.

Seeing the look on her face—that's when I knew I could do it. I could put up with all the shit of being a gay man in the NFL. It was a fantastic feeling to know that when Mama asked for money, I could give it to her. One of the best feelings in the world was to be able to give back to my mom after all she had done for me and our family, especially the way she stepped up after Daddy died. She did a great job raising us kids.

The money's not guaranteed in the NFL. You get paid only so long as you can perform. If you don't perform, they'll cut you and bring in someone else. In college, you might have a bad game, but you remain the starter. In the pros, there are ten guys waiting to take your spot. The locker room had a revolving door. Soon as you heard one guy was gone, you would see his replacement there. Every player felt the pressure to perform.

Those days, there was not a lot of protection for players. There were no repercussions for letting players go. No one questioned the team's decision. Nowadays, the NFL Players Association will demand justification. When the Dallas Cowboys cut Quincy Carter, their starting quarterback the previous year, during the first week of training camp in 2004, the NFLPA stepped in, suspecting racism because Quincy is African American. Reading stuff like that in the papers makes me think times have changed.

My rookie year, Green Bay had become a place of employment. This was a job I wanted to keep. If I didn't perform, I would go home. The stress caused more sleepless nights.

I felt extra pressure when I took over the starting nose guard position. I knew some of the veterans questioned the decision to put a rookie at a core position in the middle of the defense. The message some of them sent was, "You better pull your weight." That wasn't easy for any rookie, let alone a two-hundred-ninety-pound rookie like me. I felt the pressure to play well every single week.

During a routine weightlifting session before one midseason game, I dropped four hundred pounds on my chest. Whoever was spotting me helped me raise the bar off the stand, but he lifted it too high. The bar slipped out of my hands and crashed onto my chest and bruised my sternum. It bounced up, and I managed to slide my arms up to fend it off. The pain was excruciating, but I pretended it wasn't. I could barely breathe with my pads on, but I played the game.

I didn't want to miss a game and give another guy an opportunity. You're happy to see another guy do well but not your replacement. I know it's this way for every player. There's a little thing inside that hopes your replacement doesn't do well. That's why a lot of players play hurt. They don't want to lose their job.

The type of performance I gave on Sunday set the mood for the following week. If I had a good game, the following week went fast. If I had a horrible game, it was a long-ass week. Not only would I hear it from the coaches, I could feel it from the other players judging my every move. I had to prove myself all week long. I feared the team would cut me if I had another bad game.

Going from college to pro ball, the main adjustment a player has to make is mental. I had to decide as a young player, *Would I fold or go for it?* You must have strength and speed, but you also need determination. That's mental. I had to remember what got me to the Packers: the ability to play through pain and the fire in my belly. I had to draw on those mental strengths to keep going.

Still, the stress is unbelievable. Not only do professional football players take a physical pounding, the mental stress—the anxiety, worries, fear—takes its toll. It ages a man. They say you can add ten years to the life of an NFL football player. If you're thirty-five, it's like you're really forty-five. It wasn't just what I went through as a gay man; it's what all players experience, the job insecurity. A lot of players don't have anything else they can do. The majority of players don't come from wealthy families. If they get cut, they go home to nothing.

Once it's over, there's often nothing left. More than a quarter of 1,425 former NFL players surveyed by *Newsday* said they experienced financial problems in their first year out of football. They had made bad investments or hadn't invested at all. They had nothing to fall back on when their career ended.

The average NFL career lasts three years. Three years! What do you do after that? How many players do you see earning a living in football as announcers or coaches after their playing days are over? Very few, other than the Joe Montanas and Troy Aikmans.

You watch celebrity movies like *Mommy Dearest.* Joan Crawford was a famous actress winning awards, but when the band stopped playing, she had nothing left. She sank into anxiety, depression, pills, and alcohol. It's a vicious spiral down unless you have something else. Professional football players face the same thing.

That's why the life expectancy of the NFL player is so short. Look at Reggie White, the Packers' future Hall of Fame defensive end, who died suddenly in January 2005. He had just turned forty-three. Don't tell me that his death had nothing to do with playing fifteen years in the NFL.

A lot of players suffer from depression once their careers end. The suicide rate for former NFL players is higher than that of the general population. It's also higher for football players than other former athletes. Since 1980, seven former NFL players have committed suicide, higher than the number for the other three major sports combined during the same period, according to *Newsday.*

Growing up, I lived in a world that considered homosexuality an abomination. People thought that we were all drag queens sleeping with anybody. Guys beat up other kids for calling them "sissies." Now, there are more positive images out there for gay, lesbian, bisexual, and transgender youth. We've taken baby steps forward.

But we still have a long ways to go. We still need to feel more comfortable. For instance, a person can still lose his or her job because of sexual orientation. You can't fire someone because of her race or gender, but it happens because of orientation. I sure felt that when we were playing. One accidental slip that let out my true identity, and I was gone.

⁓

Alcohol and drugs eased the stress.

The heavy drinking started in my rookie year. I hung out with Don Davey, my fellow rookie defensive lineman, and some of the other players, but I was not a close friend with anybody. I pounded shots of Jack Daniels and tequila with teammates at McSwiggin's or went out with Robert Brown, the veteran who had taken me under his wing during training camp. Even though Robert was married, he still went to the nightclubs. Mostly, I kept to myself. Some nights I drank until I passed out.

Sometimes I took shots of tequila before games to calm my nerves, but I never showed up drunk. We had a star linebacker who came to play one Sunday all fucked up on alcohol. It was his birthday. He had started celebrating. He went into the game, sacked the quarterback a couple of times, then sat down on the bench and fell asleep. The coaches didn't say anything. He was a superstar.

I smoked pot, too. Marijuana is so common in Hawaii—it's a part of life—you grow up thinking it's not a drug. In college, there were times I couldn't afford pot, but I always had some my rookie year. Friends cultivated marijuana fields on the government land in the hills above our banana farm. They would give me pot when I came back to Hawaii. I snuck it back on the plane in shrink-wrapped plastic bags. I smoked joints after games—sometimes with teammates, but mostly alone—to relax and take off the edge.

Painkillers helped, too. The trainers gave them out like candy. It was easy to fake an injury. I would tell the trainer or doctor that something—my shoulder, my leg, whatever—hurt, and they would give me Vicodin or Percocet. They took care of their players.

When people ask me what I miss about playing in the NFL, I obviously miss the money, but I also miss the way teams take care of players. Anything you needed was at your disposal. If you needed something to get rid of a cold, it was there. If you needed something to ease the pain of an injury, it was there. If you needed a cortisone shot, it was there. Now teams are more cautious. For example, you must document a specific medical reason for cortisone shots. As players have gotten busted or addicted to drugs, the league has cracked down.

I can understand how easily someone like Brett Favre, the Packers' superstar quarterback, could become addicted when the pain pills were so easily available. Of course, the more famous you are, the more people take care of you. Whether you're the CEO or the superstar quarterback, people want to please you. They'll give you anything you want.

I don't think you can fault anybody for it. The doctors and trainers are part of the system. At the time, players did need pain pills. The doctors and trainers intended to help—it's just the stuff they handed out was addictive. Now, the question for them when a guy is injured or had surgery is do they have the best interest of the player or of the organization in mind when deciding how fast they try to bring the player back to the field? Maybe the owners are putting pressure on the medical staff, but nobody knows how fast someone can heal. A lot of times, I think players are rushed back before they are ready.

I took home the pills they gave me and washed them down with a bottle of tequila.

I was in awe playing against great players that I'd read about in *Sports Illustrated* or watched on TV. I would look across the line and see quarterback Dan Marino of the Miami Dolphins or running back Emmitt Smith of the Dallas Cowboys, both eventual Hall of Famers. I had tremendous respect for them, but I was trying to kill them, too.

My first year, I just wanted to earn the respect of my teammates. I did gain their respect by not screwing up too much. By the middle of the season, the veterans started complimenting me on my play. My welcome-to-the-NFL moment occurred in a restaurant.

In keeping with Packer tradition, Don Davey and I, as rookies, had to take all of the veteran linemen to dinner. They were happy that we were second and third rounders because it meant larger signing bonuses and a nicer place for dinner. They told Don and me to meet them at one of Green Bay's fanciest steakhouses at 7:00 p.m. By that time, they had drained eleven bottles of Dom Perignon and the bill was already over a thousand dollars. They had arrived two hours earlier and started drinking martinis and doing shots of expensive tequila.

The veterans all ordered the biggest steak and lobster on the menu along with more drinks. The defensive linemen had invited the outside linebackers as well, making them honorary members of the defensive line for the evening. There were twelve guys, including Don and me. Don and I split the bill, which came to more than forty-seven hundred dollars, including tip. I couldn't believe it. But you know what? We could pay it. That was the crazy thing to me. I could afford it. That's when I felt, *Now it's true, this isn't a dream.*

Practical jokes are another Packer tradition. At Thanksgiving, the veterans told us rookies that the local Piggly Wiggly supermarket was giving away free turkeys to Packer players. Head Coach Lindy Infante told us at a team meeting that we would find a voucher in our lockers. All we had to do was present the voucher at Piggly Wiggly and we would receive our free turkeys.

My friend Sai from OSU was coming in for the weekend. I picked him up at the airport and stopped at the Piggly Wiggly on the way home. The veteran defensive linemen had asked me to pick up their turkeys for them. "Get me a big one," they all had said. "I want to be sure to have enough for my family to eat." I piled seven of the biggest turkeys I could find into my cart. I explained to Sai that the store was giving them away to Packers. Wasn't that great?

At the checkout, I handed the clerk my voucher. She studied it. "What's this?"

"I play for the Packers. Your store is giving us free turkeys."

She didn't know anything about it. I demanded to see the manager. He came over. I explained the promotion to him. He didn't know anything about it.

I was getting pissed. "Our head coach gave us these vouchers that say we'll get free turkeys here."

He looked at the paper and shook his head. "Must be some other store."

"Isn't that your name on the paper?!" I demanded.

I worried, *What will the veterans say if I fail to show up with their turkeys?* I yelled at the manager. I was ready to kick his ass. Sai grabbed my arm and tried to calm me down.

Suddenly, the manager started laughing. "You've been gagged," he said. "This happens every year."

He showed me the camera that had filmed the entire scene. It was right out of *Candid Camera*. I was dumbfounded.

At the next team meeting, we watched film of the rookies try-ing to collect their free turkeys at Piggly Wiggly. We had all fallen for the prank. Mine was "bleep, bleep, bleep." All the players laughed their asses off.

Once you make the team, there's still competition between the offense and the defense, like two rival gangs. You don't talk about it, but you know it's there. You never let a hog get the best of you in practice. That's taboo.

We called the offensive linemen "hogs" because those of us on defense considered them nonathletes. In actuality, they're great athletes to absorb all of those hits and move the way they do. They have great footwork, hands, and strength.

We had some crazy hogs at Green Bay, the last of the old-school guys. It wasn't unusual for one of them to take a dump in a defen-sive lineman's shoes or dip a rookie's clothes in water and throw them outside to freeze up stiff as boards.

One time, a bunch of guys were in this humongous whirlpool that held about twenty-five guys after practice when Mike Compton, our center, walked in reading the newspaper. He sat on the edge of the pool, naked, and started peeing into the water. Everybody jumped out, shouting at him. He kept reading like nothing had happened. He had done the same thing in the sauna on the rocks.

In October, we played the Chicago Bears in a Thursday night home game broadcast on TNT. Somebody in the network's promotions department asked me to sing the national anthem. My first question was, "Where will it be televised?"

Only on the Lambeau Field monitors, they said. The national anthem wouldn't be part of the nationwide cable television broadcast. I asked my coaches and the players. They didn't have a problem with it, so I agreed.

I stood out on the fifty-yard line in my pads. I was in awe to see the Bears' future Hall of Fame linebacker Mike Singletary standing on the other side. He was one of the players whose career I had followed. He stood at attention to listen to me. When I hit the high part on "land of the free," the crowd of 58,435 people went crazy. I had sung when I was in college, but this was much, much bigger.

I think I'm the answer to a trivia question, "Who's the first player to sing the national anthem and then start a National Football League game?" We lost the game, but it was incredible to see Mike Singletary lined up there, to sing the national anthem, and then to start.

I went to McSwiggin's with my teammates afterward. When I arrived home, my answering machine was filled with messages. Friends and family members had called to tell me, "We saw you singing on TV!" Obviously, it had aired nationwide. The fear hit.

With every new message, I worried, *Who is this going to be?* I worried that it would be one of the men I'd slept with saying, "Oh, there you are."

I pulled out a bottle. I couldn't get through the messages. I listened to my mom and brothers but erased the rest.

The days that followed, I was afraid to read the papers or go into the locker room. I would see a photographer and think, *Shit, they've got the story.* Finally, by the middle of the next week I was able to relax and feel safe—until the next panic attack.

I set a record by starting all sixteen games—the first rookie nose guard to do so. I also made thirty solo tackles, which would be the most I ever made in a single NFL season. Probably my biggest play of the season came against the Tampa Bay Buccaneers on September 15, when I sacked the Bucs quarterback Vinny Testaverde for a ten-yard loss deep in their end late in the game and set up the winning field goal.

I even made my first interception as a lineman. In our October rematch against Tampa Bay, the ball was deflected and ended up in my hands. I started running. One of my teammates at my side was yelling, "Pitch it! Pitch it!" I didn't want to. I wanted to use my high school fullback skills to run the ball in for my first NFL touchdown. If I had been twenty pounds lighter, I might have made it, but this was in Tampa. It was something like a hundred degrees with high humidity. I bulled over the Bucs' running back, but I didn't make it to the end zone.

The more I played my rookie year, the more wonderful it felt to be a starter for the Green Bay Packers. At the same time, I felt more exposed. The NFL's storied team drew far more attention than the Pac-10's doormat ever had.

Before our final game, I learned that *Football News* and *College & Pro Football Newsweekly* had named me to their All-Rookie teams. That was a huge accomplishment—right up there with winning the Morris Trophy in college. I was in good company on that All-Rookie team. That's when I felt like I had arrived in the NFL and survived.

I would soon learn that success at the highest level could be brief and came to understand the players' grim joke that NFL stood for "Not For Long."

# CHAPTER NINE

## Mississippi Brawling

**A**S MY ROOKIE YEAR WOUND DOWN in the dead of winter, I couldn't wait to get home to Hawaii. I'd had enough of Green Bay's freezing cold. I longed for warmer weather.

Despite my personal success, the team had not had a good year. We finished 4–12, even worse than the previous season. Those were lean years for the Packers. There were no playoff games to keep us in town.

Once the season finally ended, it was great to be back in Hawaii. I hadn't been home since I left for training camp in July. In Hawaii, I could relax. I no longer felt the pressure of the workouts and the weekly combat. I felt free there, like the young boy running along the beach that I had once been.

The island would not have been my refuge if I had attended the University of Hawaii. I would have gone there, but they hadn't recruited me. They said I was too small. Since I played high school football in California, a lot of people in Hawaii didn't realize I had grown up on the island. Hawaii became a place where I could be myself, not the football star in the spotlight.

I had a blast. I hung out with my friends. I cruised the gay bars. I was able to hook up with tourists. It was a great feeling to have the money to buy drinks and have a good time.

Money allowed me to do things I couldn't have done before. For the first time in my life, I could afford a vacation like my wealthy friends. I admit that I did not always exercise the best judgment. That can be difficult for young athletes. Money suddenly presents all of these opportunities, but athletes don't always have the maturity at age twenty-three to responsibly exercise their newfound freedom. I know I didn't.

The Packers' defensive line coach Greg Blache wanted the rookie position players back in February to work out for a month. I liked Blache, and I know he liked me. He told me recently that I had been one of his favorites for my toughness and playing ability but also for my "smile, friendliness, and kindness." I didn't like the idea of returning to Green Bay in February.

I packed my bags dreading the cold. Before I left, I checked the weather report and saw temperatures in Wisconsin were below zero. The day I arrived, the wind-chill was minus twenty degrees Fahrenheit. I flew in on a Friday, dropped my bags at my townhome, and drove my Pathfinder over to the Packers' facility to check in.

When I came back, I looked around the empty house, thought about how cold it was outside, and considered my bags, still packed. I picked them up, headed back to the airport, and bought a ticket to Hawaii that Friday night.

Back home, I found out that some of my gay friends were headed to Carnival in Brazil. They asked if I wanted to join them. Carnival in Brazil? That Sunday I was on a plane headed south.

By the time Coach Blache found out on Monday that I wasn't in Green Bay, I was partying at Carnival. He called my home on Tuesday. Mama told him I was in Brazil. That wasn't exactly the most responsible way to take my first vacation, I know. I still had some growing up to do.

Meanwhile, we had a great time. We started in Sao Paolo, hit Rio de Janeiro, and partied all the way down to Argentina. We took a helicopter over Iguazu Falls, Brazil's Niagara. It was cool to know I could afford this type of extravagant trip.

Carnival was wild, as you might imagine. I tried cocaine, but I was too afraid to act out sexually. It was crazy. Brazil has the most beautiful men in the world. I was at Carnival with a group of gay friends—they were all hooking up with guys—but I was too paranoid, too scared someone might recognize me.

The Brazilians called me "Tyson," as in Mike Tyson, the boxer who was at his prime then. I'm not talking one or two people but lots of people wherever I went, "Hey, Tyson." There are not too many big guys down there. I stood out. I think that freaked me out, knowing I couldn't just blend in the way I did in Hawaii.

I had fun and was glad to take my first vacation, but my bad judgment would come back to haunt me.

Later in the spring, I reported to—and stayed for—mini-camp along with all of the other players. Coach Blache chewed me out for leaving in February. I felt awkward around the other coaches, who gave me the evil eye but didn't say anything. Management had fired Head Coach Lindy Infante in the off-season and brought in Mike Holmgren—now the Seattle Seahawks' head coach—who had been an assistant coach for the San Francisco 49ers during their dynasty years.

I also saw they had brought in several nose guards. One of them was Dewey Tucker, a big dude, something like six foot eight and three hundred fifty pounds. Seeing the other nose guards there made me think maybe I shouldn't have gone to Brazil.

Dewey was huge even by today's standards, when it's commonplace for guys to weigh over three hundred pounds. The NFL's players have grown larger in the past decade due to a combination of a lot of things. The food we eat is pumped with chemicals such as the growth hormones given to beef. Football has long been big entertainment, but now because of the money and the exposure, more kids are gunning to make it to the big time. They are spending more hours and days honing their skills and potential. Big guys who thought they would never have a chance now see that they do. It's incredible to see how they game has progressed. You see three hundred fifty-pound guys running down running backs from behind.

Steroids played a major role in supersizing the NFL, especially in the eighties. I could always tell if a guy was on steroids. His muscles were overdeveloped. For bodybuilders to be ungodly huge, I'm sorry, that's not natural. They're using some sort of muscle enhancer. I've lifted and know that weights alone won't get you to look like that.

Lyle Alzado, the All-Pro defensive end who played from 1971 to 1985, died in 1992 from brain cancer that he believed was caused by the steroids and human growth hormone he used to bulk up. After that, the NFL really tried to crack down on the use of stuff like steroids and human growth hormone. There are other substances not detected by tests that players can take. I'm not so knowledgeable about them because I never tried enhancing drugs, but I heard other players talking about them. I don't think the NFL is 100 percent drug free, but it has cleaned up the league with its policies and random testing.

My rookie year, they woke us up at 6:00 a.m. and lined us up to take a urine test. A league representative entered the stall with us, which was awkward, as you can imagine, especially for someone like me who was already shy about peeing in front of others. The league didn't want someone turning in a sample of someone else's urine. Some guys would claim they couldn't pee. It was always the ones you thought were on steroids. I mean, come on, who can't pee in the morning? That's why they woke us up so early.

Overall, I think the NFL has done a great job in cracking down. Its steroid policy is the strictest in professional sports. The league is tougher on players busted for steroid use than for recreational drug use. The first dirty test a player has, he sits out for four games. Second violation, he's suspended for six games. Third, he's out for a year.

I met quarterback Brett Favre at mini-camp. In February, the Atlanta Falcons traded him to the Packers for a first round pick. The Falcons had drafted Brett out of the University of Southern Mississippi the year before in the second round, just two picks before the Packers took me. He had played in only two games for the Falcons, didn't complete any of the five passes he attempted, and was sacked once for an eleven-yard loss. I didn't know any of this at the time. I didn't know anything about Brett other than that we were both second-year players—and that he spoke with a southern drawl.

We hit it off right away. The first question is always, "Where are you from?" When he said "Mississippi, " I told him I'd just seen *Mississippi Burning,* the crime thriller about two FBI agents investigating the murder of civil rights workers in a racially divided Mississippi town. He started laughing. He was from the country down South. I was from the country in Hawaii. We talked about our families. His family was as important to him as mine was to me. We discovered we had common interests.

The first day of practice we stood on the sidelines, talking and laughing. I was watching the Majik Man, our starting quarterback Don Majkowski, throw the ball on the field. Then the coaches sent Brett in. I had never seen him throw. He threw the ball so hard that his first pass nearly knocked down the receiver. I'd never seen anybody throw the ball that hard.

Brett came back to the sidelines smiling. I said, "Dude, you're going to be The Man." He shrugged me off in his "aw shucks," Southern way. I said, "No, really, you're going to be The Man."

Maybe Brett liked me so much because I stroked his ego. Seriously, he was cool about the praise. He was laid-back, like me. We became good friends right away.

Brett was humble about his abilities, but I could see his confidence in the smirk on his face. Even then, before he became the star that he is today, he had that confidence. I had it, too. I had been successful in college, like Brett. I had become a starter my rookie year. But fear attacked my confidence. I think being gay put a block on me achieving my full potential.

At the time, Brett was learning to golf. Just to show you what an amazing athlete Brett is, fifteen years later, he now plays with a handicap of two. He asked me and Dewey Tucker, the big nose guard, to go golfing. I had also hit it off with Dewey. I had never golfed before but figured, *If it's something Brett wants to do, it should be fun.*

I don't think Dewey had played either. He wanted to buy some clubs at the pro shop. He got measured and bought a set of expensive Ping clubs. I rented mine.

I had brought along some beer and a bottle of tequila. Whoever lost the hole had to take a shot. Dewey and I ended up trading shots. I didn't really care how I played. But Dewey had a temper. Every time he misplayed a ball, he banged the ground with his brand new Ping clubs or sent one flying into the trees. After a while, I forgot about golf. I just took shots of tequila and watched Dewey, which was entertainment enough. The three of us cut the round short and wound up in the clubhouse buying everyone drinks.

That spring, after mini-camp, Brett invited me to his home in Kiln, Mississippi, where he grew up. The Favres have a beautiful place on a couple of acres. They also have a wonderful family. Brett's father, Irvin, who died of a heart attack in late 2003, was one of the nicest men I ever met. He was a coach most of his life, including Brett's football coach in high school. Irvin was always joking around. He insisted I call him "Hammer," the nickname everybody used for him.

Brett's mom, Bonita, was special, too. Talk about Southern hospitality—that lady had it. She showed me the aloha spirit. She practiced *ohana,* which means family. She made me feel I was one of theirs.

I felt comfortable at the Favres' place, like I was back on the banana farm in Hawaii. Their place was tucked away, like the home where I had grown up. They had the swamp; we had the tropics. They had alligators; we had geckos. The two places weren't identical, but similar enough to make me feel at home.

The first day I was there, Brett's family had this huge crawfish boil. It was the first time I ever ate crawfish. His family teased me, "What? You've never eaten crawfish?"

"No," I said. "We have them in Hawaii, but we would never eat them."

Everybody was drinking a lot, too. One thing I found out about Brett was that he could drink as much as I could. We had that in common, too. He just loved life.

As the barbecue wore on, Brett said suddenly, "Let's take Esera to Hattiesburg." That's where his alma mater, Southern Miss, was.

"Yeah, good idea," others said. We tossed some beers into the car and took off. We drank on the way. It started getting dark. The way Brett had said, "Let's go to Hattiesburg," made it seem like the town was just up the road, but we'd been driving for over an hour and still weren't there. I asked, "Where the hell are we going?"

By the time we arrived in Hattiesburg, I was pretty lit up. We pulled up to what looked like a big barn but turned out to be Ropers Nightclub, a country bar. When we walked in, the D.J. was playing country music. By the time we sat down, he was playing M.C. Hammer's "Can't Touch This." I don't think he did it on purpose, but the whole mood changed.

Everybody noticed that Brett Favre had come to visit. Brett Favre was the biggest thing that ever came out of Hattiesburg. It was great hanging out with him. People treated him like the president of the United States. But there are also jealous people who can't be happy for someone else's success. They think everything is handed to us on a silver platter. They don't see the sweat and hard work it takes to achieve that success. One of those guys caused us some trouble.

We started doing shots of tequila. I was drunk and having a

good time. Suddenly, the place erupted into a big fight. Brett had talked to some guy's girlfriend. The guy was jealous. I think that's how it started. We each took a couple of swings before I grabbed Brett and pulled him outside.

Sure enough, the cops came. They had us sit on the sidewalk. I weighed three hundred thirty pounds then—the Packers had wanted me to beef up, and I had. That's not hard for us Samoans—all we have to do is smell food, and we gain weight. The cops couldn't handcuff me with my hands behind my back like the other guys because my wrists wouldn't come together, so they had me put my hands on top of my head to handcuff me. They were saying, "Oh my gosh, we got ourselves a big one." They asked Brett, "Where'd you get this one?"

The cops took us downtown. Brett stayed with them. They tossed me in a cell with about fifteen African American guys. I'm thinking, *Oh, shit. What's going to happen to us?* Remember, the last movie I saw was *Mississippi Burning*. I was scared, so I struck my fighting-cock pose. I was trying to keep to myself. One guy kept talking to me. I was still drunk and didn't understand all he said, but I remember him saying, "They're going to bring food for us in the morning." I was like, *What? I hope we're not in here for that long.* Sure enough, they brought in some bread.

Finally, a white cop brought me into his office to question me. I was still seeing *Mississippi Burning* in my mind.

The cop asked, "Where you from, boy?"

"Hawaii," I said.

"Hawhya? Me and the missus just came back from there."

I thought, *I hope you had a good time.*

"We had a good time," he said.

I felt some relief, but not much.

"Don't you worry about Brett," he continued. "This was his second home in college."

He told me Brett had called his agent, who was coming to pick us up. The cop took me back to the cell to wait. Still, I was anxious. The cell reeked of urine. That started to get to me.

Brett's agent showed up as promised. I promptly puked in his Lexus. I don't think I made a good impression.

He told me, "You better call home."

"Why?" I asked. "We're in Mississippi. How's anyone back home going to know?"

Brett's parents also told me I should call my mom. I just didn't think word of our arrest was going to get back to Hawaii. I was naïve.

The next day, it was in the papers: "Brett Favre and Esera Tuaolo Arrested in Barroom Brawl." The *Associated Press* sent the news out over the wire—everybody picked it up. *USA Today* ran the story on its front page.

When I called home, Mama was livid. She cried on the phone and told me I had embarrassed her and the family. I felt really, really bad.

That was only the beginning of my vacation with Brett Favre. One night, his family took me gambling on the casino boats. Laws forbid gambling on shore, so they have these huge boats in the harbor with casinos where you can gamble, because technically they're offshore. Brett, Bonita, and Irvin—excuse me, Hammer—and I played blackjack and drank. It was my first time playing blackjack. Sitting at the table, I thought I had more chips than I saw before me. My chips seemed to be disappearing faster than I was betting them. On our way home, Bonita handed me something like four hundred dollars. That's what she had taken in my chips. Every time I wasn't looking, she had slipped some into her purse. She told me she did that so I wouldn't leave broke. It was that aloha spirit again, her *ohana*. She was like my mom, watching out for me.

Brett and I also road-tripped to Pensacola, Florida, about a hundred miles away. His posse—a group of Brett's friends from high school and college—filled a five-car caravan. Every time Brett and I ran out of beer in our car, we pulled alongside one of his posse's pickup trucks. They passed us beer through the window while we flew down the highway.

We had a blast. For a while there, I forgot that I was gay. Maybe that's why I cherished Brett's friendship so much—we just had a fantastic time together. Little did I know that his friendship would soon save my life.

# CHAPTER TEN

# My Brother Tua

TUA DIED THE SUMMER OF 1992, right before training camp opened.

My mom didn't want me to tell you Tua's story, but I must because his story is my story, too. Forgive me, Mama. I know that you were never ashamed of him, you were proud.

That summer, Robert Brown, my Packers' teammate, had invited me to his home in Fairfax, Virginia, to train with him and his personal trainer. I had never worked out like that before the season. I figured it couldn't hurt. It was also a chance to explore nearby Washington, D.C. I would be able to see my cousin, Eni Falemavagena, a congressman from American

Samoa, and attend the wedding of Don Young, a buddy from Hawaii.

When Don heard I was coming, he asked me to sing at the reception. The wedding and reception were at a prestigious country club that had denied Harry Truman membership. I showed up in my formal Hawaiian attire, which means a Hawaiian shirt and slacks. The maitre d' pulled me aside and told me the dress code required a coat and tie. He took me to a room where they had a rack of coats and ties. I ended up singing in my Hawaiian shirt and an ugly coat and tie.

My cousin Eni introduced me to Senator Daniel Inouye from Hawaii, the senior senator who had been on the Watergate Committee. He was a celebrity to me. I was thinking, *Look what the NFL is bringing me, the chance to meet celebrities and great people like Senator Inouye.*

I stayed by myself in Georgetown in an apartment that belonged to Don's grandmother. It took me a while to talk myself into going out to a gay club in a strange city. That was new for me. I walked in and felt eyes on me, this big guy trying to be incognito. My heart pounded. A good-looking Frenchman came over to talk to me. He had long brown hair, green eyes, and told me all the things I wanted to hear. I had always heard that the French are great lovers. We went back to the apartment, and I found out that was true.

He wanted to take me out to dinner, but I said no. I figured it was safest to stick to my routine of one-night stands. I had told him my name was Kavika. I didn't dare get close to another man. He kept calling. I told him he had to stop because I didn't live there.

During the time I was training with Robert Brown, he took me sightseeing. I noticed people looking at us while we waited in line at the Washington Monument. I figured we stood out as two big guys, or thought maybe they recognized Robert. He had played in the NFL for nine years. Once we stepped inside, the elevator operator stared at me. Robert said, "We got a problem here?"

The operator said, "No." Then he asked me, "Did you sing the national anthem before a game your rookie year?"

I was surprised. I'm thinking, *Here I am, somewhere I've never been before, and this stranger recognizes me.*

Robert said, "Yeah, that's my boy."

The operator said, "I hate you."

"Why?" I asked.

"You made me cry in front of my family," he said. "I've heard that song so many times, but I have never been as moved by it as I was when you sang it."

That was cool, but it also made me panic. Here's this guy I don't know who identifies me out of the blue. *Who else recognized me?* I wondered. For the rest of my stay, I limited my time going to the bars and went only on mixed nights, open to both gay and straight people, just in case someone else recognized me. *If I didn't have to hide who I was,* I thought, *how beautiful it would have been to be able to enjoy playing in the NFL and hearing people's comments like that.*

My brother Tua, who was seven years older than me, called while I was in Fairfax.

"I have some bad news," he said.

"What's wrong?"

"I got diagnosed with AIDS."

"No. You're fucking joking."

"Yeah. I have it. I wanted you to know."

Tua thought he had a cold he couldn't shake. He went to the doctor and was diagnosed with AIDS. Back then, in the early nineties, medicine was just becoming available to treat AIDS, but the diagnosis was still seen as a death sentence.

"What do you mean? How bad is it?"

"I don't know."

I could hear the fear in his voice. "I'm coming home," I said.

"No. No."

"Yes. I'm coming home."

"Thanks. I'll wait for you."

I hung up and headed to the airport. I heard the fear. I knew it was bad. I didn't tell Robert about Tua's call. I didn't even pack anything. I brought only the clothes I was wearing and my wallet. I bought a ticket at the counter and caught the first flight to Hawaii. For twelve hours I was alone with my thoughts, fears, and memories.

Tua was the kind of person who would fill up a truck with bananas, coconuts, and *ulu* (bread fruit) and deliver them to older aunts and uncles who lived in the city, some of them in housing projects. He wanted to make sure they had enough to eat. This was also his way of bringing a bit of Samoa to those who had left their native island. He would visit for hours. He did the same for others in need. Mama sometimes got angry with him for giving away so much. Tua told her, "We have to. This is the way."

He touched people by remembering them. A lot of people forget someone's name right after they meet them. Tua not only remembered the person's name, he sent them a Christmas card every year—even if he had only met them once. He had a huge list.

Tua was close to Mama. We were her favorites. Me, because I was the youngest, Tua, because of who he was. He never cussed at Mama like she was a teenager. Not Tua. He treated her with respect.

He always helped me out when I needed money. He wasn't wealthy, but he would find a way. The guys in our fraternity used to go to Shasta Lake in northern California every spring and party on a rented houseboat. That was the kind of thing I couldn't afford. I would call Tua. He might complain, but he knew that trip with my frat brothers was important to me. Within a week, an envelope would arrive with money to pay my way.

Everybody loved Tua. When he came to visit me in college, my fraternity brothers were happy to see him. He was so much fun to party with.

A lot of guys in our frat house thought they were big pot smokers and that Oregon weed was as strong as any other. They would pull out these skinny, toothpick joints. Tua would laugh. "Your Oregon weed is shit, not like Hawaiian weed."

Always happy to share what he had, Tua would break out a joint that looked like a cigar. His potent doobie would only make it once around the circle—the guys couldn't handle any more of his stuff.

My senior year, Tua came with us to party on the Shasta Lake houseboat. On the drive down, Tua, Sai, another frat brother, and I smoked some of Tua's Hawaiian weed. We got wasted. I was driving, thinking I was doing a hundred miles per hour down this mountain road. Suddenly, *whack*. Tua, who was sitting behind me, smacked me on the side of the head. "What?!"

"What are you doing?" he asked. "You're driving so slow."

"No, I'm going fast."

I looked down at the speedometer. It read fifteen miles per hour.

"Pull over," Tua said. "Let me drive."

He was the only one who could handle his weed.

Another time, a friend from Connecticut visited us in Hawaii. Tua showed him some tiny marijuana plants. The friend said, "Wow. This is great. These are huge plants." Tua and I laughed. We've got this all on tape because the guy was recording it with his video camera. We hiked up the hills where my brother had planted an open field. He sold some of what he grew, smoked some himself, and gave away the rest. We parted the bushes that opened to reveal these enormous marijuana trees. The friend was saying, "Holy shit. Oh my god." The camera was going every which way. "You've got to be kidding." Tua and I laughed.

Tua came out to me while I was still in high school and he was twenty-three. We were planting bananas in the field one summer. Tua told me he was gay. He said it in a way that didn't leave room for me to say, "Me, too." I said, "Okay. That's cool. You're my brother. I'm not going to disown you." That was it. No big deal, but no bond either.

Tua was fascinated by our history and culture. As a kid, he read books about Samoan history and language in his tree house. He learned about the tattoos given to chiefs in the old days. A tattoo master designed a pattern from the chief's knees to navel that carried the story of the Samoan people and our traditions. It's an ancient art form.

When he was eighteen, Tua traveled to American Samoa with Mama for her mother's funeral. Tua snuck over to Samoa to get one of the chief's tattoos. He wasn't a chief, but he had the money to pay for the tattoo. The master consented. In the traditional custom, the man's family accompanies him and supports him through the tattooing ordeal. One of our cousins stayed with Tua.

The master dips a shark's tooth into ink. The tooth is sharpened into a needle and attached to a stick. He then hits the stick with a wooden club to stamp the design into the flesh. It causes a lot of bleeding. Sometimes people die because they lose so much blood. At night, Tua had to sleep on banana leaves; his bloody flesh would have stuck to regular bed sheets. After each day's session, Tua had to bathe in the ocean. The salt water stung his open wounds.

It's a very painful process. When I got the tattoo that rings my bicep, it burned like fire ants—Tua's must have felt like piranhas. Some people take weeks or months to finish the traditional Samoan tattoo. It all depends on how strong you are. Tua completed his in four days. He had that sort of bravery and mental toughness.

Tua described the tattoo process as a spiritual journey, much like the vision quests of Native Americans. One night, he felt the walls of the hut shake where he and our cousin slept. He opened his eyes but couldn't move his body. He could only move his head. He heard a woman outside the hut telling a man, "*Ave le cama!*—take the boy now."

"No," the man said. "We need to wait."

Tua panicked. His body felt paralyzed. Somebody banged against the hut's walls. No one else inside was awake.

"If you do not hurry up, we're going to lose him," the woman's voice said.

"No, wait," said the man.

Tua scooted his pillow with his head over the side of his cot. It fell onto the face of our cousin, sleeping on the floor beside him, and woke him up. Suddenly, Tua was released from the hold on his body. He jumped out of bed and screamed, "There are ghosts out there trying to take me!"

Our cousin ran outside. In the Polynesian belief, you have to yell at ghosts to show them you are not afraid. Our cousin shouted, "Don't you dare take my cousin now!"

Everybody woke up. The tattoo master explained, "Those are the jealous people trying to take you. The man must have been a family member trying to buy you some time."

I didn't know what to expect when my flight landed in Hawaii. I called my family. My sister Tusi told me that the doctors had put Tua under. I started yelling into the phone, "Put under? Why?" Tusi explained that they had sedated him because he had been getting too worked up.

I bawled on the drive to the hospital, the same one where my daddy died. I had wanted Tua to come to Green Bay so he could see me play in the NFL. He had been too busy running the family farm.

Tua was unconscious, but he knew I was there when I walked into his room. I could see on the monitor that his heart rate picked up. I rubbed his hand. It was hard to see him like that. His generous spirit and mental toughness were no match for the AIDS virus that ravaged his body. The doctors told me he was fine now that he was sedated. I didn't believe them. I had the feeling he wasn't going to make it.

I was upset that he couldn't talk to me. "You promised," I said. "You said you would wait for me."

His heart rate soared on the monitor. The nurses made me step outside the room because Tua was getting too excited. I sobbed.

Why had I gone to train in D.C.? Why hadn't I talked to him more often? Why hadn't he talked to me more about being gay? Why, why, why?

Tua died the next day, July 7, 1992. He was twenty-nine.

I was hurt and angry. I had wanted him to talk to me.

We gave Tua a traditional Polynesian funeral fit for a high chief. My family set up a large tent in the yard of the banana farm. We covered the ground with *tapa* mats, which are made out of bark pounded smooth and covered with designs. We decorated the walls around his casket with *iea koga*—fine mats handwoven out of *lahala* leaves. It requires great skill to weave the rough-edged leaves smooth as a fabric. Back in the old days before money, *iea koga* mats served as a sign of a family's strength and prestige, like sheep or cattle. Tua rested in full view at the center of the tent.

The funeral lasted several days, from Wednesday to Sunday. In the old days, it took people a long time to get to the island where the funeral took place, so funerals lasted a long time. A traditional Polynesian funeral can be a lot of work for the family, but it's a way of preserving our culture, honoring our ancestors, and remembering our family's origins. The effort emphasizes how much we value family and traditions in our culture.

Every evening, our family and guests gathered for a prayer service. A preacher gave a sermon. A different church choir sang hymns throughout the night, punctured by crying and wailing from the mourners.

Friends and family came from all over the Hawaiian and Samoan islands to pay their respects. People from California to Connecticut signed the guestbook. Friends of mine from high school joined people who had met Tua only once but received his Christmas cards annually. Entire families—including aunts, uncles, grandparents—and church groups journeyed there to honor my brother. All told, about four thousand people came to say goodbye to Tua. That didn't surprise me. He was a special person who had touched so many people.

The guests arrived in groups of twenty to fifty, bearing gifts. In the Polynesian culture, people pay their respects to the grieving family with money and gifts. They presented our family with gifts ranging from *iea koga* mats to buckets of salted pork. In return, the family responds to their generosity by feeding the guests. We roasted thirty pigs to feed everyone and gave them bread fruit to eat on the journey home.

Each family appoints a talking chief that stands up, identifies himself by his ancestors or group, explains what gifts they brought, and tells the family how they mourn for their loss. Our family's talking chief—at Tua's funeral it was my uncle, one of my mom's brothers—then stands to thank the groups on behalf of the family for their gifts and support.

The talking chiefs and guests spoke about how Tua had touched their lives. Sometimes at a funeral, you can't tell whether people are sincere or if they're simply speaking for the occasion, but at Tua's funeral, they spoke with such passion and conviction, I could tell they meant the generous things they said. I already knew Tua was a special person, but I was overwhelmed when so many people praised him.

No one spoke about AIDS at the funeral. People thought Tua died of pneumonia. His friends all knew he was gay, but some of the people in the various church groups didn't. Mama knew, but she didn't want people to talk about it. AIDS was viewed then as something negative. She didn't want to dishonor Tua, nor disgrace the family.

In Polynesian culture, it's okay to be a *faafafine,* an effeminate and affected gay man who dresses and acts like a woman. That's what people expected of gay men. People still teased or beat up the *faafafines*—they weren't completely accepted—but they were able to hold responsible positions as witch doctors and the like.

Tua was a man's man. To be masculine *and* gay was not okay. We Samoans were supposed to be feared throughout the Pacific as powerful warriors. For someone like Tua or me to be gay undermined that warrior image because being gay meant someone was weak. Our being gay threatened the Samoan cultural ideal.

It's similar with the stereotypes for various sports. No one seems surprised if a figure skater or a gymnast is gay—those athletes are stereotyped as more feminine, probably because their sports require such grace and finesse. Football players, on the other hand, are supposed to be warriors. Being gay—which is equated with being weak—threatens that tough image.

Music has always helped me cope with difficult times. I needed a song for my brother Tua. While we were making the funeral preparations, I heard a song on the radio that was perfect, as though it was written for Tua. I rushed to buy the CD so that I could learn the words and melody.

I sang it at the funeral:

If you ever stumble, I'll be there to carry you.

I'll bear all your burden, until you're as strong as before.

Whatever you do, I'll be there for you until your strength is restored

'Cause after all, that's what a brother's for.

—————

We buried Tua on my birthday, July 11. We placed him to rest in the Oahu cemetery, next to Daddy. I watched Tua go down into the ground and realized I would never see him again. I was not going to see his face. I would not see him come in from the banana patch after a hard day's work. I would not see him hug and kiss my mom. I would not hear his laugh or see his smile. Once they put him down into the ground, I thought of all of the questions I wanted to ask him. I thought of things I had wanted to say but didn't.

Watching my father's burial, I had wanted to jump down there with him. With Tua, I felt a void. It's still there.

I haven't forgotten him. Every time I see one of his friends, it's a crying fest. We still miss him so much. I was talking to my cousin the other day, and we started crying. He told me that a day does not go by without him thinking about Tua. That's the type of presence he had. He wasn't an icon like a celebrity you see on TV, but he had a huge impact on people's lives.

I know he's in my heart. That feels good.

Never in a million years did I think my brother, someone so young, would die. When my aunt was killed, I was too young to understand death. I heard the screaming and shouting at night and wondered, *Why did she leave us?* When Daddy died, I was ten years old. I'd heard in church that God has a master plan for us. I learned that Daddy was in heaven. I thought, *Okay.* But I think when Tua died, I was profoundly sad. By then I understood the permanence of death.

I was angry with God. He took away my dad, now my brother. I was not cussing out God so much as wondering why. Why take someone so young with so much responsibility? The Book of Job popped into my head. God gives the devil permission to tempt Job. He does so by stripping away everything from Job just so he would denounce God's name. But Job doesn't. I think of that every time in my life when I get to the point of wanting to give up. I can't denounce God's name either. It would be easy to blame God, but the bad things that happen aren't God's fault.

I was grateful that God took Tua fast. AIDS haunts people with pain and suffering, but God spared Tua most of that, maybe because of who he was and the good life he lived. That was a blessing.

I was touched by all of the things people said about Tua at the funeral, but I was also angry with Tua. I blamed him for not waiting for me to say goodbye. I think maybe I was making something up to be mad about because I missed him so much already. Regret tinged our relationship.

Tua knew I was gay. My senior year of high school, I had lied about my age to Billy, an older man who picked me up at Hula's. Turned out Billy and Tua paddled together on the same canoe club. At a party Billy hosted for the canoe club, he sent Tua into his bedroom to fetch his stash. My brother spotted a photo of me on Billy's dresser along with a letter I had written him. Tua told me this at my high school graduation party in California.

"I saw your letter." He said it in a way that intimidated me. "That's fine and all," he said. "Just don't tell Mama."

That was the only advice I got from my older brother. I'm not sure why he didn't want me to be open with Mama. Maybe he thought it would break her heart to have two gay sons in her family. I didn't question him. As the younger brother, I figured he knew what was right, but that shoved me deeper in the closet.

I was a young kid trying to be who I was. I was trying to find some clarity. I know Tua loved me, yet for some reason he wasn't able to help me. He probably bragged about me being a football player. But as a gay kid I needed more than that from my big brother.

I would see him at gay clubs like Hula's, but it felt weird, strained. It was almost like he didn't accept that I was gay, like he thought I was pretending. I was looking for more conversation—answers—but he didn't offer it.

After a while, I gave up seeking help from him. As long as I didn't ask him for anything, it was cool between us. During that time, the pain hadn't swollen too great because I wasn't yet the star football player. I was more of a normal person.

Today, I receive emails from kids all over the world asking me for advice. I'm no Dr. Phil, but I do tell them, "If you decide to come out, make sure of two things: First, make sure you're in a safe environment where you won't get beaten up. Second, make sure you have support from others who care about you." Both are so important.

Tua had told my mom he was gay, but I don't think he did a good job of explaining to her what that meant. Even though they were close, he kept his sexuality to himself. For instance, his boyfriend, Dan, came to stay on the farm with us for over a year, but Tua pretended they were just roommates. The two of them never showed any open affection. Tua never explained to Mama what Dan meant to him.

He could have done a better job educating her about homosexuality. Her lack of understanding what it meant to be homosexual made it harder for me when I eventually told her that I, too, was gay.

# CHAPTER ELEVEN

⌁

# If You Make the Team

I HAD NO IDEA THAT our Mississippi barroom brawl would make such big news in Green Bay, but it did. As soon as I returned for training camp in July, Greg Blache, our defensive line coach, called to chew me out.

At camp, I could feel something different in the air, like I had done something wrong. You know that feeling when you're a kid and your parents don't talk to you? That's how it was. Apart from Blache's phone call, the coaches gave me the silent treatment.

In our first team meeting, once we had broken into our separate offense and defense meetings, I noticed all of the new guys management had brought in, including the other nose guards. Everybody was looking around, sizing up one another. So much for job security.

One good thing about training camp that year was that I didn't have to sing at dinner. That was left to the rookies. Also, I roomed with Brett Favre at Saint Norbert. We had our usual good time.

In the exhibition games, I didn't start. The coaches didn't play me much at all. When they don't play you, you know you're on your way out. They don't want you to get hurt. If you get hurt, you go on the injured reserve list, where they have to pay you. They want you healthy so they can release you without pay.

The coaches wouldn't tell me what was wrong. I figured it was the Mississippi incident. I think I was labeled a "bad boy" because of the fight with Brett. Even though both Brett and I were there, they blamed me. They weren't going to let Brett Favre go. Maybe they thought I was a bad influence on their budding star quarterback.

The praises that I had heard since high school stopped. That hurt.

Every week, I waited for that cocky assistant coach to tap me on the shoulder and tell me that Coach wanted to see me, that my days as a Packer were over.

Off the field, my second season with the Packers was more fun than my first. I had met people like Brett, Dewey Tucker, and the rookies. I hung out more with them and other second-year guys, like my Wisconsin buddy, Don Davey.

When we went out, Brett would start buying drinks for everybody after he had a few of his own. This was before Brett started making the big money. The bills would top a thousand dollars. In Green Bay, that's like spending ten thousand dollars because drinks were only a buck a shot. It's just the kind of guy Brett was, generous and fun-loving. I used to steal his wallet to save him the expense. He couldn't buy everyone drinks without his credit cards.

Often, we partied at my townhouse. Brett's wife, Deanna, who was his girlfriend back then, would come over when she was in town. So would Don's girlfriend and some of the other guys' girlfriends. We played "quarters" and other beer-drinking games.

For a while, my place became the hangout. I would cook up my famous teriyaki chicken and macaroni salad or rice dishes—all recipes from my mom. When I was a child, I helped her in the kitchen because I was the youngest. Now, I love to cook. I contributed one of Mama's recipes to the Packers' cookbook: dishwasher fish. I know it sounds crazy, but it's really good. You wrap fish—I like salmon—in tinfoil with coconut milk, onions, salt, pepper, and a pinch of curry, place it on the rack and run the cycle—without soap, of course. The dishwasher steams the fish. It turns out moist and delicious. The recipe was Mama's; the idea to steam the packet in the dishwasher was mine. When I was growing up, we didn't have a dishwasher other than me.

We ate and drank and laughed at Brett's impersonations. One of his favorites is the lion from *The Wizard of Oz*. "Come on, put 'em up. Put 'em up," Brett would say with his paws out in front of him. I've got him doing that on film. He was hilarious.

Brett made his Packer debut on September 13, 1992, against the Tampa Bay Buccaneers during our second game of the season. Going in to relieve Dan Majkowski in the second half, Brett completed his first NFL pass—to himself. The ball was deflected back into his hands.
Majik Man hurt his ankle in the first quarter of the next game against the Cincinnati Bengals. That injury cost him his job. Brett went in and completed twenty-two of thirty-nine passes for 289

yards, including a thirty-five-yard touchdown pass with only thirteen seconds remaining to give us a come-from-behind 24–23 win. Brett started the following week against the Pittsburgh Steelers— and has started every game since, a string of 241 games through the end of the 2005 season. That's an NFL record for quarterbacks.

Meanwhile, I made only five tackles in the first four games of the season. In the fourth game, we trailed Pittsburgh. The coaches put me in at defensive end. I had played nose guard in college and with the Packers my rookie year. That was my position. I had not practiced at defensive end. It was an awkward feeling. I was used to being in the middle. It was like the coaches set me up to fail. As soon as that happened, I knew I was gone.

Sure enough, the following Monday, the cocky assistant coach told me after we finished watching the game film that Coach Blache wanted to see me in his office. As a starter, I never thought that would happen to me, but now it had. I wasn't surprised. I'd seen it coming. Still, I was pissed. I had played well as a starter the previous season. I had made the All-Rookie team.

Coach Blache told me, "Your play has been lacking. The performance is not there."

I knew Blache liked me as an athlete and believed in my talent. He was trying to say that the team was releasing me because of the way I had played, that it was my fault.

"You haven't given me the chance to show you my play this season," I said.

But I could see in his eyes and hear in the tone of his voice that it wasn't his decision. He wasn't the one releasing me; the decision came from the top.

Mike Holmgren, the new head coach, saw me next in his office. He told me things weren't going to work out for me in Green Bay. It was short and quick. I was gone.

The hardest part was the walk back to my locker. I saw my teammates look away. They didn't say anything. It was cold. What can you say to someone who has just been released? It's like the person just lost a loved one.

Don Davey approached me. He said the decision was fucked up. I appreciated that, but it didn't change anything.

I cleaned out my locker and headed to my townhouse. I felt I had failed. Since going into college, I had always felt confident that I would be a starter. This was the first time playing football that I felt vulnerable, like I'd been put out on an island. I thought I was going to become a statistic. At the time, the average career in the NFL was two years.

The doubts started, too. I wondered, *What if I weren't gay? Could I have done better without this monkey on my back?* I was angry with myself. The anxiety had caught up with me.

I was depressed. I sat alone in my house and cried. I didn't know how to make that phone call to my mom. I didn't know how to tell my friends.

The phone rang. It was Brett. "Keep your head up," he said. "It's going to be all right. You're a good player. You'll get picked up."

That helped. If he hadn't called, I was in such a bad place . . . I don't know. I might not be here. I don't think he realized how much that call meant to me. It saved my life.

⌐──────⌐

I packed up all of my stuff and headed to Oregon. I didn't want to go back to Hawaii. I was too embarrassed that I had been released. I didn't want to be seen as a failure. Oregon was familiar; I liked it there. I bought a condo in Lake Oswego, a Portland suburb.

I didn't just sit around. I looked for work. Ken Kramer, my agent, had also called me in Green Bay. "Don't worry," he said. "We're going to find you another team." He arranged tryouts with the Philadelphia Eagles and the Washington Redskins.

The tryout is a job interview. It's run like a mini-Combine. There are usually two or three other guys there. You're all gunning for one spot. The doctors give each player physicals, just like they did in Indianapolis. They tugged at my knee. The coaches put us through agility and speed drills side by side. Competing for a job is stressful.

I didn't have a good feeling about those tryouts. I sensed neither one of those teams would pick me up. I think they were just looking at us in case someone got hurt, so they knew who was available. They were just browsing the merchandise.

Then somebody on the Minnesota Vikings got hurt, and the Vikings needed a backup nose guard. Their coach, Denny Green, remembered me from his days coaching at Stanford. My junior year, I had been the defensive Player of the Week against Stanford when we debuted Brady Hoke's slanted nose guard defense. The Vikings brought me in for the weekend.

I had the feeling when I got there that I was going to stay. I hadn't felt that way in Philadelphia or Washington. Maybe it's because I saw the Mall of America right across from the airport, but I got excited.

I had an excellent workout against two or three other guys. The coaches called me up to the office afterward and asked me not to leave. "We're talking to your agent," they said. Ken worked out a contract with the team, and I was a Viking.

It felt good to be part of the Vikings. The quality of players on their team at that time impressed me, including defensive linemen such as John Randle, Henry Thomas, Chris Doleman, and Al Noga. Al was a fellow Samoan. He had put Hawaii on the map in 1988 when he became a starter for the Vikings right out of the University of Hawaii. I was happy to be on a team with another Polynesian.

The first guy I met was Roy Barker, a rookie defensive end. Roy called me at the Hotel Seville, where I was staying. He said, "Let's go party."

Roy took me to Solid Gold, an upscale strip club. In Green Bay, I'd gone to strip clubs with Brett and Dewey, but the girls there were so ugly that one of our teammates used to offer them twenty dollars to get off the stage. Solid Gold was high class, with private rooms. Roy knew all of the girls there. We drank tequila all night and got wasted. I was hungover the next day for my first team meeting.

Roy almost didn't show up. The night before, he made it inside his house but not to his room. He collapsed on the floor and told me he could see the door of his room, but it was like *Poltergeist* where the hallway stretched away from him—the door out of his reach. He slept on the hallway floor. He showed up late for the meeting and jokingly said, "I can't mess with you and that tequila any more."

The other guys on the team were married. Roy was a young, single guy. I partied with him that first year.

Al Noga, the other Samoan on the team, invited me over to his house. I hung out some with him and his wife but didn't want to get too close to anyone. After being released by Green Bay, I felt vulnerable. That could happen again at any time.

People don't realize how much being released hurts. You lose friends fast. It's like any friend who leaves town. You say, "Let's keep in touch," but you don't. Those friendships fade. When players leave a team, they are cut off. Once you join a new team, it's almost taboo to communicate with your old teammates. Being Mr. Aloha, I said hi to my former teammates when we played the Packers, but the Vikings' John Randle reprimanded me, "You're talking to the enemy."

My new Viking teammates were friendly enough but cool. They may have questioned my ability because I was heavy. I had lost some weight in Oregon, but I still weighed around three hundred pounds. That was large by Viking standards. Minnesota wanted fast and quick linemen. It didn't have any three hundred-pounders on its line.

Green Bay had wanted big, heavy linemen. That's why the Packers had asked me to gain weight. Once I learned what the Vikings were about, I thought it would have been great to go to Minnesota right out of college. I was not naturally a big, heavy lineman. My forté was my quickness and speed. I would have liked to play right away for a team that emphasized my strengths.

John Teerlinck was the Vikings' defensive line coach at the time. He knew the key to success for a defensive lineman was sacks. You don't see defensive linemen pulling down multimillion-dollar contracts for the number of tackles they make. Teerlinck preached the truth: sacks equaled money. He wanted his players to do well. That made him look good. He was all about sacks. Even if we lost a game but had a lot of sacks, he was happy. He wanted to win the team sack title every year. Unfortunately, when I got there, I was behind a lot of sack leaders. Ten sacks a year is an incredible year. Make fifteen, and that's worth millions. Chris Doleman had twenty-one a couple of years before I arrived.

I was brought in as a backup. It was tough to go from being a starter to being a backup, but I was willing to put pride aside and simply be grateful that I was still in the league. I was working. I hadn't become a statistic.

Being a backup made it easier on me as a gay man. I could hide out in the shadows. There was less chance of someone recognizing me.

I also saw an opportunity where I could start again. I knew money was always a factor for a team. Every team faced the challenge of keeping its top players. An opportunity might come if the Vikings could no longer afford its starting nose guard, Henry Thomas.

I tried to do well in the present so I would have my chance in the future. That kept me hopeful—somewhat.

The Vikings had a lot of entertaining personalities in the early nineties. One time when we returned from an away game, one of the team's stars and I drove over to his apartment. He pulled out a pipe and a bag. I sat there thinking, *Wow. Here I am getting stoned with a guy I watched play in the Super Bowl when I was in high school.* That was another one of the unexpected twists of playing in the NFL.

Jack del Rio, now the Jacksonville Jaguars' head coach, was a Pro Bowl linebacker for the Vikings then. He was a great guy and a great athlete. He knew what it meant to play with a good nose guard. He encouraged me because he knew if I played a good game, he played a good game. He used to give me a pat on the back.

John Randle, a defensive lineman who was a seven-time Pro Bowl selection, was on fire all the time, on and off the field. Seeing him, you would swear he was on some narcotic. He wasn't, but it seemed like it. He was like that 24/7. John always went 100 percent. Didn't matter if it was practice or a game, he went all out.

He took the rivalry between the offensive and the defensive lines to the limit. If a defensive lineman lost out to a hog in a drill during practice, the rest of the defensive line would haze him. John led the charge. The competition was intense. The opposing lines traded talk and taunts. The Vikings were more verbal than other places I've played. That intensity sometimes boiled over into fights.

John was strong and quick. He was also into the technical part of the game, the mechanics. He knew how to use his hands and feet. He was able to use his short, stocky build to his advantage. Barry Sanders, the Detroit Lions' great running back, stood five foot eight and ran so low that he was extremely difficult to tackle. John was the equivalent of Barry Sanders as a pass rusher. He was a tree stump that blockers couldn't knock off balance. At just over six feet tall, he was considered too small even to be drafted in 1990, yet he became one of the game's great defensive linemen.

Once John got the taste of success as a starter in 1992, he never let go. He grew up poor in Texas. He told me that his house had a dirt floor and no indoor plumbing. He walked to school. The way he went from nothing to everything was inspiring. If anybody deserved success, John Randle did. It was great to be able to play alongside him.

He used to say crazy stuff on the field. On the line against different teams, John would suddenly explode at the guy lined up across from him. "You call me a nigger? What? You call me a nigger?!"

Or, he would say, "You going to be my bitch tonight. I'm going to make you my bitch, yeah!"

One game, I was lined up across from a rookie. Suddenly, John said, "Esera, this dude just called you a big wetback."

"What?!" I said.

"He just called you a big wetback," he said, trying to get me riled up.

"No, I didn't," the rookie said.

John liked to quote movies. He would shout out things like the line from the final gunfight in *Tombstone:* "I'll be your huckleberry." Or, settling into his stance, he'd bark out the line from *American Me* that the inmates say to the guy they want to kill: "Hey, *ese,* you coming out to play?"

It's one thing to talk shit. It's another to talk it and be able to back it up. John could back it up. He got blocked but not often. Every single time he did a move, he had a smile on his face. John lived and breathed for sacks. He was John Teerlinck's protégé. He averaged twelve sacks a season during my time with the Vikings. After he brought down the quarterback, he had a crazy sack dance where he strutted back and forth with his hands close together in front of him. We teased him. "What are you doing, driving a little car?"

If I got a sack, he was all over the quarterback, yelling in his face, "You going to be *his* bitch tonight." He was crazy.

John and I hung out together some at South Beach, a downtown Minneapolis club. I was a buddy to him when he went through his divorce.

The Vikings had signed me in the middle of the 1992 season to fill in for an injured player. I played seven games with them. I knew if I wanted to keep a place on the roster, I had to prove myself at training camp in 1993.

Training camp is always hard. You can't prepare yourself for the mental stress of the competition and crap from coaches and other players along with the physical demands of two-a-day practices. You may become friends with the other guys, but they're also the competition.

Minnesota played a four-man front with a nose guard—sometimes called a nose tackle—lined up across from the center and shaded to one side. The other inside lineman, the under tackle, lined up across from the guard. Henry Thomas was the Vikings' starting nose guard. He had played in the Pro Bowl in 1991 and 1992. He knew I was trying to take his job.

During training camp, I would ask Henry how to do things. He would say, "If you make the team, I'll show you." He'd say it with a smirk. I'd ask him something else, and he'd say, "If you make the team." It became a joke between us.

Henry was very smart, a great player. Once I made the team and proved myself to Henry, he taught me some of the tricks. I learned a lot from him, such as listening to the quarterback's cadence and what number a team liked to snap the ball on for each down. For instance, about 80 percent of the time, an offense will go on "one"—the first "hut"—on first down. Some quarterbacks would try to throw off the defense with their rhythm; others would never stray from it. Henry taught me to study the quarterback on film. Some quarterbacks would look right and left, and as soon as they looked forward, you knew they were going to get the ball. I had never paid much attention to details like that.

In early August 1993, we played an exhibition game against the Buffalo Bills in Berlin. When I thought about Berlin, I thought about the German propaganda films we watched in seventh grade history class of the Nazi soldiers marching and Hitler giving speeches in Olympic Stadium. We played on that field.

Before we headed to Berlin, the team officials told us which parts of the city were safe for us to visit and which areas we should avoid. They told us not to venture off by ourselves. They also told us that 90 percent of Germans in the city spoke English.

I went to a restaurant with three teammates. One of them asked the waiter when he brought us menus, "Do you speak English?" The waiter gave him an odd look. My teammate got frustrated and yelled at him, "You cocksucker!" I think the waiter knew what that meant. He turned and walked away.

I stood up to leave. "Where are you going?" my teammates asked.

"They're either going to come after us or spit in our food," I said. "I'm not staying for that." They left with me.

Berlin had sex clubs that I also visited with my teammates. The clubs had back rooms where you could watch live performances of a man and woman having sex together. I was nervous that I would get a hard-on and my teammates would know I had been looking at the man. I only went twice.

I almost went to a gay club in Berlin, but I chickened out. I asked a cab driver to take me to a gay bar. I thought being in Berlin, so far away from Minnesota, it might be safe for me to go incognito. When we pulled up to the gay section of town, there were a lot of people walking around on the street. I didn't get out of the cab. What if one of the players' relatives along for the trip saw me there? I asked the cab driver to take me back to the hotel.

I showed up very early for the game with a few other players, about four hours before kickoff. We had some beers at a huge party hosted by MTV. It was incredible to play in the same stadium where Jesse Owens had run and Hitler had refused to give him his medals. We beat the Bills 20–6. I played a good game. I wished my mom had been there to watch.

In the first half, I broke my thumb. It bent all the way to the back of my hand. On the sideline, the trainer tugged on my thumb and taped it. I was back on the field for the second half.

There's a difference between being injured and being hurt. If you're injured, you can't play. But when you're hurt, you can play. That's where the mental toughness comes in. Mental toughness and the fear of losing your job let you do superhuman things.

We played an exhibition game in Japan the following year, but I didn't have the chance to see my friend Chad Rowan. He grew up in Waimanalo. We went to grade school and middle school together until I left for the mainland. He became a sumo wrestler in Japan, where they call him *Akebono*. He is the first non-Japanese person ever to achieve the title of grand champion. Chad's got a statue in our hometown. I don't.

In Minnesota, I dated women. I could hide behind my relationships with them.

Al Noga, my Samoan teammate, introduced me to Elizabeth Wolfgramm, the lead singer for the Jets, a Tongan family band. Al was married to Kathi, the Jets' keyboard player. He took me to hear them play. I was star struck. I had listened to their hits "Crush on You" and "You Got It All" in college. In fact, I signed their song "Make It Real" for my final exam in a sign language course.

It wasn't love at first sight with Elizabeth, but I liked her right off. She was a wholesome woman who came from a really nice family. We started dating. It was like having a best friend. I enjoyed that. She was a virgin, which made it easier for me. She was waiting to get married. We kissed, but there was no pressure to perform sexually.

After a couple of years, dating became difficult. Elizabeth wanted to take our relationship to the next level, marriage. I felt the pressure from her. She wrote songs for me and slipped me her love poems. I also felt the pressure from society. There are thousands of guys in the United States who get married each year even though they are gay. I almost proposed.

I tried to love Elizabeth the way she wanted to be loved, but I couldn't. For someone like Elizabeth—who was beautiful, nice, and talented—not to be able to "convert" me proves again that being gay is not a choice.

I didn't want to get trapped into a marriage that wouldn't work. We had "the talk."

The breakup didn't go so well for her. I'm glad to see that she's happy now. She found another Samoan guy to marry. Last I heard, they lived in Utah.

Even if I had been straight, things would not have worked out with Elizabeth, who was raised in the Church of Jesus Christ of Latter-day Saints. Our beliefs clashed. I believed in the Bible; she believed in the Book of Mormon. If I had converted to her faith, my mom would not have been able to enter the temple to attend our wedding because she wasn't Mormon herself. I couldn't have lived with that.

I met Patty, a beautiful Hispanic woman, at one of the clubs in downtown Minneapolis. She was wonderful. We became good friends. Eventually, Patty wanted to take our relationship further, but I couldn't. I told her that after my breakup with Elizabeth, I wasn't ready to get serious.

I took Patty to one of the Viking Christmas parties at Glam Slam, Prince's nightclub. She bought an expensive beaded dress and looked stunning that night. When she walked in, all of the players said, "Whoa!" The party had an open bar, and we both drank plenty. We ended up at her house in the same bed. With our clothes on. Nothing happened. I passed out. The next morning, she woke up and had the imprints of those beads all over her body.

We're friends now and laugh about that. She says, "I should have figured you were gay because you let me sleep in that beaded dress."

When I was with Green Bay, the team didn't have a lot of superstars. Even All-Pro wide receiver Sterling Sharpe, as good as he was, encouraged people. Minnesota had a lot of superstars, some nice, some not. I didn't like some of the guys—guys who tried to lead by degrading others or guys who cried like a baby when they didn't get attention. Even though I hung out with some of my teammates, I didn't feel close to any of them. I didn't feel at home in the locker room.

Speaking of that, people always ask me, "How did you function in the locker room? Was it like a buffet for you?" Those people haven't been in a professional football team's locker room. It's not a glamorous place. There's garbage tossed on the floor and the stench of sweat. It's always packed, not just with athletes but with reporters, too. You shower and leave. I'd leave especially quickly after a loss, when I worried about how I would look on film the next day. I was not thinking erotic thoughts there.

It's not like going to the gym where you might spot an attractive stranger. I worked with these guys. In the locker room, there's all the drama of a family. You hear about your teammates' problems at home. You know their troubles on the job. It's the perfect reality show.

Some people might see the locker room as an erotic place, but we see it differently; it's where we work. Once you make the team, those forty players are brothers. It's an us-against-the-world mentality. Everybody knows his role in the family. I get tired of reporters bringing it back to the showers. If anybody was talking about somebody's dick, it was a straight guy. For a paranoid, anxious, depressed guy like me, sex was the last thing on my mind in the locker room.

The Vikings had some guys who ran their mouth. Their jokes were harder for me to take. There was a lot more drama in the Vikings' locker room than anywhere else I played—even fights.

While I was with the Vikings, a rumor broke out that the Dallas Cowboys' superstar quarterback Troy Aikman was gay. He's not, but the rumor spread. The day I heard that, I walked into the locker room panicked and afraid. I didn't know what to expect, wasn't sure what I would have to endure.

Some of the players started saying nasty, graphic things about Troy and his supposed sexual habits. I was going along with it, laughing with the others. The talk turned into speculation about other players. My stomach knotted. I hoped no one would point the finger at me.

One of the tight ends on our team at the time was a cocky guy that others picked on—they knew they could get a reaction out of him. John Randle said to him, "You must be gay." The tight end freaked out. He attacked Randle. A brawl broke out in the locker room.

These two big guys threw blows at one another. Everybody else tried to break it up, including me. John's locker was right next to mine. I tried to pull him off the other guy and got hit in the back of the head. I felt the adrenaline surge of the fight. I also felt tremendous pain. That could have been me getting teased and in a fight. I was thinking, *I am in such a fucked up nightmare. I wish I could wake up.*

Coach Denny Green called a team meeting. Sitting there, my mind kept returning to the fight. I should have said something. "I'm gay. So what?!" *Why can't they accept me for who I am and who I love? I don't make jokes about them or judge them for what they do with their wives or girlfriends.* I was a coward.

Green was angry that someone could have gotten hurt. He called the fight selfish. "We depend on each other as teammates," he said. "This is supposed to be a team." I was thinking, *Fuck that shit. I don't feel part of the team.* I wanted to die.

The next day, I didn't want to wake up. I didn't want to go to practice. I questioned myself. *Can I do this?* But football was the profession I chose. I was stuck with it.

Life got harder for me each year in the NFL. My dreams of suicide became more frequent.

There's a point in time when you need somebody. My prayer at that time was, "God, let your will be done, and please send someone for me to spend the rest of my life with."

My big fear was that I would never find someone. I saw the other players happy with their families. It hurt to see them have what I wanted. It hurt worse to think I might never have a family of my own.

I did more acting during that time. I took home more women. I made sure people saw me kiss a woman in public. I played the cover-up game harder.

Each year when I returned from Hawaii for a new season, I thought, *How am I going to do this?* My prayer became a bit more desperate.

It really hurt to see some of these players smiling with their families one night and cheating on their wives the next. They took their families for granted. I would go home and scream at the walls. They treated so lightly what I wanted so badly. When you have something, you don't realize how precious it is until you lose it. I wanted to have that to lose. Pain pills and alcohol became my closest friends those days and long, lonely nights.

My first full season with Minnesota, I rented an apartment in downtown Minneapolis. Most of the players lived in the suburbs, close to the Vikings' suburban Eden Prairie training facility. I was the only one who lived downtown. I thought it might make things better to live near the action.

After one night of partying, I came home alone, drunk, and depressed. I was frustrated with my life, angry I was not able to be myself with my teammates. I slammed my fist through the wall. I sobbed, a cry from deep in my belly.

I lived on the fifteenth floor. The windows were built to not open all the way. I forced open a window. I leaned out and looked down. I was bawling. This was it. I was going to jump and end the pain and panic attacks. End the lies and masquerade. End the loneliness and hopelessness. Jump.

My mom popped into my mind. Tua, too. Daddy. I wanted to jump but felt someone pulling me back.

I passed out on the floor by the window.

There were many times like that, especially when I was drunk.

I never thought about quitting football because I didn't want to be a quitter. I didn't want to feel forever the failure I felt after Green Bay released me.

I didn't jump that night, but I was convinced life would be easier if I were dead.

# CHAPTER TWELVE

# Play through the Pain

**M**Y OPPORTUNITY ARRIVED IN 1995, when the Vikings did not renew Henry Thomas' contract. The Detroit Lions picked him up. Going into training camp that year, I knew I would be the starting nose guard.

During my first two and a half seasons with the Vikings, I had played whenever Henry was tired or hurt. He didn't let me play on third-and-long downs, though. Those are passing downs; he didn't want to miss a sack possibility. Now, with Henry in Detroit, I had the chance to shine.

That recharged me. I felt I had accomplished something. I could be The Man again.

At the same time, the anxiety returned in a bigger way. I was in the limelight, out of the shadows. Those games, after a sack, I panicked. Success brought fear. In the off-season, I had been going back to Hawaii. A larger number of guys knew my secret. There was a greater possibility one of them could out me.

People noticed defensive linemen in Minnesota. During the late seventies, the Vikings' Jim Marshall, Carl Eller, Gary Larsen, and Alan Page—the famed "Purple People Eaters"—became household names. Even their backup, "Benchwarmer Bob" Lurtsema, became a celebrity. They were great athletes. Page and Eller made it to the Hall of Fame. But they played in a different era. The game then was totally different from what it is now.

I tired of the comparison. When we played well, the media and fans likened us to the Purple People Eaters. When we didn't, we weren't considered in their league. We had fantastic athletes who deserved credit in their own right—big, strong guys who could run. People seemed to overlook that.

I didn't grow tired of the playoffs while in Minnesota. We went every season I played with the Vikings except one. I hadn't had that chance in Green Bay. Everybody loves the playoffs. The atmosphere becomes more exciting for the fans and the players. Everybody's up, happy.

The playoffs meant more money. The farther you advance, the more money you make. The Vikings had great teams those years, but for some reason we never made it past the first round. The rap against Head Coach Denny Green was that he could not take his team deep into the playoffs.

Maybe his playoff tactics could have been different. He had us practicing in full pads and going full speed. After already playing sixteen regular season games, all the players' bodies hurt. Guys were bruised and injured. In the locker room, they complained about the hard practices. That took away some of the enjoyment of having made the playoffs. But I guess when you're set in your ways as a coach, it is hard to change.

Green was not a personal coach unless you were a superstar—I never had a one-on-one conversation with him—but I don't think he was the only reason for the Vikings' playoff jinx. One individual does not win or lose a football game. He took the blame as the head coach, but there's always a combination of factors that contribute to the outcome. I felt bad for him.

I started all sixteen games in 1995, the year Henry Thomas left. I had a decent season, putting up numbers comparable to my rookie year. We played Dallas in our third game. Emmitt Smith, who became the NFL's all-time leading rusher, was their running back behind an incredible offensive line that included Pro Bowlers Larry Allen, Ray Donaldson, and Mark Tunei. The Cowboys ran the ball a lot. They didn't care if you knew. They were so good, they had the attitude, "Here we come. Try to stop us."

It wasn't easy, especially in the middle. They had a play where they triple-teamed the nose guard. I felt like I ran into a wall on every single play. After that game, I had the meanest headache. Smith ran for a hundred and fifty yards and scored a touchdown in overtime to give Dallas the win. For the most part, though, I held my ground against them, and my coach complimented me afterward.

I don't remember many specific incidents from the games I played. The stress and depression I felt at that time caused me to black out on the field. I wanted to erase all of the bad feelings. One play does stand out, though.

On Christmas Eve, our last game of the season against the Cincinnati Bengals was meaningless. If our division rival, the Chicago Bears, won their final game, they would go to the playoffs instead of us. They had won earlier in the day. That was the only year during my time in Minnesota that we didn't make the playoffs.

There were about fifty seconds left in the game. I hit the Bengals' quarterback Jeff Blake as he released the ball. This was in the Bengals' old stadium where the artificial turf was as hard as asphalt. It was a cold day. I stood up. Walking back to the huddle, I heard a loud "pop!" I thought Blake, the quarterback, had kicked me in the back of the leg. I turned around, but saw no one there. I sat down right away. The trainers came and carried me off. I had shredded my Achilles tendon.

I loved to play volleyball. That's how I stayed in shape during the off-season. When I got injured with only fifty seconds left in the season, my first thought was, *Damn, I won't be able to play volleyball this year.* But the consequences would be much worse than that.

I got a boot cast for Christmas that year. Some of my family had moved to Minneapolis: my mom, my sister Tusi, and my sister Sina and her family. We had a Christmas party at my place. I was living in a log cabin in Waconia, about a forty-minute drive from the stadium downtown. I invited one of my Viking teammates to our family Christmas party.

The teammate—I'll call him Derek—and I had become close. The Vikings had picked him up from another team. We hit it off. We hung out, partied, went to clubs. My place in Waconia was on the lake. We water-skied and relaxed on the boat. We had deep talks about all sorts of stuff.

It was great to have a buddy. I hadn't had a hang-out friend like that other than Brett Favre.

Derek was funny. We laughed a lot together. He had this joke about a gorilla with a muzzle. It was a stupid joke, but to him it was the funniest joke in the world. He loved to tell it.

I helped him buy clothes. I threw out his entire wardrobe. It was the whole "queer eye for the straight guy" thing. He used to wear flannel shirts. They looked terrible. I told him he had to get rid of those. He said he liked the way I dressed. So I said, "Let's go shopping. You've got to dress like a professional."

That upset his fiancée because she had bought him those flannel shirts. I think she was jealous that Derek and I had become such close friends. The more he talked about me, the less she liked me. A lot of players' wives didn't like me because I was a single guy taking their husbands out to party. Little did they know that I was the one reminding them when they flirted with other women, "Don't do that. You're married."

As the season progressed, I felt there was something more between Derek and me. You know when you can feel that extra something, an unspoken feeling? He was very attractive. Yet, I knew I could never go there.

After a night of drinking, we wound up back at his apartment. I said, "I'll sleep on the couch."

"No, sleep in the bed," he said.

It was a friendly gesture. He had a king-size bed. There was plenty of room. He wanted me to be comfortable.

I woke up in the middle of the night with him on top of my chest. I don't know if it was because he was drunk or because he was dreaming that he was with his fiancée or what. I sensed the invitation to respond sexually, that the door had been opened. But I couldn't.

I shook him. "Dude, wake up. Get off of me."

I pushed him off and rolled away.

That happened more than once. Derek was straight, but I sensed he felt something more for me.

Derek came to my family Christmas party with his fiancée Carla (not her real name). Everybody had a fantastic time except her. Derek and I were drinking and singing with my family. Suddenly, he decided he wanted to go sledding.

"Are you crazy?" I said. "I'm in a cast."

"I'll carry you," he said.

He grabbed me, and we headed outside. We had the best time sledding down the hill in back of my house. We laughed like little kids.

On our final run, we climbed on the sled together, flew down the hill, and crashed at the bottom. Derek ended up on top of me. I was flat on my back. We giggled. I looked up. He looked into my eyes.

We both paused. If I would have committed, I think we would have kissed.

Then—this happened just like it would in a movie—Carla shouted from the house, "Derek! Come on. We've got to go home."

There was a moment of sudden nervousness between us. He hopped off and helped me up.

"Esera," he said. "I don't want to go. I'm having a good time with you and your family."

I wanted to say, "Then stay." By this time, Carla was almost in the car. "Derek, you've got to go with her," I said. "She's not having a good time."

They left.

I went inside. The house had a basement walkout. I spent a moment alone downstairs. *What just happened?* I asked myself. *Did we just have a moment between us?*

I started feeling sorry for myself. *Why didn't I kiss him? Why am I such a chickenshit? Why do I have to be unhappy this holiday season?* Again, I fell short. Again, I felt miserable. I wanted to scream. I wanted to smash my fist through something. But I couldn't with my family upstairs.

I heard a pounding on the door, like someone was trying to break it down. I opened the door. Derek stood there, out of breath.

"Are you okay?" I asked.

"Yeah." He told me he had jumped out of the car while Carla was driving and run back across the frozen lake. She had followed him down to the lake and yelled after him. "I told her how much you and your family mean to me," he said.

We were in the laundry room. I sat on the dryer, listening to his story. He walked over to hug me.

Again, we had a moment.

My sister Tusi knocked on the laundry room door. "Carla's upstairs."

Carla was cold and angry. She had followed Derek across the lake.

"You've got to go," I said. "That's your fiancée up there. You've got to take care of her."

He kept saying, "I don't want to go."

I wanted him to say, "I love you." He didn't.

"Derek, don't do this again," I said.

After that night, our friendship was never the same. I don't know if he wigged out over those moments, if Carla had a talk with him, or if my reaction turned him away, but things changed. Maybe he thought he had crossed the line too far and had to retreat. The next day, he was cold toward me. Stone cold.

That hurt so much. I had opened myself up to someone—the best I could at the time—and he shut the door on our friendship.

We had had so much fun together. That ended. That cut me to the core.

I couldn't help but wonder, *What if?* That night I almost felt I could come out of my shell. Maybe he was someone I could have shared my secret with. I don't know what would have developed between us. I had never had that type of intimate relationship. It would have made a world of difference to have someone who understood and was in the same profession. We could have fed off of one another.

In the end, Derek married Carla. They have children and live in the South.

He was the only teammate I ever played with in the pros who I thought might have been gay or bisexual. I was never able to get close enough to anyone else to find out otherwise.

---

I had surgery after Christmas to repair my Achilles tendon. The surgeon stitched it back together with wires and pins. If I had blown out my Achilles two years previously, the injury would have ended my career. Lucky for me, advances in medicine and technology made it possible for me to have the chance to play again.

When I sat up after surgery to look at my leg, the nurse said, "You may want to lie down."

"Why?" I asked.

"Because I don't want you to faint when you see your leg," she said. "I don't want to have to catch a three hundred-pound guy falling out of bed."

She was right. My leg looked like Frankenstein's monster, all discolored and ragged with stitches. It was ugly.

They put me in a cast up to my crotch. It was hard to shower. The crutches rubbed my underarms raw. That lasted eight weeks.

There was nothing I could do to rehabilitate my leg while the cast was still on, so I went home to Hawaii. At least I could do nothing in paradise.

This was my first major injury. The doctors told me it was a big setback. They put the recovery time at eight months.

Injury is the kiss of death. Remember what happened when Dan Majkowski got hurt and Brett Favre filled in? So long, Majik Man. Somebody comes in and does better. That tells the front office people maybe they don't have to pay the star millions. They can pay the replacement guy less. It's all about cutting corners, saving money.

I returned to Minnesota once my cast came off. The operation was considered a success, but I had to get back the strength I had lost in my leg while it was in the cast and allow the tendon to fuse back together. I worked out at Winter Park, the Vikings' training facility. I ran in the pool, pushed golf carts, ran stairs, lifted weights. It was a lonely road back.

The front office and coaching staff give players the message to fight through the pain; that's the NFL way. Be tough. I could handle the physical pain. Having been through what I had as a gay man, that was nothing. It was the emotional bullshit that was hard.

I feared losing my job. I felt coaches and management pressuring me, "We need you back." Yet, I didn't know if they would still believe in me. I didn't want to let down the coaches and my teammates. I feared being released again.

An injury takes time to heal, but there's always a sense of urgency in the NFL. There's no margin for sympathy. It's not like a corporate job where you can take the time you need to get well

165

from a sickness or injury. We NFL football players can't afford that time. The team made an investment. Management wants you back on the field. It's hard to see the looks on their faces when the doctors say you're only 70 percent. "That's not enough," they say. "We need you 100 percent."

It's almost a point of pride to come back fast. "Takes other guys six weeks to heal from this injury? I can do it in four." That's the twisted macho pride you find in the NFL. I think a lot of athletes come back early and ruin their chances because they are not fully healed. The body can only heal so fast.

By the start of the season, I was back in uniform. Within several weeks, I had won back my starting job. My leg hurt the whole time, but I played through the pain. I pretended it didn't hurt. You can't show it. If you do, you're gone. You become a big actor. I was practiced in doing that.

I came back too soon. I still wasn't 100 percent. I think because they didn't give me enough time to heal, I wasn't able to perform the way I wanted to. I should have waited a couple more months.

But I always felt I had to get back in there and prove I could still do my job. I was so terrified of losing it. I didn't want my injury to be the kiss of death.

# CHAPTER THIRTEEN

# A McDonald's Wedding

**A**FTER THE 1996 SEASON, I went home to Hawaii the way I usually did. I always stayed with Calvin Ro. Calvin was a mentor and friend who looked out for me. He never let me get away with placing myself above others as an NFL football player. He knocked me back down to earth when I needed it. If he thought I had hurt someone's feelings, he made me apologize. As an older gay man, Calvin was to me what my brother Tua wasn't able to be.

We had a mutual friend in Jack Law, who owned Hula's and another nightclub, the Wave. Calvin and Jack formed part of the small circle in Hawaii who knew my secret.

I was going through a tough time that winter. I hadn't been happy with the season after coming back from my injury. I was depressed that my prayer for a lifetime partner had not been answered. Calvin observed my struggles and mentioned them to Jack. Through his clubs, Jack had met a lot of closeted gay men.

He gave me a book, *The David Kopay Story.* David Kopay was a running back who played for five teams over ten years in the NFL. He retired in 1972 and came out four years later. His story was a *New York Times* bestseller in 1977. It was reissued in 1988, but I had not heard of Kopay or his book until Jack gave me a copy.

I cried when I read his book. For so long, I had felt isolated as a gay man in the NFL. I hadn't known that there had been someone else like me. It was fantastic to discover I wasn't the only one.

Kopay's book gave me hope. Someone else had gone through what I was going through. He had survived. I didn't want his playboy lifestyle. The one-night stands hadn't filled the empty space in me. I wanted a lifetime partner, someone I could wake up with in the morning and know I was going to spend the day with, and the next day, and the day after that. I wanted a family. But I felt like a woman who hears her biological clock ticking. As I snuck up on thirty, I feared time was running out on me meeting someone.

David Kopay's book let me know that it might be possible for me to find that special someone. His book gave me the strength to think that if something did happen, if someone did come along, I would pursue a relationship with him. Kopay's book gave me courage.

Ever since I had listened to my mom and dad play the ukulele and sing traditional Samoan songs around the campfire on the beach, I had loved music. I started singing for them and their friends when I was five years old. Later, being able to sing the national anthem at football games was great, but I had always wanted to record my passion, to be able to hear myself sing on a

CD. I found the chance to do so when I met Rob Rivera at a Minneapolis club. He was a music producer who liked my voice. He agreed to produce my *One Man Island* CD.

This was during the period when I was dating Elizabeth, the lead singer for the Jets. Seeing her perform inspired me, but I did not want to ask her for favors. I didn't ask her to listen to my songs. We didn't discuss my singing.

Rob wrote a couple of original songs. My friend Paul Jones, also a music producer, wrote another. We included a remix of "Lady in Red." The CD had five songs total. It was more of a demo than an album meant for record stores. Several Twin Cities radio stations played it.

This was before a lot of football players and professional athletes started cutting their own albums. I hadn't planned the CD's release as a strategic career move. I recorded it more to fulfill a personal desire. Turns out, the exposure it gave me would change my life.

People in the NFL caught on that I could sing. Rick Garson, the concept developer who was with Gridiron Records at the time, asked me to be part of a project that paired an NFL player with a popular musical talent. The idea was to put out two albums, a country one and a hip-hop one. All-Pro quarterbacks Brett Favre, Troy Aikman, and Terry Bradshaw were among those who sang on the country album; running back Ricky Watters and wide receiver Andre Rison—both five-time Pro Bowlers—sang on the hip-hop album. I was the only NFL player to sing on both.

Rick Garson flew me down to Nashville for an audition with some other players at the studio of James Burton, who had been

Elvis Presley's lead guitar player. I sang last. I was nervous. In addition to Burton, there were some big-time players on the music scene, including one of Aretha Franklin's songwriters. Since I didn't have anyone to accompany me, Burton did. I sang a soulful version of "Somewhere Over the Rainbow" that impressed Rick. "We've got one who can *sing*," he said.

He paired me with the famous country singer Lari White, who had written hits such as "That's How You Know (When You're in Love)" and "That's My Baby." She sent me a tape and asked what key I wanted for the song. I suggested we sing it in the key on the tape, which was high. She didn't know I was a high tenor. She thought a big nose guard would have a deep voice and not be able to sing that high. "Be sure that's the key you want," she said, "because I have the Garth Brooks A band playing backup."

That happens a lot. People see me and think, *He's a football player. He can't sing.* They are surprised to hear a sweet voice coming out of an elephant. I've used those negative comments to make myself better, whether it be playing football or singing. The criticism fuels my desire.

Once Lari heard me sing, she apologized for stereotyping me. We ended up making a video together of her song "Another Broken Heart." We filmed it in Hawaii on the islands of Oahu and Maui on top of a mountain and by a waterfall. We had a $170,000 budget, three helicopters with cameras, and separate crews for wardrobe, sound, and makeup. If I wanted anything, say, a cheeseburger, somebody would get it for me. It was incredible. After recording my five-song CD on a shoestring budget, this production made me feel like Prince.

Music has the power to connect us with others and with ourselves. On the banana farm, the only radio station we could pick up was an oldies station. These days, when I hear Motown oldies, those songs take me back to the farm. I'm gliding on the tire swing my daddy hung for me, sliding down hills on tealeaf branches, or climbing mango trees. Music puts me in touch with that young boy I was.

~

After I had released my *One Man Island* CD, a Minneapolis radio station invited listeners to write an essay that explained why they should be the one to get married at McDonald's on Valentine's Day. The radio station not only paid for the wedding, it arranged for Ronald McDonald to stand up for the couple and the Minnesota Vikings' Esera Tuaolo to sing. I was a little embarrassed by the radio station's goofy promotion. Doing a gig at a McDonald's wedding seemed a step below an airport hotel lounge act. I agreed, though, and was glad I did.

I flew to Minneapolis from Hawaii with my two-year-old niece. My mom had brought her to Hawaii for a visit. I was bringing her back to her mom, my sister Tusi. We arrived at 6:00 a.m. on February 14. The wedding was at 8:00 a.m.

My friend Paul Jones picked us up and rushed us straight to the McDonald's. Everyone was dressed in frilly ruffles—they looked like the cast from *Little House on the Prairie.* One guy stood out—a handsome man dressed stylishly in a sharp suit. His friend, the bride, had won the contest. I noticed him right away.

This handsome stranger mesmerized me. My eyes followed him around the room. I wanted to get to know him. Meanwhile, I was trying to look after my niece, who was jet-lagged and crying. I felt like a hobo myself, having just stepped off the plane. I kept staring at this handsome stranger who looked like someone I might see in my fantasies.

We traded glances and brief hello's. My heart skipped, but it would be months before I saw him again.

⁓

Not long after that, I was invited to an appreciation party at La Costa Resort and Spa in San Diego for athletes who promoted No Fear apparel. On the flight there, I met Paul Molitor, the future Hall of Fame baseball player who was with the Minnesota Twins at the time, and his wife, Linda. She and I struck up a conversation and realized we were headed to the same party.

Linda is a fantastic woman. We hit it off and had a great week together at La Costa.

⁓

In April, I attended the opening of *The King & I* at the Orpheum, a Minneapolis theatre. My friend Calvin Ro had called and told me that Simion, a gay actor friend of his from Hawaii, was in the show. Simion and I had dinner afterward with a straight friend, Patrick. Simion wanted to go dancing at a gay bar. Patrick was willing to go, but I said no way.

"I can't do that in Minnesota," I said. "All I need is someone talking."

Simion finally convinced me. "If someone recognizes you, you can blame it on me," he said. "Everybody's got gay friends."

Even though I feared the idea was dangerous, I went along with it. I think Kopay's book gave me the strength to take the risk.

We crossed the street to the Saloon. I felt paranoid. I stood tall like I was a straight man. I didn't smile at anyone. Everybody seemed to notice Patrick, who is very good-looking.

I spotted someone familiar across the bar. I knew I had met him but couldn't remember where. He looked in my direction. At first, I thought he was staring at Patrick, but then our eyes met.

Simion noticed. He nudged me. "Go talk to him."

"No," I said.

"Okay, let's get out of here," Simion said. "Or else, I'll go talk to him."

"No, don't," I said.

I didn't want to leave, but I couldn't cross that floor. I don't know why, but finally I pointed at Mitchell and beckoned him. He headed toward me.

My heart pounded. He could have shaken his head, could've flipped me off. But he didn't. He was walking toward me. It was like a *Seinfeld* episode. I thought, *Oh my god, it's working. What do I do now?*

I was sweating. I felt excited, nervous.

"Aren't you a football player?" he said.

That was the last thing I wanted to hear in a gay bar. "No," I said.

"You're not that singer?"

"No."

"What's your name?" he asked.

I panicked. This guy was going to tell someone. I said, "David," the English version of Kavika, the Samoan name I often used in gay bars.

"Oh. I thought you were that Minnesota Vikings singer."

Suddenly, I realized where I had seen him before. He was the handsome stranger from the McDonald's wedding. My heart pounded faster.

There was a silence. We were like a couple of junior high kids standing there awkwardly.

"Okay," I said. "What do we do now?"

"I think this is where we exchange phone numbers."

I jotted "David" on a slip of paper. I was about to write down a bogus number, but I decided at the last second to give him my actual number.

He handed me a piece of paper that said, "Mitchell" and his number.

I headed home feeling giddy and worried. My worst nightmare might come true. I imagined the headline on the next day's sports page: "Esera Tuaolo Gay."

Still, this handsome stranger—Mitchell—had wanted to meet me. For someone like me, who had never liked his appearance, who considered himself ugly, it was a huge self-esteem boost. I was so happy I drove home at a hundred miles per hour.

That was April 4, 1997. I didn't sleep that night.

Mitchell didn't call the next day. Instead, Linda Molitor called me out of the blue. My mom answered the phone and passed it to me. "Hey, Esera, it's Linda Molitor. I just called to see if you want to have dinner and go to a baseball game. I have a couple of tickets."

"Great," I said, even though I didn't like baseball. "Whenever. Let me know."

We chatted for a while and said goodbye.

Later that evening, I called Mitchell.

"I have a confession," he said. "I know who you are. I had a mutual friend dial your number."

He had told his mom and trusted friends that he had met a guy. He was talking about me—the guy he met—with Linda Molitor at the salon he owns. He wanted to find out who "David" really was. "I think I met a gay Viking," he told her.

"Who? Which one?" she asked.

"I think his name is Esera, but he gave me his number and told me his name was David."

"Esera?" she said. "I just met him at La Costa. Let me call him."
She snatched my number out of Mitchell's hand. That's why she
offered me the baseball tickets. She had asked to speak to "Esera,"
not "David."

Mitchell was sweet on the phone. "I want you to know I would
never tell anyone your secret," he said.

But I was scared about someone else knowing. There was so
much pressure not to let anyone know about my sexuality. A heterosexual couple didn't have to face the drama of a high profile
gay man still in the closet. "No, I wanted your number for my
friend," I told Mitchell.

"Oh, well. I just want you to know I would never tell anyone."

The more he comforted me, the more at ease I felt. The people
he had talked to before he knew my real name were close friends
of his. I needn't worry about them. The sincerity in his voice convinced me he was trustworthy. He had worked with celebrities. He
understood the need for discretion. After years of being alone and
wanting a relationship, I sensed the possibility of one with this
man. I decided I would take the risk.

I finally admitted I was interested. I had been attending services at Speak the Word church since I had moved to Minneapolis. I
invited Mitchell to church the next day, Sunday.

I drove over to his place to pick him up. He lived in a cute cottage house. We sat and talked. And talked. I felt so comfortable
with him. We talked so much that we missed church. We went out
for brunch instead.

Afterward, we went back to his house. I started to feel nervous.
"Do you have any tequila?" I asked. He did. Petron, one of my
favorites. I took a couple of shots. He took one. We talked some
more.

After that, we talked a lot on the phone. I had never talked that much on the phone with anyone. We talked for hours, late into the night. One of us would fall asleep and wake up to the other saying, "Are you there?"

We talked about everything. Our families. Growing up. Football. His salon. We asked questions back and forth. We were learning each other's stories.

He had been born in California but grew up in several places around Minnesota and Texas. He attended a suburban Minneapolis high school. Mitchell was a loner, often teased by other kids for being different. He had the business sense and ambition to manage a Mexican chain restaurant when he was sixteen. Later, after college, he worked as a set decorator for Prince, designing sets for music videos and decorating his house in Los Angeles. Then, he and his mom bought Spalon Montage, a chic salon on the verge of bankruptcy. He turned it into a thriving business, expanding from twenty employees at one location to four hundred at three locations.

I told him my story. It felt so good to unleash everything, to find someone I could tell my secrets and deepest fears.

Straight friends who had found their life partners used to tell me, "You'll know when you meet the right person."

"Whatever," I responded.

That's the way it was, though, for me with Mitchell. When I first walked into his house and saw him, I knew he was the one I had been looking for. He was the answer to my prayers.

Our meeting was fate. It was my first time at a gay bar in Minneapolis. It was Mitchell's first time in nine months going back to the bar. He had just broken off a relationship, and a friend had dragged him out.

Not only did I feel the fireworks with Mitchell, I fell in love with who he was. He was honest, kind, and humble. The fact he loved his mom and was close to her told me he was a good person. I went down the checklist, and he had it all, including husband potential.

Some of the guys I met, all they wanted was to jump in my pants. Mitchell wasn't like that. He wanted to get to know me first. That's another thing I loved about him. We talked so much that we developed a closeness. When we finally did make love, it was fantastic.

Three days after our first date, Mitchell wanted me to meet his mom. Driving over to her house, he said, "You have to help me. I've heard your name pronounced so many ways. What's the correct way?"

"'A-sarah,' like the girl's name with an A in front," I said. "The English pronunciation is 'Es-e-ra.'"

He was quiet the rest of the drive. I asked him questions, but he gave me only one-word answers.

I started getting nervous. I was still with the Vikings, still afraid of being outed. I was wrapped up in the emotional whirlwind of having just met Mitchell. *Was this moving too fast, too recklessly?*

He pulled into a fancy neighborhood where the likes of Carl Pohlad, the Twins billionaire owner lived. *Who are these people I'm going to meet?* I wondered. I hoped none of the Viking owners were neighbors of Mitchell's mom.

We parked in the driveway. Rang the doorbell. His mom, Shelly, answered. "Mom, I'd like to introduce you to A-sarah," Mitchell said.

"Nice to meet you," she said politely.

"No, Mom," Mitchell said. She didn't seem to understand something Mitchell was trying to tell her. "This is *A-Sarah.*"

Shelly suddenly became very emotional, almost hysterical. She hugged me and nearly tackled me.

I was dumbfounded. "Okay, let me in on this," I said. "Why are you so happy?"

We went inside, and Shelly told me the story.

Mitchell had come out to her when he was eighteen (he was thirty-one when I met him). She was in shock, trying to be understanding but afraid of the unknown. She sent Mitchell to therapy.

One day, as she was trying to sort through what it meant to have a son that was gay, she was driving home from work and looked in the rearview mirror. She saw her parents, who had died ten years earlier. They had both died of alcoholism, but in the rearview mirror they looked beautiful.

She had a conversation with them. "Why are you here?" she asked. "Are you here to tell me that Mitchell is sick? That he is going to die of AIDS? What?"

Her mom talked to her, consoled her. The last thing she told Shelly was, "Don't worry. He's going to be all right once he meets a Sarah."

All along, for thirteen years, Shelly thought Mitchell was going to meet a woman named Sarah who would straighten him out. She had told this story to Mitchell, her cousins, her friends—everyone she knew. She had come to accept Mitchell and the fact he was gay—she did not want to change him. But she never forgot what her mother had said in the rearview mirror.

So, when I showed up and she heard my name, it was as though a prophecy had come true. For me to find someone with whom I seemed to fit so perfectly in a supernatural way was amazing—especially after my prayers to find a lifetime partner.

Shelly is the most supportive person I've met. I wasn't sure what to expect from Mitchell's stepdad, Dan. He owns a large construction firm. I worried he might be a close-minded person. He was the opposite. He gave me a big hug right away.

Both Dan and Shelly assured me that my secret was safe with them. That night, they invited me to go to Italy with them. Turned out Linda Molitor, our mutual friend, backed out to make room for me on the trip.

A few days after I first met her, Shelly invited Mitchell and me to her house. Mitchell's Aunt Janice and his cousin Tiffany were coming over, too. When they arrived and Tiffany looked at me, a big smile crossed her face. "You don't know me, right?" she said.

"No," I said.

"I used to hand you your room key," she said. She had worked at the downtown Hilton hotel where the Vikings stayed the night before each home game.

Right away, I panicked.

"Don't worry," Mitchell said. "You're safe."

Meeting his family was like winning the lottery. They were educated and sensitive about what it meant to be gay. I went into a very supportive environment. Not everyone is so lucky.

I think the secret to happy families is unconditional love for one another, especially for the children. That's what Mitchell's parents had for him and what they poured out to me. They made me feel special.

Two weeks later, we headed to Italy. It was a fairy tale to go from being closeted and depressed to flying first class to a romantic place with my handsome new boyfriend. I felt like Cinderfella.

Seriously, for the first time in my life, I felt whole, like a complete person. My prayers had been answered. I thought, *There must be a God in heaven who heard me.*

We stopped first in London and stayed at a Knightsbridge hotel a block from Harrods, the world-famous department store. Mitchell and I had a huge, beautiful suite with our own private butler.

I couldn't believe how terrific my life had suddenly become. Here I was, making love to this wonderful man in a fantastic place. I would wake up at night and sit in a chair and watch Mitchell sleep. I hoped it wasn't all a dream. So much of my life had been bad to that point. I wondered, *Can this be true? Is this the beginning of something great for me?*

From London, we traveled to Lake Como, where we stayed in a romantic hotel with a view of the Swiss Alps. Then, it was on to Venice with its charming canals. I felt blessed to sit with Mitchell at a café on the Piazza San Marco.

From Venice, we headed to Bologna, where Mitchell attended a salon convention. I was nervous to meet the five team captains from Spalon Montage. They seemed so cool that I decided I didn't care if they knew I was gay. Mitchell's parents were also wonderful to travel with. The little bubble that I had been living in was growing bigger. I still wasn't ready to bust out of it, but it felt better.

We took a day trip to Florence, where we marveled at Michelangelo's *David,* and Mitchell bought me a gold locket with the *David's* face pictured on front because I had first told him my name was David.

I freaked out in Florence. Mitchell and I were shopping, going in and out of boutiques, when I noticed a group of college-age guys following us. Each time we came out of a shop, I spotted them waiting for us. Finally, after trailing us for three blocks, one of the guys approached and asked, "Are you Esera Tooalowaloh?"

I panicked. *Had I been holding Mitchell's hand? Had they seen that?*

I hadn't expected someone to recognize me halfway around the world. It turned out they were art students from Minnesota. They were simply excited to spot and meet a professional football player. I introduced Mitchell as a friend.

After the convention in Bologna ended, we headed to Rome, where we saw Pope John Paul II bless the crowd. I bought a cross for Fred Zamberletti, the Vikings' head trainer whose family came from Italy, and took a picture of me dipping the cross into holy water. At the Colosseum, I could sympathize with the Christians eaten by the lions. All of my life, I had feared I would be thrown to the lions if I came out.

The honeymoon ended on our flight home. We had our first argument. I didn't want our incredible time together to end, yet I feared it would when we returned to Minnesota. I didn't know how to express that to Mitchell. I wanted him to rescue me by saying he wanted me to come home with him. He didn't say that, so I figured he wanted some space from me. I think he wanted me to tell him that I wanted to come home with him, but I didn't want to invite myself. Since I didn't, he figured I wanted space. Our thoughts got tangled up, and the words grew heated.

Standing at the baggage carousel in the Minneapolis airport, he finally said, "I don't want you to leave."

I started crying. "That's what I've been trying to say. From our first date, I've known I want to spend the rest of my life with you."

I had never felt wanted by someone. I didn't want our relationship to end. We went back to his cottage.

Shortly after, the Vikings released me. I don't think it had anything to do with my new relationship. I think it was my Achilles injury. Management didn't trust my leg. The front office feared I wouldn't be able to return to my previous level of play. Also, it was about money. I don't think the Vikings wanted to pay me the last year of my contract, which was worth $1.2 million. That would have been the first time I earned over one million in a season.

This time, there was no talk. Just a phone call to my agent. I didn't care. I had met Mitchell.

# CHAPTER FOURTEEN

∼

# The Past Can
# Destroy the Future

THE SPRING OF 1997, I spent pretty much all of my
time with Mitchell. I had bought a house in
Chanhassen, an outer suburb, where I lived with my
mom. She had moved to Minnesota two years earlier.
After Tua died, no one was looking after her in Hawaii. I had
remodeled the house on the banana farm, but my brother Fale
had moved his family in. I visited one time and discovered
Mama living in Tua's abandoned shack out back. She deserved
better.

I bought her the house in Chanhassen so I could take care of
her. I had rented the log cabin in Waconia for myself, but after the
1996 season, Mama convinced me to move in with her. "Why are
you paying rent when you could be living in the house you
bought?" she asked me.

Mama had been very grateful for the way I treated her. When I bought the house for her, she told me she appreciated her baby taking care of her. In most Polynesian families, that's the responsibility of the oldest child, not the youngest. I stopped her. "Mama, you have nothing to thank me for," I said. "In this lifetime, I can never thank you for all that you've done for me."

My mom is a humble woman. She gives so much but doesn't act like she has done anything for anyone. She had cared for me and my siblings, and she had been the one who was always there for me with a hug. Her care and steadfast love had meant more to me than I could ever express.

After I met Mitchell, I had been going home every day to change my clothes, but that was about it. One day, when I stopped home, my mom asked me in Samoan, "Are you ashamed of me?"

"What do you mean, Mama?" I asked. "Why do you say that?"

"Why don't you bring her home to meet me?" she said.

My heart dropped. "Mama, I'm not ashamed of you."

"Then bring her home so I can meet her."

I went upstairs to my room and cried. I called Mitchell. "I have to tell her."

I waited almost two weeks for the right moment. My older brother Tua had said, "Don't let Mama know." He didn't want me to hurt her. That was the last thing I wanted to do, but I needed to tell Mama. She meant so much to me. I had to let her know. I didn't want this secret to be a barrier between us. Yet, I feared that her age and fundamental religion might prevent her from accepting me being gay.

I also feared she and my sisters might reject me. I had heard of people whose families had tossed them out on the street for being gay. A person grows up with brothers and sisters and develops that family bond. Knowing that you could lose your family because of your secret makes being gay so hard. Just that risk—knowing you could lose them—hurts. That's one of the fears of every gay person who has not yet come out to his or her family.

The right moment came on Mother's Day. After lunch, my sisters, Mama, and I were sitting in the living room of the Chanhassen home. Ever since Mama had asked me if I was ashamed of her, I had been wanting to tell her. My secret had been weighing on me.

I had told my oldest sister Gene when I met Mitchell. She had always been a sort of best friend/mother figure to me. As kids, I used to call her Auntie Gene because she was so much older than I was—sixteen years—which used to tick her off. Gene had been close to Tua. I had never heard her say anything negative about homosexuality. I trusted her with my secret. I figured Gene, Sina, and Tusi could comfort Mama if she had a hard time.

Sitting in the living room, I realized the moment had arrived to tell Mama. I started bawling. Gene knew why right away. But Mama didn't. "What's wrong?" she asked in Samoan. It always seemed more dramatic when she spoke to me in Samoan because that was the language of my childhood and it is so beautiful. "It seems there is something heavy in your heart."

"Yes, there is," I said. "I really need to tell you something."

I told them that it was something big, something about me that had been true my whole life, something that had caused me hard times, even made me want to kill myself. I was setting them up. They were saying, "Okay, okay. What is it?"

Finally, I said, "I'm gay."

Mama and my sisters Sina and Tusi were shocked. They had met Elizabeth and other girlfriends I'd had. But they didn't reject me.

Mama buried her face in her hands and sobbed like she had at Tua's funeral. I think a lot of parents wish their kids would marry someone of the opposite sex. That's their dream for their children. When they hear their child is gay, all of the negative things they've heard about homosexuality run through their heads. Mama had lost a son to AIDS. She didn't want to lose me. I was her baby.

She sobbed from a place so deep that it scared me. I was afraid that my news might harm her health or send her into a depression. I held her and told her everything was going to be all right. My sisters also comforted her.

Mama cried for a long time. Then, we had the best conversation we had ever had. We talked together in a new, intimate way. I didn't have to pretend or cover up anything. I could be myself with her.

She wanted to know everything about my life. I explained to her the pain that I had experienced. She cried again.

I tried to be careful about what I said. Most parents aren't educated about homosexuality. She didn't understand completely. She had known Tua was gay, but he hadn't educated her. "All I want is to be happy, Mama," I said. "I want what my other brothers have: a partner, a family. I've met someone who I want to be my life partner."

"Bring him over," she said. "I want to meet him."

The next day, Mitchell came to dinner. He was nervous as hell. So was I. My sisters were uncomfortable, too. It was awkward. I had just shocked them with my news. Now they were meeting their brother's boyfriend. I knew it would take them some time to process it all.

There was a bit of a language barrier with my mom. She speaks broken English, and, of course, Mitchell didn't speak Samoan. Yet, I could tell Mama liked him.

We sat on the deck and had drinks. My sisters and mom asked Mitchell the kind of questions you might ask any new boyfriend or girlfriend a sibling has just introduced you to: Where are you from? Do you come from a big family? How did you two meet? Mitchell managed some questions of his own, such as How do you like the weather here? and Why would you leave a beautiful island for Minnesota? The mood remained somewhat awkward, but the evening went better than I had expected. We were able to laugh some, like when my sisters teased me, "That's why you wanted an Easy-Bake oven," and we all laughed. Mama could see I was happy. That made her happy.

A couple of months later, on my birthday in July, Mama met Mitchell's family. She giggled while I was opening my gifts. "What's going on?" Mitchell asked me.

I didn't know. I found out when I opened her gift, a statue of two guys wrestling. It was her confirmation of me.

She had more questions for me, like, "How does Mitchell's stepdad Dan feel about you two?" I think his family taught my mom that love is love. We made our love look normal. Society's definition of a couple is of a man and woman. For us, a couple meant two men. Mitchell's family's love and support of him helped my mom see our love as a good thing. We did not fit the negative stereotype of promiscuous gay men engaging in endless one-night stands. Gay love was presented to my mom in a beautiful way. I think she thought that some people in Mitchell's family would be angry or judgmental, but she saw that his stepdad, mom, aunts, and brother—everybody—embraced him. She saw our love and joy.

Her questions continued. The whole year was a learning experience for her. She was as supportive as she could be.

"If this is the life you've chosen, you have to make it right," she said.

"It's not a choice, Mama," I said.

I explained the difference between sexual preference and sexual orientation. She came to understand that being gay is the way a person is created.

When Mitchell and I argued, I would go home to Mama. She never told me to leave him or that I would be better off without him. Instead, she would ask, "What did you do?" She would tell me in Samoan, "Do what it takes to make your family right."

That wasn't easy. Mitchell was my first relationship. Up until that point, my "relationships" had been one-night stands, often with strangers. I had a lot to learn about being intimate with someone in a committed relationship. The lessons were often difficult and painful for both of us.

I went back to work in July. My new agent, Mitch Frankel, landed me an invitation to the Buffalo Bills' training camp. I had fired Ken Kramer, my agent from the International Management Group, because it seemed to me that IMG had grown too big for someone like me who wasn't a superstar. In retrospect, it might not have been the best move, but at the time my phone calls were not being returned, and I wanted an agent who was interested in me.

The Bills held their training camp at State University at Fredonia, halfway between Buffalo, New York and Erie, Pennsylvania. Mitchell could not come with me. He had to run his business. We had been together almost every day since our first date three months earlier. I was glad that another team was interested in me but sad to leave him behind.

I knew when I arrived at the Bills' training camp that I wasn't going to stay with the team. It was the opposite of how I felt when

I had arrived in Minnesota, only with the same certainty. The coaches had already set the team. They had some great defensive linemen such as Pro Bowlers Bruce Smith and Ted Washington. There was no opening for a nose guard, not even as a backup. I think they brought guys in to have a look at them for the scout team, the players that mimic the next week's opponent in practice but don't suit up for Sunday's game. I had the feeling that no matter how well I did in practice or games, I still wouldn't make the team.

The workouts themselves were easy. Marv Levy, in what would be his last year as the Bills' head coach, did not work his players hard in training camp. The superstars on the team did nothing. They didn't listen to the coaches. Even though the practices were light, my Achilles tendon was killing me. I didn't tell anyone. I played through the pain, pretended it didn't hurt—the way I was accustomed to.

I had a roommate, so I called Mitchell secretly on my cell phone. I feared that rumors about me would trickle from the Vikings to the Bills. Some of the Vikings' wives were regular customers at Spalon Montage. It seemed only a matter of time before they heard gossip about the owner's new boyfriend. I trusted Mitchell to be discreet. He wasn't going to walk up to me at practice and say, "Hi, honey," or give me a kiss. It's just that I knew talk flowed freely among salon workers and customers.

Though I had to call Mitchell secretly, I was grateful to have someone to call. It made me feel like one of the other players. They called their girlfriends and wives. I called my boyfriend. I felt almost like a straight athlete.

I had a hard time concentrating on my job at training camp. My mind kept wandering back to Mitchell. I thought he was cheating on me. We argued heatedly on the phone. I called him names. He denied being unfaithful. I accused him of lying. I was convinced he was hiding a lover in the house.

My fears and insecurities almost sabotaged our love.

For starters, I lacked confidence in myself. I was confident on the field, but not about my looks. I had never liked my physical appearance. I didn't see why anyone would be interested in me. That was a byproduct of growing up without anyone complimenting me other than for my football performance. I suffered from low self-esteem. I wondered if Mitchell was attracted to me only because I was a football player. It took me quite a while to realize that I could be somebody's type. To realize that someone could love me for who I was. Mitchell reassured me that he found me handsome.

My suspicions also arose out of my jealousy, which I mistakenly equated with love. Growing up, I had learned that love wasn't true love unless someone was jealous. That was based on seeing my daddy cheat on my mom. He had been my role model in relationships. I learned that men in love weren't to be trusted. They left their loved ones jealous.

I also lacked a healthy image of a gay couple. Society subscribed to the stereotype of the promiscuous gay man—a stereotype perpetuated by television and other media. Church reinforced the image of gay men as sinners, guilty of promiscuity and rape, as in the story of Sodom and Gomorrah, where men attempted to rape God's angels. My own experience of my homosexuality had consisted primarily of cruising for men in clubs, starting as a young, impressionable teenager. I had known only the promiscuous side of being gay. That's what I had come to expect of other gay men, including Mitchell. I had met someone truthful and faithful, but I didn't realize it. Instead, I accused him of being unfaithful.

Since we met in the off-season, Mitchell had not been to one of my games. I wanted him to see me play football. I invited him to attend one of Buffalo's exhibition games.

Mitchell battled anxieties of his own that I didn't understand. He was borderline agoraphobic. The thought of boarding a plane on his own terrified him. He couldn't do it without alcohol or medication.

I was not sympathetic. I had developed the jock mentality: if you've got a problem, you deal with it and move on. That left no room for crybabies. I had no patience for him at first. Why can't you just suck it up and get on a plane? Like a spoiled child, I whined for him to visit me. I couldn't see the situation from his perspective. He talked about his anxieties with me, but I didn't understand. By default, I reverted back to the jock mentality. There was so much I needed to learn about being in a relationship

Mitchell came to visit but was sick. Maybe that resulted from the anxiety of flying alone. He had such a high fever that he was hallucinating. He couldn't get out of bed. I had to leave him in the hotel while I played the exhibition game. Even then, I feared he was cheating on me—that somehow, sick as he was, he had snuck someone into his hotel room.

My suspicions were irrational. That's the way it often is for people who have been sexually abused as children. We have difficulty trusting even trustworthy people.

The first time it happened, my parents went shopping with my older brothers and sisters. They left me home alone with my uncle, who had come from Samoa to live with us. I was six at the time. Uncle Fafawia led me out to the banana patch. He made it

seem like we were playing a game. He pulled down his pants. He told me to touch him. To fondle him. To pump him until he spurted goo. I did what he told me.

I sensed that what he had me do was wrong, but I thought that everything he told me was right. Uncle Fafawia—my dad's cousin—had told my parents that he would watch me. I was under his care. I was supposed to respect my elders. Polynesian culture is all about respecting those older than you. Yet, he was making me do things that I didn't want to do. I was scared of my uncle. He was so much bigger than me. He had me suck his penis like a popsicle.

He commanded me to do these things like he was telling me to do a chore. But he pretended we were playing a game. It was fun. The sexual part was exciting, even enjoyable. I struggled to understand this for the longest time as an adult.

Afterward, Uncle Fafawia told me not to tell my mom and dad about our game. "If they find out, they will be angry and beat you," he said.

This happened for a while. My parents left me with him, and we played Uncle Fafawia's game. I began to think this was just the way life was for a child.

One night, after my uncle had been molesting me for about a year, we all slept together in the hut—my family, my uncle, and me. That was the first time I cried when Uncle Fafawia did what he wanted with me. It was the first time he penetrated me. He was forceful, and it hurt. Uncle Fafawia held his hand over my mouth, so I wouldn't wake up anyone. He kept ramming. That was the most painful thing I ever experienced.

Afterward, I ran out to the banana patch. I was crying. I hurt so bad where he had rammed me. I didn't know what to do; I was scared. I knelt down and prayed, "Please, God, take the pain away."

I was terrified of Uncle Fafawia after that. Up until then, what we'd done had been fun and games. Everything changed when he forcefully had intercourse with me. He became evil.

After that, when my parents left, I cried and told them I didn't want to stay alone with my uncle. I couldn't tell them why. When I started to resist, Uncle Fafawia threatened to tell my parents what we had done. He said they would take me to a foster home. I was more afraid of that than the things he did. After he molested me, he beat me so I wouldn't tell.

I don't know how long he would have continued to molest me if he had not been killed. Uncle Fafawia is the uncle that was beaten to death beyond recognition. The one my parents identified at the morgue by his name tattooed on his arm.

When I heard that he had been killed, I was relieved. I could start living my life again. Uncle Fafawia wasn't coming home. The pain was not going to happen again. I no longer had to live in fear of him. I didn't have to tell my mom. Instead of feeling sorry he had been killed, I thought he deserved what happened to him.

I felt guilty about my uncle's death, like maybe I had caused it. My prayers had turned into, "Please, God, let it stop." I felt God had helped me. Now, as an adult, I know God doesn't answer prayers in that way; but then, as an eight-year-old child, the timing of my uncle's death made me think it resulted from my prayers.

I look at my children now, see how vulnerable they are, and I can't believe my uncle molested someone so young. The abuse confused me deeply. Sensual touching is pleasurable. I enjoyed that part. As a young child, I didn't know what he did was wrong. I respected him as my elder. He robbed me of feeling the love that goes with sex when I was older and ready for the experience.

If you ask me one thing I would change in my life, it would be what my uncle did to me. I wish I could have experienced the innocence of puppy love. I'm thankful that I had somebody solid like my mom who I could hold onto. With her, I felt the honesty and safety of a mother's love.

I had thought the sexual abuse was my fault because it had felt good at first. I believed I had sinned with my uncle. I think many victims feel that way. My religious upbringing contributed to my feelings of guilt and shame. A lot of the preaching I heard relied on the fear factor. The pastor tried to scare us with all of the negative things that could happen to us if we didn't behave. He invoked the image of the all-powerful and destructive God by saying things like, "Look what happened to Sodom and Gomorrah." So I lived in silent fear with my guilt and shame.

In college, I attended a bible camp. One night after being moved by a sermon, I answered the altar call. I approached the altar and confessed my sins, including the sexual abuse. I cried. People prayed over me. But afterward, I still didn't feel washed clean. I sought out the pastor and told him what had happened with my uncle. He basically told me I needed to repent. I told him I had answered the altar call and confessed but still did not feel right inside. Instead of referring me for professional counseling or talking to me more in a way that might help, he just repeated that I needed to repent.

I carried my guilt and shame through the early years of my relationship with Mitchell. It wasn't until I was a guest on *The Oprah Show* after I had come out publicly that I found relief in something Oprah said. Most predators make a game out of the sexual abuse so that it seems fun. "The victims end up feeling guilty about enjoying the abuse," Oprah said. That's the way it happened with me. For the longest time, I thought what my uncle did to me was my fault because it felt good. Hearing Oprah explain it helped relieve me of my guilt and shame.

Mitchell returned to visit me at the Bills' training camp with his mom and my mom. The practices were open to the public. Several hundred people usually gathered to watch the team run through its drills and plays. I spotted Mitchell in the crowd.

Immediately, I panicked. My old fear had come true. I had spotted in the crowd the face of a man I had slept with—that person, I feared, would out me.

*Wait a minute,* I told myself. *That's Mitchell.* I had to reason past my reflex. He was in on the secret. He wasn't going to tell. Gradually, I let myself relax.

Later in the week, during the exhibition game he attended, it was cool having someone special up in the stands watching me. I felt like the other players who had their girlfriends or wives there to cheer them on. I caught myself looking up at Mitchell, wondering how he felt at that moment. Maybe now that I had found someone, it would be easier for me to play in the NFL. I would not feel so alienated and alone.

Shelly had to return home, but Mama and Mitchell stayed on for an extra day. The three of us went to Niagara Falls on my day off after the game. We ate a picnic lunch. I wandered off and returned to find Mitchell in tears. Mama had told him the sad story of her youth, which had moved Mitchell to tears. She had opened up to him, and he, being the sweet guy that he was, had accepted her. It was wonderful for me to see the two of them bonding.

The fear I could not trust Mitchell haunted me. I still suspected he was cheating on me. We had that argument many times. I threatened to leave. Shelly, Mitchell's mom, told me he would never betray me, but I couldn't believe it. My relationship with Mitchell was what I had wanted for so long. Once I found it, my past prevented me from believing it could be possible.

Buffalo released me at the end of training camp. I wasn't surprised. In a way, I was happy to go back to Minnesota, which meant going back to Mitchell. But I wasn't ready to retire. Football was still in my blood.

The Bills kept me until the final cut. At that point, all of the other teams were set. I had to wait for someone on another team to get hurt before I would be called for a tryout. I waited a long time, over two months.

I didn't take well to the prospect of being forced into early retirement. I was only twenty-nine, and I knew I could still play. I wanted to play. But no one was giving me the chance.

Once again, I felt I had failed. Two teams—the Vikings and the Bills—had released me since I had played my last game. They had dismissed me, judged me not worthy to play for them. I sank into depression.

Mitchell tried to encourage me, but I wouldn't have it. I didn't think he could understand.

One time when we were at his mom's house, he asked me about football. He admitted he didn't know anything about the game. Because I was raised with that warrior mentality, I thought every man should know about football. "What's wrong with you?" I asked nastily. Even his mom saw how roughly I had treated him.

Mitchell went out and bought a book about football. Isn't that sad, that he thought he needed to know about football for me to consider him okay? I felt bad about that afterward. I had so much to learn about accepting and loving someone.

As the weeks went by without any job offers, I became increasingly irritable and hard to be around. Mitchell tried to be supportive, but my negative attitude wore him down.

I struggled with the trust. He finally suggested that I date other people. "If you want to come back, I'll be here," he said. It was like that saying, "If you love something, let it go. If it comes back, it's yours forever. If not, it was not meant to be."

He was letting go, but I wasn't able to see that. "Why do you want me to date other people?" I asked. "Do you have someone else?" I couldn't get over that jealousy.

I wanted to be in control. I wanted to be The Man. I decided who could come into our circle. I dictated who Mitchell could tell about us. I got angry if he told someone without clearing it first with me. I was afraid someone would find out, and I would never play in the NFL again.

This need for control can be another consequence of sexual abuse, just like not being able to trust. I wanted to control the relationship so it wouldn't hurt me.

Mitchell wanted me to see a therapist. At first I said, "No way." I couldn't admit to a stranger that I was gay. No NFL team would give me a chance if my secret was out. Mitchell explained that therapists are bound to confidentiality, that whatever I said in therapy would not become public knowledge. I realized I needed to try therapy if I wanted to stay in the relationship.

I was really nervous for my first appointment. The therapist was nice, but not a good fit. I sensed from the moment I walked in that she wasn't comfortable. Maybe my size intimidated her. When I talked about my experience, she seemed to discount what I said. "You're not gay," she said. "You're just acting out a fantasy."

I didn't feel any better when I walked out.

After a couple of sessions like that, I stopped. Therapy with her was not going to do me any good.

Mitchell and I talked about breaking up. My life with him seemed as uncertain as my football future.

# CHAPTER FIFTEEN

## Champions for Christ

FOOTBALL GAVE ME ANOTHER CHANCE when Jacksonville called in November of 1997 and invited me for a tryout. I had a good workout and signed on for the final six games of the season with the Jaguars. I was glad to have the chance to work, even though it meant leaving Mitchell in Minnesota again.

I rented a room at an extended-stay roadside hotel until I knew I had the job. For the first couple of weeks, I wasn't sure, so I didn't want to commit to an apartment. The room was outfitted with a kitchenette and drab, outdated furniture. It was a lonely place without Mitchell. I had grown accustomed to having him around.

I felt isolated in many ways. Jacksonville seemed even more culturally remote than Green Bay had been. People were friendly enough, but a Samoan might as well have been an alien. I was coming out of a store one day when a redneck in a pickup yelled at me as he sped by, "Hey, nigger!" I thought, *Dude, you're so igno-rant you can't even get your slurs right.*

I did find a familiar face there in Don Davey. Jacksonville had selected my Wisconsin buddy from the Packers' roster in the 1995 expansion draft. It was great to be reunited with him. We partied some together, but by then Don had married his girlfriend and started a family. He was in love with his wife and kids and put them first in his life. I hadn't had many healthy role models for relationships, but Don proved to be one.

Jacksonville was playing its third season. Tom Coughlin, now the New York Giants' coach, was the Jaguars' head coach at the time. He led a young team. I signed as a backup but ended up playing a lot.

Jacksonville is the land of Holy Rollers. I have never been any-where else like that, where religion has taken over the entire city. It extended to the football team. The Jaguars were known as a Christian team. About half of the players were involved in some way with an organization known as Champions for Christ. I had seen Christian groups on other teams but nothing like this. The CFC members seemed to accept only the guys who attended their weekly Bible study. I was my usual Mr. Aloha, always happy-go-lucky in the locker room and able to get along with everyone. But I could feel the tension between the CFC guys and the rest of the players. It was as though you had to choose between two cliques that divided the team.

A lot of the team's stars belonged to CFC, including Mark Brunell, the quarterback who had upset John Elway and the Denver Broncos in the AFC Central Division playoffs the previous season, and Tony Boselli, an offensive lineman and the first player the franchise drafted. They were the two biggest stars on the team. They really pressured guys, especially the younger players. An older player might start preaching to a younger guy in the locker room that he needed to change his ways because the end was near. You could feel the threat of rejection. Don Davey told me the star players and other CFC members had shunned him because he hadn't accepted their invitation. It felt like if you didn't go to their Bible study, you weren't part of the team.

The Holy Rollers carried the attitude, *Either you're with us or you're against us.* That took me back to the Pentecostal days of my childhood when the pastor preached, "If your friends don't go to church, you should de-friend them and find some Christian friends."

When I arrived in Jacksonville, they thought that I would automatically gravitate toward Champions for Christ because I was a Christian. They had seen me kneel in the center of the field with other players after games. I always went to chapel on game days with the Vikings and Packers. But CFC's militant approach rubbed me the wrong way.

In a way, CFC seemed like a cult to me. Any religion that excludes a certain group is a cult. True religion accepts everyone as they are. That's my understanding of God's love. I also don't think you should pressure someone into faith. I think we should teach people about our faith by the way we live. Our job as Christians is not to convert; our job is to introduce the idea that Jesus Christ can help someone in his life. I leave it to the Holy Spirit to convert and to the individual to feel the conviction in his heart. When players try to push their religion on others, it tears a team apart. I could see that in the Jaguars' locker room.

My hunch that something wasn't quite right with Champions for Christ later proved correct. When running back Curtis Enis, the Chicago Bears' top draft pick in 1998, fired his agent after attending CFC Bible studies and hired a friend of CFC president Greg Ball, the media started questioning the group's practices. Reports speculated that CFC, which endorses the biblical practice of tithing, preyed upon the NFL's high-paid players. Brunell, who made more than $6 million a year, and Boselli, who made more than $2 million annually, both admitted that they gave 10 percent of their income to CFC. The NFL, which had acted in the past to protect players against scams, launched its own investigation. Much of the talk focused on the Jaguars. This all happened after I had left the team.

While with the Jaguars, I felt the pressure to join Champions for Christ. Not long after I had been in Jacksonville, a teammate and CFC member asked me if I believed in God. I said yes. Then he asked me if I had accepted Jesus Christ as my personal savior. I again said yes. He invited me to the Bible study. I balked.

An experience at my church in Minneapolis made me cautious.

I had attended services regularly at Speak the Word since 1992, when I had come to play with Minnesota. In all of those times, I hadn't heard a word spoken about homosexuality.

The week after my first date with Mitchell, I went to the Sunday morning service at Speak the Word on my own. The topic of the sermon was homosexuality. I had admired the pastor. He had preached about love and discipline, topics that spoke to me and bolstered my faith; but that Sunday he spoke about homosexuality as a sinful choice, as though someone could choose his or her sexual orientation.

I felt like Fred Flintstone, the way he shrinks when someone yells at him. The more the pastor railed against homosexuality, the smaller I felt in the big church, as though everyone was pushed away from me.

The pastor proclaimed that he was going to raise his children to be straight. He said the way to do that was to raise them "the Christian way." That meant he would be involved in their lives and teach them to be great children of God. I had been raised the Christian way, with the Bible, and I was gay. Yet the pastor thought he could dictate his children's sexual orientation.

I couldn't believe these words coming out of his mouth. This church was a place where I had felt at home. I had given money to support its ministry. Yet the pastor was talking about me as someone who was not one of God's children.

I didn't want to listen to any more of this negative talk. His message said nothing about love. *Stop this talk,* I was saying to him in my mind. *Please stop.*

Then something surprising happened. As I listened, a peace came over me. I had the revelation, *He's not telling the truth.*

I started crying. The people around me consoled me, saying, "The Spirit has touched you."

*Yeah, He did,* I thought, *but not like you think.* The Spirit said, "I do love you." He told me the truth. God opened my eyes as to what kind of church that was. I wanted a church that preached God's love, a church that made me—and everyone—feel like part of the family.

That was the last day I set foot in Speak the Word.

Needless to say, I had reservations about attending the Champions for Christ Bible study. One day, I saw a CFC flier in the locker room that listed Darryl Flowers as the guest speaker. I knew Darryl from Oregon State, where he had been a star basketball player along with future NBA point guard Gary Payton.

Darryl had later become our football team's chaplain. I had liked Darryl. I figured I could please my CFC teammates and catch up with Darryl by attending that week's Bible study.

I had attended other teams' Bible studies, where a handful of guys sat in a circle and talked about scripture. This one wasn't like that. It was held in the conference room of an airport hotel. There must have been a hundred people there: my teammates with their wives and their friends from church.

Beforehand, I greeted Darryl. We hugged. He seemed happy to see me.

The Bible study started like many others. We introduced ourselves and said some prayers. Then Darryl started to speak. I expected his message to be like those I had heard in the past. I expected him to talk about drawing inspiration from the Good Book or about finding our strength in God. I hadn't expected him to speak against homosexuality as an abomination. He sounded like the preacher at the church I attended as a child, saying that such sinners would spend eternity in the lake of fire.

The anger started to rise within me. I was fed up with this kind of misinformed talk. Tua came to mind. I had not let myself think of him since his funeral. I missed him too much. I had tried to block out the pain. That night with Darryl speaking, I couldn't help but think of Tua and what a wonderful, kind person he was. I thought of the way he had helped others and the way he treated my mother so well. A person like that could not end up in Hell, could they?

I thought about Mitchell. I had finally met a wonderful man, who I thought was the answer to my prayers, yet this kind of talk forced us to live a secret life. I wanted to stand up and shout, "I'm not going to Hell!" Instead, I stewed in my seat, torn between what I heard and what I lived.

After Darryl's sermon, we broke into small discussion groups. Darryl was in my group. I said to him, "I had a gay brother who died of AIDS." The other guys in my group leaned back with worried expressions on their faces, like my brother had contaminated me.

"You're telling me that if Hitler in his last breath asked God for forgiveness, that he would be forgiven," I continued, "but my brother, who was gay, would not be forgiven?"

"Yes," Darryl said. "Murder is different from abomination. Murder is a sin that can be forgiven. Homosexuality can't be forgiven because it is an abomination."

"That does not sit right with me," I said to Darryl. "If you knew my brother Tua and how many people he helped, you would know like I do that he has a place in heaven."

I stood up to leave. "I can't accept that."

"That's what the Word of God says." Darryl quoted Leviticus 18:22, "You will not have intercourse with a man as you would with a woman. This is a hateful thing." (New Jerusalem Bible)

"If you're going to follow Leviticus, then every NFL player should be put to death for working on the Sabbath and touching pigskin," I shot back. (In addition to the passage Darryl quoted, the book of Leviticus also mandates resting on the Sabbath and not contacting pigs, which are considered unclean. What's more, Exodus 35:2 states, "Work must be done for six days, but the seventh must be a holy day for you, a day of complete rest, in honor of Yahweh. Anyone who does any work on that day will be put to death." New Jerusalem Bible)

They looked at me like I was crazy. I walked out.

I drove back to the hotel irate. When the Vikings played the exhibition game in Berlin, I had visited a concentration camp near the city. I had seen Hitler's legacy of horror. *He* was going to be forgiven but not my brother? Why did Tua need to be forgiven in the first place?

Back in my drab room, I started to drink tequila. The more I thought about what had happened and the more I drank, the more upset I became.

What if Darryl and all of the guys there—my teammates and the star players—were right? Maybe Tua wasn't in heaven. Maybe I was headed to the lake of fire. That's what pastors had been telling me about homosexuality since I was a child. My heart didn't believe it, but my head was filled with their preaching. I was confused about what I truly believed.

I had spoken up about Tua, but I hadn't had the guts to tell the other guys about me. Once again, I was a coward. Why must I always deny who I was? How long would I have to feel ashamed of myself?

All of my confusion and conflict came out in a rage. I drove my fist through the wall.

I wanted to kill myself. I felt the despair and defeat that I had known so many times in Minnesota. Once again, I was alone and confused and wanted to die. If I had had a gun that night, I would have used it.

I called Mitchell. Instead of letting him comfort me, I blamed him for the miserable way I felt. I told him that I could not be happy with him, that I didn't want to see him again. In my confusion and despair, I rambled on about being a sinner and not deserving him in my life. In the next breath, I begged him not to leave. Eventually, I hung up on him.

He called back. I hung up.

I immediately called him to tell him why I had hung up on him. He wasn't sympathetic enough. He couldn't understand. I hung up again.

This went on for three or four hours.

Mitchell kept calling and talking until he got through to me. I think he realized how serious this was, that I really was suicidal, that he could lose me. He didn't panic. He was able to look past all of the rotten things I said about him. He managed to calm me down. His persistence and love kept me alive.

He told me to sleep before making a decision about our relationship. Finally, exhausted, I surrendered to sleep at about 2:00 a.m.

The next morning, I woke up drained. I was grateful to have football practice. It gave me somewhere to go.

Some of the players who had not been in my small discussion group had not seen me leave. One of those guys approached me in the locker room and asked, "What did you think of the Bible study?"

"I consider myself a Christian," I said. "But you guys are stuck in the Old Testament practice of condemning certain groups. In the New Testament, Jesus brings love, forgiveness, and compassion to everyone. To live like Christ is not to cast out another group. That's what happened at the Bible study."

We had a long conversation.

The New Testament was the new revelation; it gave us a new understanding of God through the person of Jesus Christ. I'm not saying we should throw out the Old Testament. I'm saying we should read it in context of the New Testament. To stick with some of the teachings in the Old Testament can cause people to live in the past.

I think many of the Old Testament's comments on homosexuality are teachings from the past that Jesus did not endorse. I heard Robin Williams deliver a great line: "If homosexuality is an abomination, why didn't it make the top ten list of sins?"

Jesus would not dismiss me from his presence. He saw the beauty in everyone. Look who Jesus hung out with: tax collectors and prostitutes. He never discriminated against anyone. His message was to treat others with respect, not to pass judgment on Earth.

Jesus loved everyone. He died on the cross for everyone—not just for straight people, but for *all* people. Some Christians try to exclude some groups from the blood of Christ, but Jesus didn't. No, he died for all of us. During tough times, I held onto that.

The Bible says in Leviticus 18:22 that it's unnatural for a man to lie with a man. God created me—you, all people—in his image. I am not a mistake. God doesn't make mistakes. My own belief is that if God doesn't make mistakes and God made me gay—I was born gay—it would be unnatural for me to lie with a woman. Since God created me gay—with a desire to be intimate with men—it is natural for me to lie with a man.

It bothers me that people are selective in their scripture readings. They only pick the passages they want to use for their own purposes. If you're going to read one passage, you've got to read them all. If you're going to read Leviticus 18:22, you've got to read the whole book, which says, among other things, that "Whenever a woman has a discharge and the discharge from her body is of blood, she will remain in a state of menstrual pollution for seven days. Anyone who touches her will be unclean until evening." (Leviticus 15:19–20, New Jerusalem Bible) Are you going to cast out your wife when she has her period? We have to consider the context and use common sense.

Some people blame gay men for the destruction of Sodom and Gomorrah, but there were also men raping women and other sins taking place there. God destroyed the people in those cities for doing evil. A lot of people are stuck on men trying to rape the angels, but the place was long gone before the angels arrived.

Critics view homosexuals as a group. If a man goes on a shooting binge, you don't read in the paper that a heterosexual man went on a shooting binge. But if a homosexual man molests a child, you read that a "gay man" molested a child. There are bad homosexuals just like there are bad heterosexuals. Please don't judge us as a group.

I don't understand how religious people can read the Bible and know that there's only one judge, yet take the responsibility for being that judge. They condemn all homosexuals simply because of the way we are created. I see a little lesbian girl or gay boy listening and becoming afraid like I was, believing there is something wrong with them. These people tell these gay kids that there is no place in this world or God's kingdom for them. It breaks my heart to hear that. I cannot imagine that God would hate anyone. Remember, Jesus shed his blood for *all* of us.

I want the gay, lesbian, bisexual, and transgender people who have turned their back on God to return to their faith. Ignore the misinformed people; don't ignore God. When I speak at colleges, I want to make sure that those who hear me know God loves them. I speak out of my Christian faith, but I tell them, "Whether you are a Jew, Buddhist, Hindu, or whatever, hold onto your faith. Religion is supposed to bring comfort and joy to your life. It's not supposed to scare the hell out of you."

Religion involves a personal relationship between you and God. People can give you advice, criticize you, say what they want, but in the end, when you stand before God on Judgment Day, you'll stand alone. We each need to decide for ourselves what we believe and live out that faith.

People ask me, "How can you believe in God after all of the negative things you've heard in church and Bible studies about homosexuality?" I know those negative things others have said don't come from God. I still believe because God has always been there for me. If it weren't for God, I would be six feet under. My faith has made me explore the Bible even more. I found out God loves me the way He created me. I've held onto that love. That's all you need.

I don't want to come across as holier than thou. I'm not perfect; no one is. I've got skeletons in my closet. We all have our weaknesses. We all fall short of God's glory because we're all human. I'm not an expert, and I don't claim to be a scholar, but I know the Bible and what I believe. I simply want to spread the word about God's true love the way the book of Wisdom describes it: "Yes, you love everything that exists, and nothing that you have made disgusts you, since, if you had hated something, you would not have made it." (Wisdom 11:24, New Jerusalem Bible)

These thoughts were not as clear in my mind the day after I attended the CFC Bible study. I was feeling wiped out and adrift. After practice, I went over to Don Davey's house. Mitchell wasn't there to comfort me in person, but Don and his wife were. I told them about the Bible study and how I couldn't accept that my brother was an abomination. They were very supportive and sympathetic.

I talked to Mitchell again on the phone. He told me he would stay in the relationship if I would. I wouldn't have blamed him if he had called it quits after the way I had treated him. I think he believed that deep down I was a good man. Even when I treated him horribly, he believed that good man would again show himself.

I tell people that Mitchell is the strongest man I know. I put him through a lot of crap, but he stayed with me. That night could have destroyed us, but instead, we took an important step forward.

# CHAPTER SIXTEEN

⁓

# We're Going to Miami

ONCE I HAD SECURED a spot on the Jaguars' roster, I rented a beautiful condo on Jacksonville Beach. Mitchell flew down for Thanksgiving. He bought new dishes and cooked me a full turkey dinner. I had a lot to be grateful for that year.

For starters, I wasn't alone on the holidays. Before my mom and two sisters moved to Minnesota, I had been by myself on the football season holidays, Thanksgiving and Christmas. Even with them around, those days had lacked that special someone. It was wonderful to be able to share holidays with Mitchell.

I was also grateful to be playing football again after those long, dark weeks in Minnesota when I feared I would be forced into early retirement. Even if the Jaguars were a divided team, they gave me the chance to play, which I appreciated.

Mitchell returned to Jacksonville for our first Christmas together. I surprised him with two trees in my beachfront condo, one in the master bedroom and another in the living room that was over twelve feet tall. We gave one another Rolex watches without knowing what the other had bought.

The Jaguars made the playoffs, and I started the first game against Denver. The Broncos had a great team that year. They blew us out 42–17. Mitchell and I went to the Super Bowl in San Diego, where the Broncos beat the defending champion Green Bay Packers. It was an exciting matchup between two great quarterbacks, Denver's John Elway and my buddy from Green Bay, Brett Favre.

I introduced Mitchell to people as a friend. He is not a girlie man, so he passed easily for a buddy. I don't think it raised suspicions for me to attend the Super Bowl with another guy. Lots of guys do that.

I had sprained my ankle toward the end of the season. Even though I was healthy enough to start in the playoffs, the Jaguars did not renew my contract. Once again, I was out of work.

I had long dreamed of singing the lead in a church choir. I fulfilled that dream in a big way at First Baptist Church of Jacksonville, one of the largest churches in America.

The church invited me to sing at its Easter service in 1998, even though the Jaguars had let me go. At first, I was reluctant. I had the chance to fulfill a dream and to share my gifts, but I resisted. As a gay man, I have wanted to avoid the spotlight. I panic at the thought of being thrust in front of everyone.

I'm like Jonah when God summoned him to tell the people of Nineveh his message and Jonah resisted. Only after a large fish swallowed him did Jonah consent to God's will. The lesson is,

"When God calls you to do something, do it." I believed God wanted me to use my voice to reach people. My parents had taught me not to hide this gift God had given me. I agreed before I met the large fish.

First Baptist was huge. The church campus covered over nine city blocks in downtown Jacksonville. The worship center auditorium seated nearly ten thousand people—it seemed as big as the Metrodome, where the Vikings play. Two very large screens flanked the altar so the people in the back could see. It was a powerful feeling to be in front of that many people, backed by a mighty choir, on Easter Sunday, celebrating our Lord's resurrection. I felt truly blessed that God was using me as his instrument with the gift of my voice.

I sang "Day Star." I could feel the Holy Spirit in me. When the choir came in to back me up, it felt like a huge hand cradled me. I sang, "Lead me, Lord, and I will follow. Anywhere, I will go." The song's message is to let God take control, the way Jonah finally did. I could see people in the audience crying. My voice reached them. I felt so empowered to be part of other people's religious experience. I believe God is with us all of the time, but when I sang that song, I felt his presence in a special, powerful way.

If I had had more religious experiences like that as a child—more experiences of feeling God's love in church, instead of hearing the negative messages and feeling the fear—I would have understood at a younger age that religion is about giving of yourself to help and inspire other people. It's not about fear; it's about love.

I still wasn't ready to retire when Jacksonville released me. I was thirty years old and in the later years of my career—the injuries, pounding, and stress were taking their toll—but I still thought I could play in the NFL. I was grateful that the Atlanta Falcons invited me to training camp. They were coming off a 7–9 losing season, but I was glad to have another chance to play.

I had heard of "Hotlanta," but I wasn't prepared for the suffocating weather at the training camp in Suwanee, Georgia. Man, it was hot. Georgia in the summertime was the most humid place I had ever been. I don't know how people who live there can stand it. You can't even own a convertible down there because you would never drive it—the place is just too hot.

Training camp was really hard in that humid heat. That was the first time in all of my days playing football that I saw someone quit. A seventh-round defensive lineman at his first training camp just walked off the field one day during practice. He quit the team and walked away from all the money he could have made. It was just too damn hot for him.

Every player was pushing himself, but you have to know your body and not drive it too hard. You have to know when to ease up. I always listened to my body. When it was time to turn it off, I slowed down. You couldn't go full speed all of the time in that heat.

I survived the heat and final cuts of training camp. I liked the Falcons, and they seemed to like me. Ever Mr. Aloha, I managed to make friends wherever I went. I went out with running back Jamal Anderson and defensive lineman Travis Hall. Sometimes a large group of the guys would grab a meal together on the road at a steakhouse.

I also hit it off with Craig Sauer, a linebacker and special teams specialist. We shared a Minnesota connection. He was from Sartell, a small town in central Minnesota, and had played at the University of Minnesota. I, of course, had played with the Vikings for five seasons and still had my home there. Craig was a part of the Christian group that attended chapel and prayed on the field after games, so we also had that in common.

Craig became my joking buddy on the team. He was married with kids, so we didn't go out much, but we were always teasing one another in the locker room or during practice. He had a large forehead, so I called him, "Five-head." I would tell him, "You don't have a forehead, you have a fivehead." He would come back with, "Hey, Esera, can you move your big head? It's blocking the sun."

That sort of banter was typical in the Falcons' locker room. Guys ragged on each other, but their jokes didn't have the negative bite that I had heard elsewhere. The players traded occasional faggot remarks but never to the point where I heard hate in their voices. Their joking didn't make me as uncomfortable as I had been in other locker rooms.

The Falcon players treated each other well. I did not experience the negative attitudes I had seen in Minnesota nor the division I had witnessed in Jacksonville. The superstars didn't act like prima donnas. Instead, the guys encouraged one another. If someone messed up, the others were there to pick him up. The Falcons had the chemistry of a successful team.

A lot of that good chemistry could probably be attributed to the head coach, Dan Reeves. He was the best head coach I ever had. He had taken the Denver Broncos to three Super Bowls and seen success with the New York Giants before he took over the Falcons in 1997. He would be named Coach of the Year in 1998, the season I played for him in Atlanta.

Having been a player himself for eight seasons with the Dallas Cowboys, Reeves was a player's coach. He set the tone by treating us as equals. He did not show favoritism. He understood our problems. He wanted us to take care of our families first. He had the philosophy that if you did not have problems at home, you would not bring problems to work.

In the Falcons' locker room, I didn't hear guys talking about cheating on their wives. They seemed to be taking care of business at home the way Coach Reeves encouraged them to.

Meanwhile, I was still having difficulty in my relationship with Mitchell. I felt the constant threat of losing my job, one made more real by the fact that four teams had already let me go. I blew a hamstring in the middle of the season that caused me to miss three games. Age and injuries had broken down my body, and the league's homophobic currents had taken their toll on my emotions. They say we hurt those closest to us. In my case, that meant Mitchell.

When we were together, I was usually happy. Separated, I couldn't overcome my jealousy. I caused him a lot of undeserved stress with my insecurities and suspicions. That started to affect him at work. His business—running a salon and spa—is all about making people feel good. That's hard to do when you don't feel good yourself. At the time, they were expanding the business, opening new locations, but our relationship hurt Mitchell's effectiveness.

Shelly, Mitchell's mom, and Katie Lundgren, his best friend from high school, expressed their concern. I think if they had just considered the relationship and not liked me so much, they would have told Mitchell to leave me. Shelly and Mitchell's brother, Robin Julien, who runs the business with him, encouraged Mitchell to take some time off and work things out with me. I didn't understand how much I had affected his business until he took a leave of absence. He came down to Atlanta for a couple of months late in the season, so we could address our issues.

As much as I gave Mitchell hell, I knew I couldn't live without him. I think he knew he couldn't live without me, too. He told me he had remained friends with his past boyfriends, but if we ever broke up, he could never talk to me again because it would hurt too much. That's the way I felt, too. We would fight until we got to the point where one of us threatened to leave. The other would crack and say, "No, don't."

We tried couples therapy in Atlanta, but the therapist didn't consider us a couple. She thought I was going through a phase of experimentation, that's all. Mitchell was small, fashionable. She could accept him being gay, but not me, like it's different for an NFL player. I guess in her view celebrities like to experiment sexually more than other people. Mitchell and I left our therapy sessions more upset than when we went into them.

Basically, if I wanted our relationship to last, I had to work on the shit from my life. I had to unlearn ways I had picked up in my youth and relearn what it meant to love someone. That wasn't easy.

People had looked to me as a leader, on the field and in my family. I had been captain of my high school and college football teams and a starter in the NFL. Even though I was the youngest in my family, I was a leader because I took care of my mom. Others— friends and family—asked me for advice. I was put in a position where I made decisions for them. I had grown used to that. It was hard to give that up in my relationship.

I struggled with the fact that I could not always be in control. That was a major adjustment after being single and independent, always able to do what I wanted when I wanted. Also, as an NFL football player, I had grown accustomed to being catered to as a mini-celebrity. It wasn't easy for me to shift my thinking to take into account what someone else wanted.

I was making a lot of money—nearly a million dollars a season—and thought that entitled me to the power. I had never been in a relationship where each person shared what he had. I had watched other players treat their wives with the attitude, "I'm the man. I bring in the money. As long as she's happy, I can do what I want." That was the modus operandi I learned when I came into the league. I'm not saying that's right, but it's what I observed and picked up.

I thought Mitchell should be like the other players' wives. He should shut up and reap the benefits. I know that sounds harsh, but that's what went through my mind in those days. Obviously, that thinking was holding us back. I learned that didn't work in the kind of relationship I wanted to have. I had to recognize that Mitchell's work was as important as mine and that he was my equal in all things.

Early on, I didn't understand the wisdom and necessity of compromise. As our relationship has grown, I've learned that there are sacrifices you need to make. It's got to be 50–50; it can't even be 55–45. For instance, with our children, I can't just say what I want. My partner and I have to find our common ground.

I think Mitchell always had hope that things would change. He was patient enough to give me the time I needed to grow up. We're still not the perfect couple, but we've come a long, long way.

My year with Atlanta, 1998, proved to be a Cinderella season for the Falcons, probably because of the closeness of the players. We sailed through the regular season with a 14–2 record and finished first in the NFC Western Division. I had been brought in as a backup but clocked a lot of playing time. I was a run-stopper, used on first and second downs, or brought in for goal-line stands. I was satisfied to have a role on a successful team.

We faced the San Francisco 49ers in the division playoffs. The 49ers were one of only two teams that had beaten us in the season. They had superstars like future Hall of Famers Steve Young and Jerry Rice, and a Pro Bowl running back in Garrison Hearst, who had rushed for a team-record 1,570 yards that season. He broke his ankle on the first play of the game. I was on the field and heard the bone snap. It was an awful sound. My heart went out to Garrison. I knew from when I had blown out my Achilles that he had a long road of rehab ahead to come back. Everybody felt bad for him.

We didn't bow to the 49ers' stars. Our team's player of the year, running back Jamal Anderson, scored two touchdowns, and we squeezed by San Francisco with a 20–18 win. The victory put us in the NFC championship game against the Vikings. The winner would advance to Super Bowl XXXIII in Miami. It was sweet to have a crack at the team that had not wanted to pay my salary.

My Falcon teammates showed new interest in me the week before the game. They turned to me for scouting reports. The offensive linemen wanted to know what they needed to do to stop John Randle. The defensive linemen wanted to learn what moves would work against the Vikings All-Pro linemen Todd Steussie and Randall McDaniel. Everybody wanted my opinion. That was cool. I was happy to be of use.

We played the Vikings in Minnesota. I invited my Falcon team-mates to dinner at Dan and Shelly's house the day before the game. They owned a beautiful house and agreed to cater a party for the team. It was gutsy, but I trusted my family and Mitchell's knew what they could and could not say about us. I told my team-mates that Dan and Shelly were my Minnesota family.

We rented limos to shuttle the players from the motel. Not everybody came, but a lot of them did. My mom was there along with Tusi and Sina, Sina's husband Mike, and a couple of my college friends, including my Polynesian buddy Sai. Mitchell's brother Robin was there. So were his stepdad's children: Jessica, Jina, Jeff, and Jaime, with his wife Libby.

It was cool to bring over NFL players to meet my family. At the same time, I was nervous. We planned to check in at the hotel, then go directly to Dan and Shelly's house. On the plane, I started to worry. What if Shelly had forgotten to take down the photographs of Mitchell and me?

Shelly worried even more than I did. She is an extremely honest and straightforward person. Having to lie was trying for her. She would ask before situations like the dinner at her house, "What are we going to say? What's the story?" It didn't help that Mitchell and I never scripted anything. We usually let the story flow and answered questions as they came up.

At Shelly's house that Saturday, I introduced Mitchell as my buddy and his family as my Minnesota family. We spun an elaborate story of how they used to come to Hawaii to visit. No one questioned it. The players seemed more interested in the food—put food in front of an NFL player and he's happy. Everything was going perfect, but I was waiting for that one slip that would expose me.

Somehow, Shelly's sister Pat had not been clued in that the Falcon players didn't know Mitchell and I were a couple. Aunt Pat noticed that we weren't close that evening, but figured we were having another argument. We watched the MTV video I made with the rap singer Richie Rich. When the players saw me kiss a woman in the video, they all went, "Oooh," because they saw me getting some action. Aunt Pat thought their reaction was sympathy for a gay man having to kiss a woman. She had an enchanting time eating dinner with Morten Andersen, the Falcons' kicker, and did not give away our secret.

All night long, Dan's son Jaime had wanted to get a picture with Jamal Anderson, the Falcons' star running back, but Jaime had been too nervous to approach Jamal. Finally, as Jamal was stepping into the limo, Jaime's wife, Libby, asked for a photograph. Jamal said, "Sure, no problem," and climbed out of the car. Jaime and Jamal posed, but Libby was so nervous that she couldn't work the camera, and it jammed. Jaime missed the opportunity to take the picture he wanted. I still tease him about that.

I was really pleased the dinner went so well. Nobody slipped up. That was the beginning of a great weekend.

I was excited to face the Vikings but scared as well. I had caught wind of rumors in Minnesota about me being gay. They had probably started at Mitchell's salon where some of the Vikings' wives heard whispers about the owner dating a professional football player. People had seen us together around town. Even though as a three hundred-pound nose guard I didn't fit the stereotype of a gay man, I was single, without a girlfriend in the three years since I had met Mitchell, and I sang in a high voice. That was enough to set tongues clucking. I didn't know what to expect back at the Metrodome, especially from the fans.

Football players head onto the field for warm-ups in an order specified by position. The kickers go out first. Then the quarterbacks and receivers appear. The running backs, defensive backs, and linebackers follow. The offensive and defensive linemen are the last groups out. Once we walk onto the field, all of the groups come together to stretch as a team.

Everybody was on the field by the time I ran out with the rest of the Falcons' defensive line. The Metrodome was packed. It was louder than hell in there, even for warm-ups. The fans were crazed with excitement, and for good reason. The Vikings had finished the season 15–1. With seven Pro Bowl players, their offense had set an NFL record for most points scored in a season. They were powered by a lethal combination of quarterback Randall Cunningham, an MVP candidate, and NFL Rookie of the Year Randy Moss, who had caught seventeen touchdown passes, the most ever by a rookie. Kicker Gary Anderson had not missed a field goal or point-after-touchdown all season.

The Vikings had been invincible at the Metrodome that year. They had won all nine of their home games by an average of twenty-three points. They were favored to beat us by eleven. This was the Vikings' year finally to return to the Super Bowl in Miami and, after four previous losses, to win it all.

I had never heard the Dome so loud.

After we stretched, we broke into groups by position. The defensive linemen headed to a section of the field close enough to the stands so that I could hear individual fans. Some of them shouted, "Welcome back." Others screamed, "You fucking traitor." Huh? Wasn't it the Vikings who didn't renew my contract? I would have been happy to continue playing in Minnesota. What did the fans want me to do, retire if I couldn't play for the Vikings?

The Viking players gave me the coldest reception I ever experienced from a former team. It's common for opponents who know each other to exchange greetings before a game. But no one on the Vikings would talk to me. They wouldn't even give me a nod. I could understand John Randle. Since I played for another team, he now classified me as the enemy. That didn't bother me, but the reaction from the others did. The Vikings' star running back Robert Smith was the only one who came over and shook my hand as I trotted off the field after warm-ups. It was like I had the plague or worse—that they knew.

The Vikings' reception really pissed me off. I had played with some of those guys for five seasons. In the locker room, I told my Falcon teammates, "No one out there talked to me. Can you believe that?"

"No way," they said. "Are you serious?"

"Yeah, let's go out and kick their fucking ass!"

I didn't start, but I could feel the electricity on the field once the game began. An incredible energy pulsed between the end zones. It was so loud out there you couldn't hear yourself think.

We took first possession. Our offense moved the ball down the field and scored on a five-yard touchdown pass from Chris Chandler to Jamal Anderson. That was a key aspect of the game. It gave us some confidence and the Vikings some doubt. We thought, "Hey, we can move the ball against this team. We can score."

Our touchdown quieted the fans a bit, but only briefly. Cunningham hit Moss for a touchdown, and the Vikings went on to score twenty straight points. We stayed disciplined, though. Our offensive line never jumped early. Meanwhile, Chandler drew the Vikings' defense off-sides four times with his altered cadence.

Another turning point occurred late in the first half when we knocked the ball out of Cunningham's hand and Travis Hall recovered on the Vikings' thirteen-yard line. Chandler threw a touchdown pass on the next play. We trailed 20–14 at the half but went into the locker room on a high note.

Minnesota led by ten points with less than four minutes to play when our kicker, Morten Andersen, a Danish guy, kicked a field goal to cut the lead to seven. The Vikings drove back, deep into our territory, and set up a thirty-eight-yard field goal attempt for Gary Anderson. He had kicked more field goals than anyone in NFL history. That season, he had been perfect. He hadn't missed a single field-goal attempt in thirty-nine tries. He had also hit sixty-seven of sixty-seven point-after-touchdown kicks. This thirty-eight-yard field goal attempt was a gimme for someone of his caliber. The extra three points would push the Vikings' lead back to ten and shove the game out of reach.

Anderson missed. His kick sailed wide by six inches. We were still in the game.

Our offense answered with a touchdown that tied the game with less than a minute remaining. You could hear the crowd groan, "Oooh," like someone had let the air out of the Dome. Minnesota got the ball with enough time to run a play or two, but Cunningham took a knee to run out the clock and send the game into overtime with the score tied 27–27. When I saw that, I turned to my Minnesota friend and Atlanta teammate Craig Sauer and said, "We're going to win."

We had our chance when Morten Andersen lined up to kick a thirty-eight-yard field goal in the sudden death overtime. The Viking fans thundered to distract him and make him miss. That was the loudest they had been all day. Soon as his kick cleared the uprights, the whole place suddenly fell silent. It was eerie.

My Falcon teammates started dancing on the field. Morten was shouting in Danish, "We're going to Miami!" I turned around and looked into the stands. The Viking fans were in shock. Some of them cried.

Minnesota fans blame their kicker, Gary Anderson, for missing his attempt in the fourth quarter, but you can't blame a loss on the guy who missed a field goal when you're still up by seven points late in the game. Atlanta deserves a lot of credit for coming back to tie the score. Blame the Vikings' loss on that.

I peered at my family and friends way up in the nosebleed seats, in the second-to-last row. They were so high up that they could touch the canvas ceiling. Their section of two hundred Falcon fans were the only ones in the place cheering. They were screaming. Perhaps they were the only ones in the building to appreciate what an amazing upset we had just pulled off. We had defied the odds and beaten the giant.

The whole season had been a fairy tale that would culminate in Miami. For the first time in Falcon history, we were headed to the Super Bowl.

# CHAPTER SEVENTEEN

—

# Super Bowl XXXIII

THE FOLLOWING TUESDAY, at our first team meeting since our victory, the excitement my teammates and I felt charged the room. Making it to the Super Bowl is one of the hardest things in the world to do. Of all the guys who play in the National Football League, very few can say they've played in the main event. We were headed to Miami to play in Super Bowl XXXIII on January 31, 1999.

Dan Reeves, our head coach, talked to us in the team meeting room that Tuesday before we headed out to practice. He had been to the Super Bowl three times before as head coach of the Denver Broncos and knew what to expect. He tried to prepare us by breaking the week down into particulars.

Coach Reeves told us that a ton of media would compete for our time. He said that there would be plenty of other distractions and we would have a midnight curfew the week before the game in Miami. He said family and friends and friends of friends were all going to want tickets, but we players would receive only two dozen each to dole out. I was as pumped as the guys around me to play in the Super Bowl, but with each detail Reeves gave us, my anxiety mounted.

Tickets. *Could I invite Mitchell? His family? Wait a minute. Of course I'm going to invite Mitchell. He's the love of my life.* But if I was to keep my secret safe, I would have to pull off an amazing juggling act.

The team arrived in Miami for Super Bowl XXXIII a week before the game. No matter what Coach Reeves had told us, we couldn't know what to expect until we experienced the Super Bowl for ourselves. The week leading up to the game turned out to be the best and worst week of my life.

We players were treated like royalty in Miami. Police escorted our bus everywhere we went. The South Beach nightclubs granted us free admission. Fans waited outside our hotel for autographs. They asked me—a second-string nose guard—to sign helmets and football cards, and to pose with them for photographs. Gifts from NFL sponsors appeared in our lockers and hotel rooms—hats, shoes, sweatshirts, water bottles, duffle bags. Whatever we wanted, someone was there to give it to us.

Except for what I wanted most: not to have to hide who I truly was.

Super Bowl week attracts celebrities from all over. The week before the game, Miami was crawling with famous people. One night, I went out to dinner with my teammates, running back Jamal Anderson and defensive lineman Travis Hall. Jamal was a celebrity in his own right. That season, he had set a club record by rushing 1,846 yards. He had also invented the "Dirty Bird," a funky dance he did in the end zone to celebrate touchdowns. I used to do the "Dirty Bird" in practice as a joke.

Jamal invited another guy to join us for dinner but didn't formally introduce us. I thought he looked familiar and tried to figure out how I knew him. He was an older guy, maybe sixty years old, with a deep scowl. I finally realized I had seen him in movies. Turned out he was in Miami filming *Any Given Sunday* with Al Pacino, Cameron Diaz, and Jamie Foxx. Toward the end of the evening, the others caught on that I didn't know the actor's name because I was saying stupid things like, "I know you're an actor, but I'm trying to figure out where else I might know you from." They snickered.

Walking out of the restaurant, I asked Jamal, "Who the hell was that?"

Jamal said, "You really don't know? No idea?"

"No."

"You just had dinner with Jim Brown."

"Who's he?"

Jim Brown played for the Cleveland Browns from 1957 to 1965. When he retired at his peak he was the leading rusher of all-time. Some say he was the greatest running back ever. I had no clue. In Hawaii, I hadn't followed football. On a Sunday as a kid, I preferred to go to the beach rather than get up at 6:00 a.m. (because of the time difference) to watch football. I could tell you who the surfers were but not the NFL greats. I knew nothing about the game's history. That's why I hadn't been impressed by the Green Bay Packers when they drafted me and why I didn't recognize Jim Brown at my dinner table.

When the families started to trickle in, I saw other players hug their kids and kiss their wives. I got depressed thinking that when Mitchell, my partner of three years, arrived, I couldn't greet him openly with the affection I felt for him. I couldn't show others my happiness at having him there with me. We had to hide in the shadows.

Mitchell couldn't stay with me. The married players on the team were able to have their wives sleep in their rooms. I booked my partner a separate room in the hotel. We had to sneak around. I hated that.

Mitchell was family to me, but I had to lie about it. I couldn't introduce Mitchell as my partner to Coach Reeves, the way the other players introduced their wives or girlfriends to him. Instead, I introduced him as my music manager and friend.

We played that charade the whole week. Mitchell dressed stylishly enough to pass for someone in the music business. Also, having worked as a set decorator for Prince, he knew enough of the inside workings of that world if questioned. We told people that he managed my singing career. But there were times that week when I thought he wasn't acting enough and we wouldn't manage to pull it off.

The size of that fishbowl in Miami heightened the extreme paranoia I already felt as a closeted gay man playing in the NFL. I feared that if anyone discovered my secret, not only would I face public humiliation of enormous proportions, I would end up with nothing back on the banana farm in Hawaii. I had played my football career in fear. It increased to fit the dimensions of the Super Bowl.

Mitchell and I took every precaution we could. We were really, really careful not to bicker like a couple in public. We didn't kiss in cars, where someone might spy us through the closed window. We didn't use our cell phones. With all of the media there—eager to give their readers, listeners and viewers an exclusive behind-the-scenes story—we figured it was too dangerous to risk someone picking up our signal. The slightest slip between us could end up world news: "Gay Football Player in Super Bowl." I didn't want to be that headline.

I planned to use only some of the two-dozen tickets I was allotted, so I sold the rest through a friend's broker. I made $12,000 on ten tickets. League officials fined Vikings' head coach Mike Tice $100,000 for scalping his tickets to Super Bowl XXXIX in 2005, but, believe me, he's not the only one scalping tickets. The league tells you you're not supposed to sell your tickets, but officials know everybody is doing it. I heard other players brag about how much they made by scalping their tickets.

In addition to Mitchell, his parents Dan and Shelly, and my mom, I invited people who had influenced and supported me as a football player over the years. That included Olivia and Mike Lee from Chino, California, where I had played football with their sons, Mikey and Brandon, at Don Lugo High. They used to drive up to Corvallis to see me play at Oregon State.

I invited Iris and Randy Butler, who had been my surrogate parents during college. They were my biggest fans from Oregon. They had collected every single article and picture since I started playing at OSU and through my retirement from the NFL.

I gave tickets to my brother Afa and his wife, Beverly. Afa had helped me out when I was younger. Afa was the one Tua went to when I asked him for money in college. Afa ran a successful orchid farm in Hawaii. I had always looked up to him.

I also invited Jill Willis, my real music manager, and her boyfriend. Jill had managed Prince. She now represents Donny Osmond, who is huge in Europe. We told people that Mitchell was part of her company, Renaissance Management.

The only people who knew about Mitchell and me were Mama, Dan, Shelly, Jill, and her boyfriend. Olivia and Mike, Iris and Randy, and Afa and Beverly didn't know. I thought I could manage a group this size. I hadn't invited more people because I thought it would become too complicated to keep our white lie going. We gave the story that Dan and Shelly were my Minnesota family, that Mitchell was their son and my music manager, and that I was a straight football player.

I probably could have trusted the others with my secret, but I hadn't told them yet and this didn't seem to be the right week to break the news. I was scared one of them might let something slip amid the media circus. Also, I realized that this was a once-in-a-lifetime opportunity for them to attend the Super Bowl as the guest of someone playing in it. I wanted to let them enjoy themselves without distracting them with my secret.

The first night everybody was there, we went to dinner at Joe's Stone Crab, which was *the* place to go. A friend of mine from Minnesota had told me to call his buddy in Miami if I needed anything. I called him to help us get a table.

"For how many?" he asked.

"Thirteen," I said.

"No problem. I'll get you in."

We arrived at the restaurant and people like John Elway, the Broncos' superstar quarterback, were waiting for a table. The line stretched out the door. I walked up to the maitre d' and said,

"Table for Tuaolo?"

He said, "Ah, yes. Your table is ready. Right this way, please."

That was cool. I had arrived in style. We had pulled up in a stretch limo and walked past all of these famous people waiting as long as two hours to be seated. The friends and family in my group were impressed.

I was feeling blessed to be at the Super Bowl with the people who mattered most to me. I felt almost normal to have friends and family sharing this major event of my life. But, of course, I wasn't normal. My husband and in-laws were there, but I couldn't even let everybody at the table know what they meant to me.

Olivia, who had looked after me in high school, began grilling Mitchell. She was trying to see where he fit in my life. We had told her that he and his family used to take annual trips to Hawaii to visit us. Olivia asked Mitchell for the fourth time since she had met him earlier that day, "Now, how come we didn't meet you when we came to Hawaii?"

She was frustrated trying to figure out our connection. Our story wasn't adding up. Mitchell caught my eye. *Help!*

Shelly, his mom, rescued him. "We have been going to Hawaii for as long as Mitchell remembers," she said.

But I wasn't sure Olivia would drop it. I couldn't be sure our secret was safe.

I hated not being able to share who Mitchell was with those close to me. This was the biggest thing that ever happened to me, but I had to lie my way through it. In order for me to succeed—and for them to enjoy the success with me—I had to pretend I was somebody else. That tore me up inside.

It was stressful to juggle the lies. I was paranoid and on edge. I lost my temper over small things that shouldn't have mattered. I threatened Mitchell that I would leave if he blew our cover.

I'd had big expectations for this week, but it turned out not to be as much fun as the Super Bowl that Mitchell and I attended the previous year. In San Diego, we could stay together in the same room. There were no family and friends to fool. I was out of the limelight as a spectator.

We couldn't party in Miami the way we had in San Diego. The parties started after 10:00 p.m. The Falcons had bed check at midnight. We were there to win the big prize, not to party. In San Diego, Mitchell and I had been able to enjoy ourselves without worrying. I didn't have a game to play at the end of the week.

My guests enjoyed themselves, and I was happy for that. I took them to team picture day at Pro Player Stadium, the Dolphins' stadium where the Super Bowl would be played. They walked the field and took photographs with players. I sat back and watched them. Mama was having a good time, giggling. It was worth a million bucks to see her and the others having fun.

Part of what was so awesome about the week was seeing my friends and family so happy. This was something I was able to give them because of football. I was able to share my success with people who were important to me. That was one of the rewards for all of the hard times I had been through. I delighted in the smiles on their faces.

Randy Butler, my surrogate father from college, provided us with some laughs. He's a muscular Kenny Rogers, a country boy carpenter from Roseburg, Oregon. He had a camera from the sixties that you had to crank to wind the film. He was taking all these pictures, but his camera wasn't working. It was so funny. He had to ask one of the professional photographers on the field how to change the film because his wife Iris was the one who always did that, but she wasn't there. The photographer looked at the camera and laughed. He'd never seen one like that. He couldn't help Randy.

We also had media day at Pro Player Stadium. Media from all over the world packed the field. Reporters came from every little town in the United States and from faraway cities like London, Berlin, and Tokyo. The Super Bowl is the largest media event in the world, and this was their day.

The marquee players spoke at podiums. The rest of us hung out on the field and talked to the roving reporters. I drew a few questions, like the one from the Minneapolis newspaper writer who asked me how it felt to make it to the Super Bowl by beating my former team.

I received some attention but not much. The reporters wanted to talk to the big name players. I couldn't help but wonder, *What if? What if I wasn't playing with this monkey on my back? What if I'd reached my potential and become a star?* I would be one of those guys everybody wanted to talk to. Or, *What if I was open about being gay and everybody accepted it?* They would want to talk to me.

Instead, my Falcon teammate Craig Sauer and I stood around and cracked jokes, acting like reporters. "I'm from the South Pacific Reporter," I said. "Tell me, how did you get a forehead that big?"

The jokes helped distract me from my pain. I was grateful for guys like Craig who I had met in the NFL. Laughing with them made my situation tolerable.

Shortly after I woke up on Super Bowl Sunday, my mom called. She told me somebody from our team had been arrested on

Saturday night. I thought, *No way. This is the Super Bowl. Who would be stupid enough to get into trouble the night before the biggest game of his life?*

Mama said, "I think his name is Robinson."

I thought her limited English had caused her to misunderstand the name. "Not Eugene Robinson," I said. "He is our spiritual leader."

The All-Pro free safety was also the leader of our defensive secondary, a key player on the team.

I turned on the television. It was all over the news. Eugene had been charged with trying to buy a blowjob from an undercover cop posing as a prostitute. On Saturday night, he had left behind his wife and their two kids, his mom and dad, aunts and uncles, and cousins—all who were there with him—to cruise one of the seediest areas of downtown Miami, Biscayne Boulevard, known for its drug dealers and prostitutes.

I was stunned. Eugene was involved in the team's Bible study. He organized the prayer on the field after games. We called him, "The Reverend." Saturday morning, the religious group Athletes in Action had presented Eugene with the Bart Starr Award to recognize his "high moral character."

I went downstairs to eat breakfast with the team. We were supposed to be pumped up for the big game, but it was quiet at the tables. Too quiet. I had the sense, *This is not good. It will be a miracle if we win this game.*

Robinson was arrested the night before the game. There was no time to bounce back. If it had happened early in the week, we would have had time to adjust, but Eugene's arrest occupied everybody's minds the morning of the game.

Coach Reeves stood by Eugene, said he loved him unconditionally and that Eugene would start. Other teammates told the press that they were sure Eugene was innocent, just in the "wrong place at the wrong time."

We had a team meeting after breakfast. Everybody was still in shock. The police had let Eugene out of jail. He walked into the room for the meeting and sat down a couple of seats ahead of me. Guys walked up to Eugene, patted him on the back, and said, "We all make mistakes. Keep your head up."

I was pissed off. Patting Eugene on the back and offering him support was probably the right thing to do—what else can you say to a teammate in that situation?—but I was thinking, *What if they had found out I was gay on the morning of the Super Bowl?* If the media were blasting me, would my teammates have patted me on the back? No way. Not based on the reaction NFL players gave me when I did come out later.

People say Eugene Robinson wasn't a factor in the game. Bullshit. We went from a team being pumped up to a quiet, meek group. Instead of going out to perform in the biggest show of our lives, it seemed we were going to a funeral. All of the media attention on Eugene was an incredible distraction. It was difficult to focus on the task at hand. We had been the number one team for scoring in the red zone (inside the twenty-yard line) that year, yet our offense only scored three times—two field goals and a touchdown. (We also returned a kickoff for a touchdown.) The team was not on track.

Eugene was one of the reasons that we were in the Super Bowl. He was the NFL career leader among active players in interceptions. In the NFC championship game against the Vikings, he had helped shut down Minnesota's prolific Randall Cunningham to Randy Moss connection. After Moss caught a touchdown pass early in the game, Eugene and his secondary held Moss to only one catch in the second half and overtime. In our first playoff game against San

Francisco, Eugene had picked off a pass at our three-yard-line and returned it seventy-seven yards to set up a field goal.

But Eugene was not at his best Sunday in Miami. The Broncos picked on him all day long. They burned him deep twice, once for an eighty-yard touchdown pass.

The loss was not all Eugene's fault. Give Denver credit, too. They had a great team that season. Running back Terrell Davis rushed for over one hundred yards. Wide receiver Rod Smith caught five passes, including the eighty-yard touchdown. Quarterback John Elway was at his best, throwing for 336 yards and running for a touchdown. He was voted the game's Most Valuable Player.

As a footnote to Eugene's story, he returned the Bart Starr Award. In a press conference after the game, he denied the charges against him and apologized to his family. Five weeks later, he agreed to submit to an AIDS test and attend an AIDS education class in exchange for the police dropping the misdemeanor charge for soliciting sex. He was and still is one of the nicest guys you'll ever meet. He's an example that we are all of the flesh. We're human. We all make mistakes and fall short of the glory of God. He deserved that award. The sad thing is that Eugene will be remembered not for being a great guy or a terrific player but as the guy who allegedly propositioned a prostitute the night before the Super Bowl.

Cher sang the national anthem. Right beforehand, I was down on the field with her. She was standing with k.d. lang and some other friends not three feet from me. I had admired Cher for a long time. I wanted to say, "I'm a huge fan of yours," but in front of my teammates that would have been the same as saying, "I'm gay." "Cher" and "macho fans" aren't often used in the same sentence. I kept my mouth shut.

I played in the game without any worries of exposure—until that last play when I tackled Elway to end the game. Eugene Robinson occupied all of the media attention. Even though we lost, playing in the Super Bowl was a thrill. The energy on the field was like no other game. We all knew that not just Atlanta and Denver fans but football and Super Bowl fans from all over the world—a billion people—were watching. It was awesome to play on a stage that large.

In the locker room afterward, the mood was grim. We knew we should have won that game. Had we been able to carry our momentum from the season and the upset against the Vikings into the Super Bowl without the Eugene Robinson fiasco, I think we would have had the emotional advantage. I really think we would have won. It had been that sort of season for us.

But we didn't. Everybody was hurting. We had missed the chance of a lifetime. You can't get that back. The bus ride to the hotel was quiet. As we unloaded, I looked out the window. I saw the players' wives embrace their husbands. They comforted their pain. I got off the bus and signaled Mitchell with a look to meet me upstairs. Only in the secrecy of my hotel room could I break down in Mitchell's arms. That's how Super Bowl XXXIII ended for me.

# CHAPTER EIGHTEEN

# I Can't Lose This Man

I WASN'T SURPRISED THAT ATLANTA did not renew my one-year contract after the 1998 season. The team had some young players the coaches wanted to develop. They didn't think it was necessary to keep me on the roster. I had expected that. Every time you go into a team, you run the numbers game in your head. You look at the other players, consider what they're paid, and calculate whether the team would rather pay your salary or theirs. I figured my stint in Atlanta would last only a year.

I returned to Minnesota with Mitchell but was not ready to give up on football. Yet again, my future hung in limbo.

The week after the Super Bowl, I sang the national anthem at the Pro Bowl, the annual NFL all-star game played in Hawaii. If I wasn't going to make it to the Pro Bowl as a player, the next best thing was to be invited as a performer. That allowed me to show people back home a different talent. I was not widely known in Hawaii because I never played for a team there. People thought I was a transplant; they didn't realize I had grown up on the island of Oahu. They didn't know how much Hawaii meant to me.

Mitchell, Jill Willis, my music manager, and Calvin Ro, my mentor friend from Hawaii, came with me to the Pro Bowl. We all had field passes, since I was singing. Everywhere we turned, we saw another superstar. These were the top players in the league. Calvin loves sports. He couldn't contain his excitement at being on the field with so many of his heroes. He would grab my arm and gush, "Oh my God! There's _____!"

Calvin is the type of person who thinks nobody would guess he is gay, but anybody can tell he is by his mannerisms and expressions, especially when he's excited, the way he was at the Pro Bowl. Here I'd been worried that people would suspect my relationship with Mitchell, yet every time Calvin grabbed my arm, it was as though he was about to tug my secret out of me.

Calvin carried a large bag onto the field. Suddenly, he reached in and pulled out helmets and footballs he wanted the players to sign. He walked around and collected autographs. The players seemed happy to sign, and no one made any remarks to me about him.

I never would have thought to ask the players I knew or went up against for their autograph. It was enough for me to carry my memories in my head. Now that I have a son, I wish I would have done that for him. I could still get some autographs—from former teammates like Brett Favre and Jamal Anderson—but I wish I had asked stars like Warren Moon, Barry Sanders, and Roger Craig when I played against them. If I'd known I would have a son, I might have so that I would have something to show him when I tell him—or my grandkids—about my playing days.

Before the Pro Bowl, Calvin, Jill, Mitchell, and I went to a karaoke bar for me to practice singing the national anthem. It's one of the hardest songs in the world to sing because it has so many octaves and the words don't flow smoothly. I had not sung it in public for a while and was nervous to perform in front of my home crowd.

Calvin appointed himself my music guru. He corrected all of my faults. "Don't sing like a big, black woman," he admonished me. "Sing it like you." He told me when to hold out a note, when not to. "Pronounce each word correctly," he said. He was so serious that Jill, Mitchell, and I couldn't stop laughing. Of course, we'd been drinking, too.

It paid off at the Pro Bowl, though. When I started singing in the middle of the field, I felt a huge sense of pride belting out the national anthem in Hawaii. For the moment, I enjoyed the spotlight.

Not long after Mitchell and I returned from Hawaii, my agent, Mitch Frankel, called. The Carolina Panthers wanted to bring me to Charlotte for a workout. I went through the physicals and competed in drills against two or three other guys—the whole routine again. I guess I did well because they signed me for the 1999 season as a backup.

The Panthers hold their training camp in Greensboro, South Carolina. I suffered through another hot, excruciating camp. On the up side, the team had incredible facilities at its headquarters in Charlotte, where we practiced and played at Bank of America Stadium. The team was in its fifth season, and everything was brand new.

Everybody on the team knew I was a singer. So was my new Panther teammate, wide receiver Rae Carruth. He and I used to joke we were going to make a record together. Then he was charged with murdering his pregnant girlfriend in the middle of the season because she refused to have an abortion. After the season ended, he was convicted of conspiracy to commit murder and sentenced to almost nineteen years in prison. Strange, you play together and think you know a guy. I never expected something like that of him.

It sparked my fears to know somebody that nice could turn and do something so horrendous just because she was pregnant. What if he—or someone like him—found out I was gay? Guys I thought were my friends could turn on me. Even if one of them didn't do something to me himself, there were people out there someone could pay to take me out like Carruth did with his girlfriend. You never know what could make them snap and turn. My being gay could be that thing.

As it turned out, I didn't have any problems in Carolina with teammates. They lived the macho, testosterone life. I stuck to myself. After work, I went home to a furnished apartment I rented in a beautiful, gated complex with specialty shops lining the streets. I didn't go out much with the other guys.

Since I met Mitchell, I had toned down my partying. Being in a relationship had taken away a lot of the loneliness and fear I would never meet someone, which had caused me to party so heavily in the past. I still feared people would discover I was gay, but I figured if I was outed, I would still have Mitchell. That took the edge off of the fear.

There was different stress involved with a relationship. I missed Mitchell. I was frustrated that I could not be openly affectionate with him when we were together in public. I hated having to lie about who he was. I hated having to lie about myself. Yet, we endured the stress together. Even when we argued and I threatened to leave, I knew I didn't really want to break up. I didn't want to be alone again.

Mitchell visited several times, but we still struggled with the difficulties of a long-distance relationship. My constant moving from one place to another proved stressful. Since I met Mitchell, I'd been in Buffalo, Jacksonville, Atlanta, and now Charlotte in a span of three years. I craved stability. I wanted Mitchell to quit his job. "Why can't you let your mom and brother run the business so you can be with me?" I pleaded.

He would respond, "If you want that, you should date a waiter or someone who doesn't have obligations."

I would take that to mean he didn't love me enough.

When I look back at it now, I can't believe I thought he had no life other than me.

The longer I stayed with Mitchell, the more it bothered me to see other players with their wives. I was angry that I couldn't be open with him. It hurt that I could not ask him to join us when the team would dine with their wives and that I had to go alone to the team Christmas parties. I blamed some of our arguments on the stress of having to play a double life. I had something wonderful, but football could kill it because of the burden it placed on our relationship.

Don't get me wrong. It wasn't all bad between Mitchell and me. We had more fun times than bad times. It's just that the pressure made the bad times seem more severe.

I had a lot of playing time in Carolina. We went 8–8 that season under the Panthers' new head coach, George Seifert, and narrowly missed picking up the wild card entry to the playoffs. I played an especially strong game on a Sunday night late in November against my former team, the Atlanta Falcons. They had beaten us earlier in the season, but we had our revenge in a prime-time national television broadcast. I was destroying Atlanta's offensive linemen. With less than three minutes remaining, I recovered a fumble inside our twenty-yard line to protect a slim lead and preserve our victory. Craig Sauer, who had been my joking buddy in Atlanta, said afterward, "You looked like a Pro Bowler the way you were tossing people around. Why didn't you play like that when you were in Atlanta?"

I was happy to play well and help the team win. At the same time, Craig's question nagged me. It seemed I couldn't play up to my potential regularly because I was so conflicted. I wanted to be big and macho so nobody knew my secret, yet I feared the spotlight would expose me as a gay man. The anxiety cramped my performance.

Maybe I could have played the way I did against the Falcons all of the time. Maybe I could have made a name for myself instead of becoming a run-stopper. It hurts to think maybe I could have really shined if I hadn't carried this monkey on my back.

I blew out my hamstring again in Carolina. I was making a tackle. That extra drive with my foot stretched the muscle at the back of my leg; I heard a "pop." I knew right away I was done for the season, but at the time, I didn't realize that tackle would be the last play of my career.

Mitchell was at the game with his parents, Shelly and Dan. Soon as I went down, my mind automatically went to Mitchell. *How can I get a message up to him to let him know I'm okay?* Once off the field and into the locker room, I couldn't call him because there were people around tending to me. I knew he was worried.

It hurt not being able to talk to him. Another player would have been able to call his spouse in the stands.

I went into rehab right away but knew with only four games left in the season, my hamstring wouldn't heal in time for me to play again that year. I watched the rest of the season from the sidelines in street clothes, visibly marked as an outsider.

Once the season ended, Carolina didn't offer me a contract for the next year. No other teams called.

Mitchell and I had some long talks. Thirteen years of football—four at OSU, nine in the NFL—had battered my body. I'd hurt my knee, ankle, hamstring, ribs, hands, and sternum. As I grew older, the physical punishment became harder to take. The emotional strain of hiding and lying had also worsened. I didn't want to be away from Mitchell, and I wasn't sure our relationship could survive the stress of another season of separation.

After blowing out my hamstring I was thinking, *I can't lose this man.* I was no longer willing to play football at the expense of our relationship. We decided it was time for me to retire. Just like that, I was done.

Retirement was a difficult decision, but by then I wasn't happy playing because it meant being apart from Mitchell. It's a sad thing for anybody to retire from a job before they're ready, but I wanted to be with Mitchell and be happy.

I thought the arguments would end, but, of course, they didn't. They just changed. Now I was home all of the time. We had to adjust to that. It was a challenge. I couldn't just go off to play football. I really had to work on myself and on the relationship. The adjustment took a while, but things improved with time.

I no longer had to live with the awful fear of being shunned from the NFL if someone found out my secret. I still lived a double life, but it was easier being out of the spotlight. We had a small circle of friends that included another couple, Tim and David, Katie, Mitchell's best friend from high school, and a few others.

During my season with Atlanta, Mitchell had given me a gold commitment ring with a two-carat diamond. My Super Bowl ring was big and beautiful—the size of four class rings and studded with diamonds—but the ring I prize most is the one Mitchell gave me. I had waited all of my life for this ring, for someone to want me the way he did. It was a sign to me that he wasn't going anywhere.

Later that year, I bought him a three-carat diamond to show him my commitment. I tend to want to do everything bigger. The commitment ring I gave him was no exception. Yet the message was the same: I wasn't going anywhere. It was a gradual thing for us to reach a harmony in our relationship, but that mutual commitment made it possible.

After I retired, I didn't have to go to practice, to watch film, to work out. That was weird, not having to do anything. I was looking for something to fill my time. A man who worked at Mitchell's salon was also an actor. He invited me to perform in *Master Class,* a play about the life of the great opera singer Maria Callas. He offered me a bit part that didn't involve any singing. I figured I had been acting all of my life, I might as well get paid for it. I didn't exactly steal the show with my two lines, but I enjoyed it enough to want to do more.

Not long after my stage debut, I secured a part in another show, a revival of the fifties musical *The Most Happy Fella.* We performed at prisons and schools. I was starting to find my niche outside of football.

Here I was, a retired NFL player doing theatre—anybody should've known I was gay, but I wasn't ready to come out of the closet. The roots of fear had sunk too deep during nine years in the macho world of professional football.

# CHAPTER NINETEEN

## That's the Big Secret

WHEN MY FORMER FALCON teammate Craig Sauer signed with the Vikings, he remembered our Minnesota connection. He asked some of his teammates, "You guys know Esera?" They looked at him weird. Their wives, who frequented Mitchell's salon, had passed along the rumors that circulated about us.

"You didn't hear about him?" they said to Craig. "He bats from the other side."

I was in my car, driving home from a *Most Happy Fella* rehearsal when my cell phone rang. It was Craig. We slipped into our usual banter. "Hey, Fivehead."

After a moment, he said, "I've got something for you."

I thought he was going to tell me a joke. Instead, he asked, "Are you gay?"

I sighed. I didn't know what to say. I knew he probably had heard the rumors. I knew people in Minnesota had been talking.

My heart sped up. The fear kicked in. I remained silent for a long time.

*Shit,* I thought. *I'm going to lose another friend.* I knew Craig was a Christian. He probably believed homosexuality was an abomination, and I feared that would separate us. He was someone who made me feel good. I didn't want to lose another friend.

All of these thoughts sped through my head. I prepared myself for the rejection. I told myself, *You've gone through this shit before. You'll be able to deal with it.*

Finally, I said, "Yes."

"So that's why you haven't called me," he replied.

Right away, I knew I would be okay with him. I sighed in relief and thanked God.

"We're friends," he said. "You know I think God is against it, but I love you like a brother."

We talked some more. I remember him saying, "You don't have to run."

When I hung up, I cried.

Craig was the first NFL player who reacted positively to me. His reaction shocked me in a good way. I had underestimated him.

I'm glad he called. Instead of listening to and accepting what others said, he wanted to check things out for himself. My sexual orientation didn't change the kind of person I was. He knew that. He could have turned his back on me, but he didn't. I appreciated that.

I went home and told Mitchell. I was so excited that a football player had accepted me the way I was. The fact he thought God was against homosexuality didn't bother me. I knew I could discuss our religious views without offending him because he knew I was a Christian.

When Craig calls now, we fall back into the old jokes. He tells me they're not getting any sun up in St. Cloud, seventy miles northwest of Minneapolis, and asks me to move my head out of the way. I tease him that his fivehead is growing larger.

* * *

Korey Stringer was a great athlete and a great guy. He was an All-Pro offensive tackle who lit up a room when he entered it. He reminded me of Fat Albert, not in a negative way at all, but because he was so "Hey, hey, hey!" We used to rib each other all the time. We played together for two years. He was my joking buddy in Minnesota the way Craig Sauer was in Atlanta.

Korey would say to me, "I'm sorry they canceled your show," meaning *Chips,* because he thought I looked like the star Erik Estrada.

Korey was a big guy, over 330 pounds. I would say to him, "I loved you in that movie where you carried that woman up the tall building and fought the planes," likening him to King Kong.

Korey suffered heatstroke on the second day of the Vikings' 2001 training camp, a day when the temperature soared to ninety-five degrees. He died later that night. He was twenty-seven and left behind a wife and a three-year-old son.

I was really sad when he passed away. Even though I hadn't seen him for several years, it tore me up because I knew he was a good man. He made people laugh and feel good about themselves. When he had a horrible game—which wasn't often—he never pointed fingers. The Billy Joel song, "Only the Good Die Young," applied to him because he was such a good person. We lost a true champion when he died.

Korey's death was one of those freak accidents. He didn't have anything to prove. He was an All-Pro. He didn't have to go full speed, but I know how hard a team can push an individual.

Having been through a couple of excruciatingly hot training camps myself, I know what it's like to think you're going to die in the heat because the coaches push you to your limits. It's harder on us big guys. That's why they call those practices "Hell week." That's the price you pay to play at that level.

His wife, Kelci, thought the Vikings may not have looked at the signs of Korey pushing himself the day before. She thought they should have backed off practicing in that heat.

As much as I love Korey and his family, I also understand the gladiator mentality in sports. The day before had also been incredibly hot, with temperatures in the nineties. Korey had vomited during the morning workout and left the field, then sat out the afternoon session. The morning of July 31, the Minneapolis *StarTribune* ran a large picture of Korey puking during practice. Maybe when the other players teased him about throwing up, he went full out so they wouldn't make fun of him again.

Whatever happened, it cost him his life.

The funeral home was about three blocks from my house. I was really nervous about going to his funeral. I had recently spoken with Craig Sauer. I didn't know if I could walk back into that macho world with all of those rumors swirling around me. At the last minute, I decided to go.

I pulled up and saw reporters gathered outside. When I stepped out of my car, I felt the eyes follow me up to the entrance. Just as I was about to walk inside, the funeral home staff closed the doors. The place was full. They said they couldn't let anyone else in. They had reached the fire code limit. Before they shut the doors, I glimpsed some of the Vikings' staff inside. I know they recognized me. If they had said, "Hey, wait, let him in. That's Esera Tuaolo," I know I would have been inside. But they didn't say anything.

I stood there a moment. I was so embarrassed. Everybody standing outside—the reporters, the camera crews, others—had seen my former team shut me out. It had taken all of my strength to reach those doors. Now I had to turn around and pass all of the people watching me. I put my head down and walked toward my car. I felt sick in my gut.

I passed a couple of Vikings. "Hey, what's up?" I managed to say. They walked by without saying anything. All I got from them was a smirk and an arched eyebrow. That really hurt.

Todd Steussie, the Vikings' All-Pro offensive tackle, had been my teammate for three years. He stopped. "Hey, Esera. Where you going?"

"Home," I said.

"You doing okay?" he asked.

"Yeah, fine," I said. I couldn't tell him that they had turned me away. I knew they would let him in.

I jumped in my car, said a prayer for Korey and his family, and drove home.

Not long after that, I saw John Randle at South Beach, the Minneapolis nightclub where we used to hang out together. He was cold. I walked up to him and said, "John, you and I have been friends for a long time. This doesn't change anything. I'm still me. I'm still the guy who was there for you when you went through your divorce."

He nodded but didn't say anything. I walked away.

Later, he came up and shook my hand. "I understand," he said. That was enough for me.

Mitchell and I had talked about kids. I always wanted a family. Mitchell was more skeptical. It's not that he didn't want to have children. He just didn't think as a gay man he could have them. My dream to have a family came true with the birth of our twins in November 2000.

All these thoughts kicked in. *Will they have ten fingers and ten toes? I finally get to be a father. Oh my gosh, am I going to love them? Will these babies love me? Will they cry the whole time?* I couldn't stop this rush of emotion.

I started thinking about Christmas. *We're going to have children for Christmas!* My thoughts raced farther ahead. I was going to be able to have grandkids, someone to tell my stories to. *It's going to be like the Waltons I watched growing up.* I pictured my grandkids running into the room at Christmas time calling me "Grandpa!"

When I first saw them, they were wrapped in white blankets, just their faces showing. I started crying all over again. I took them both in my arms. They were twins, a girl and boy, and Samoan like me. Michele's eyes were so big. Mitchell was wrinkled and skinny. I wondered what they were thinking. Did they know I was their daddy?

I'd been around my nieces and nephews a lot and had seen my brothers' and sisters' joy. That day, I knew how it felt when they held their first-born children. It was the best feeling in the world to hold mine.

Big Mitchell held little Mitchell in his hands away from his body. I don't know if he had ever held a baby before. I could tell he was nervous. Then little Mitchell smiled at him and Mitchell melted. He had thought he might not be able to love these children as his own, but after that moment, there was no question he could.

It wasn't easy early on as any parent of a newborn—or twins— knows. Mitchell and I took turns at night sleeping on the floor of the nursery because we were afraid we wouldn't hear the babies cry. I would wake up two or three times to put my ear next to their noses to make sure they were still breathing. Mitchell did the same. Knowing that you're responsible for another living being, especially when they are babies, is an incredible experience.

As they grow, it's wonderful to know that you are able to pass on everything positive that you have learned in your life. All any child wants is love, to know that they are supported and accepted no matter what. That's what Mitchell and I want to give our children, that unconditional love.

My cousin Susan gave us some good advice before we adopted Michele and Mitchell. She told us we needed to have a strong foundation between the two of us for our family to be strong. Every week, she and her husband have a date, so their relationship can bloom. "I love my children," she said. "But I'm in love with my husband. I know kids need more attention, but you can't put your husband on the back burner. You have to love him, so that your children will have a solid base."

Mitchell and I don't take anything for granted with our children. We know that Minnesota is one of only five states where both partners of same-sex couples can adopt children. In most other states, people don't have that right. One partner has to declare himself or herself the child's parent for the purposes of the adoption. If he or she dies, the other partner—their other father or mother—is not automatically granted custody of children. We thank God every morning for Michele and Mitchell.

Once Mitchell and I adopted our children, it became harder and harder for me to lie about my sexual orientation. Doing so meant I had to deny my family. I realized I could no longer do that after a rafting trip down the Colorado River with Mitchell, Shelly, and Dan. Mama stayed with our children back home.

We were with a group of eighteen people on two rafts for seven days. I had been retired for two years, but somebody in our group recognized me as a professional football player. We immediately slipped back into our story of Mitchell being my best friend and how our families had been friends in Hawaii.

I felt awkward lying again. I didn't like reverting back to that mode we thought we had left behind when I left the NFL. But we were on a raft with these people. It wasn't like meeting at Disney World where we could walk away from them.

When they found out I had children, I had to pretend that I had adopted them as a single parent. They started showering me with compliments. "Oh, how wonderful that you adopted children by yourself." They went on and on, placing me on a pedestal as an NFL player who had adopted children on his own.

I looked at Mitchell. I could see that his heart ached to say that they were his children, too. I could see Shelly hurting, too. These were her first grandchildren. She loves them so much that she can't go a day without speaking to them. She wanted to show everybody the pictures of Michele and Mitchell in her wallet. Dan was also a proud grandparent. I felt so bad when I looked at them, like I was neglecting them.

The Grand Canyon is one of the most beautiful places I've been, but our lies spoiled my view of it. Instead of being able to relax and enjoy the trip, I became uptight, worrying that one of us would slip up and reveal our secret. I had wanted to end that anxious feeling.

Before we caught our flight home, we ate at a restaurant in Las Vegas and talked about the week. Shelly said, "I think we need to prepare ourselves better the next time we go away."

"No," I said. "I can't do this again. I can't deny you being a grandmother or Mitchell being a father."

We talked some more. It was sad thinking about the way I had denied them but liberating to realize that we weren't going to lie any more. I was going to live in my truth.

Soon after, I talked with a television producer who is a friend of a friend about doing a documentary on my life. He met with various television companies to discuss funding. HBO told him that it wouldn't fund a documentary but that the producers of its show *Real Sports with Bryant Gumbel* were interested in my story.

Mitchell and I sat down to discuss whether I should tell my secret on the show. The idea scared the hell out of me. At the same time, I was tired of living in our lie, which made even routine trips to the supermarket risky. I would run into someone I knew, and Mitchell had to jump into the next aisle. While he and I talked, we each held one of our kids, who were almost two years old. I looked down at little Mitchie in my arms. He said, "I love you, Big Daddy." We decided we had to do this for our family.

We didn't want our children to grow up in a lie. We didn't want them to have to call Mitchell "Uncle." We wanted them to be able to call both of us "Daddy." We wanted to make sure they knew their fathers loved each other. We wanted to keep our windows open when we had a birthday party.

I called Nick Dolin, the producer of *Real Sports,* and told him, "I'm not coming out by myself. I'm coming out with my family, with Mitchell and our children. Are you guys comfortable with that?"

He said, "Yes."

The fear kicked in. My life would air on national television. Not the public part—me playing football—but the private part—the secret that I had protected so desperately—would air for everyone to know and judge. The time to back out would be now. Yet, Mitchell and I realized that we were not like a normal family. It would be impossible for us to remain private forever because I was known as an NFL football player. We wouldn't be able to live our lives without some tabloid or gossip columnist writing about us. Coming out on *Real Sports* gave us some control over how we would be portrayed. We wanted my disclosure to happen in a positive way.

I told Jill Willis, my music manager, our plan. She set me up with Howard Bragman, a Hollywood publicist who had helped a bunch of famous gay people when they came out of the closet. I had thought, naively, that our coming out might not be news beyond Minnesota, where Mitchell and I lived. I thought doing the show would simply allow us to live our lives without having to lie anymore.

Howard knew better. He told me that an NFL player—even a retired one—saying he was gay would be huge news and helped prepare me for the reaction. He orchestrated something very tasteful. He didn't book us on the *Jerry Springer Show*. He made sure people took seriously the fact that I was an NFL football player coming out with a family.

Every time I talked to Nick Dolin or Andrew Bennett, the producers of *Real Sports,* I became a bit more nervous. It started to become more real to me that this was going to happen, that I was going to let the world know I was gay. I was excited but afraid, too.

The plan was for them to interview us at home in October 2002. I thought there would be one man, one camera. Despite Howard's preparations, I still hadn't realized what a big event my announcement would become. The HBO crew showed up with a truckload of equipment—cameras, lights, screens, etc. They turned our house upside down. It was a huge production. Seeing that overwhelmed me.

While they set up the cameras, I hyperventilated in the back of the room. My stomach twisted inside out. They told me Bernie Goldberg, who would conduct the interview, was on his way over. I went into the bathroom and broke down. "Dear God, please help me," I prayed. "I do not know if this is the right thing to do. I feel in my heart that it is, but I'm not sure. Please let me know if we're making the right decision."

Mitchell could see what a mess I was. He was cool and calm. The support my husband showed me during the whole process that day really helped—he's such a great partner. He sat down with me on our bed, and we prayed.

We wanted Michele and Mitchell to know their fathers loved each other. We wanted them to know there are different types of families. Some children have single moms, some have single daddies, some have two mommies, and some have two daddies. That's the type of world we have. We live in a diverse society. We're not living in the Beaver Cleaver era where there are no blacks, Asians, Hispanics, or Polynesians.

Mitchell and I wanted to be able to attend PTA meetings together and both be able to talk to our children's teachers. We didn't want to have to hide in the supermarket. We didn't want to have to draw the shades for family events.

All of these thoughts rushed through our minds. They let us know we needed to go through with the interview. We agreed that it was the right thing to do for our kids.

My stomach was still twisted. The doorbell rang—Bernie. I looked at Mitchell, started crying, and couldn't stop. I was petrified. I ducked back into the bathroom to splash water on my face and compose myself.

My mom was there to take care of Michele and Mitchell. She didn't fully understand what was taking place. I had tried to explain that I needed to make this announcement for our family. She was skeptical. She worried about what other people would say. She also worried about our children's safety. But, ever supportive, she gave me her blessing. She told me in Samoan, "If you need to do this, then you should do it."

I walked into the living room and met Bernie. He seemed to be a nice guy. We sat on chairs facing one another and started the interview. I still felt panicked.

"What's the secret?" he asked.

"Um, that I'm gay," I said. "That's the big secret."

When those words came out of my mouth for the first time, I knew I had reached the point of no return. I felt a rush of peace and panic together. I felt liberated to shake off the monkey I had carried on my back since I was a child. At the same time, the fear of the unknown surged. I didn't know how people would respond. Would we receive death threats? I knew Billy Bean, the ex-Major League Baseball player, had received hate mail after he came out in 1999.

The rest of the interview was a blur. I kept excusing myself to throw up in the bathroom. I came back, answered a few more questions, then excused myself again. I battled with myself. *Is this the right thing? Yes, it has to be. I'm doing it for the children.* The devil on my other shoulder argued, *There's going to be trouble. Ask them for the tape and cancel the whole thing.* The day was a mind fuck for me.

After a while, I grew somewhat more comfortable with Bernie. He was a great interviewer who brought up some good questions.

"Why'd you retire from the NFL?" he asked. "You could've played a few more years."

"Due to, you know, knees and shoulders," I said.

"But that's not all of it," he said.

I hesitated. "Because I wanted to be happy."

"You couldn't be happy making an NFL pro athlete's salary?" Bernie pressed.

"How? They didn't know the true me. They didn't know who Esera Tuaolo is. Now, maybe after this segment, they'll know me for who I am: a gay, NFL—well, former NFL—football player."

A sense of peace followed. Everything fell into place. I finally understood why I was doing this interview. It was for Mitchell. For our children. I needed to feel like my straight friends felt with their families. I had lived like a prisoner in my own skin. Those words set me free.

When they turned off the cameras, I met Mitchell back in the bedroom. We embraced. "Great job," he said. "It's going to get better."

We had to wait a week before the show aired. Jill Willis and Howard Bragman told me to stay focused on my family. I tried, but it was a long week.

I felt exposed even before the *Real Sports* segment aired. I was working out on the treadmill at the health club, watching ESPN-TV, when the announcer reported that an NFL player who was gay planned to come out on *Real Sports*. Someone had leaked the story to ESPN. The people working out next to me started talking about the news report. I stopped and looked around. Did they know they were talking about me? I felt like I was in a *Twilight Zone* episode.

On my drive home, I listened to several talk radio stations. People were trying to guess, "Who is the gay NFL football player?"

Some people said negative things. Some joked about it. Some said there's no place for a gay person in the NFL. Some said a person's sexual orientation shouldn't matter. I started thinking, *I hope it wasn't a mistake to do that interview.*

Still, no one knew who it was. Hearing the buzz and seeing the way the media grabbed the story gave me a sense of how big my announcement would be. I was excited to know that I was the one they would all be talking about. I also realized how naïve I had been to think Mitchell and I would be able to go on quietly with our life.

Howard, my publicist, suggested I fly to Los Angeles, where he was based, to brainstorm how we would handle the media exposure once the *Real Sports* segment aired. He picked me up at the airport. My cell phone rang in the car. "Esera?" a voice said. "This is Rosie O'Donnell."

I thought it was a prank. "No."

"Yes, this is Rosie O'Donnell." After we spoke for a while, I recognized her voice. I couldn't believe that Rosie O'Donnell—Rosie O'Donnell!—had called me on my cell phone.

She had learned I was the gay NFL football player everyone was talking about. She had called to tell me that coming out with her partner Kelli had been wonderful. She said they would be there for me if I ever needed anything and so would a lot of other gay people. "I want you to know you are loved and supported," she said.

She helped calm some of my fears. I thanked her. I was impressed that someone of her status, respected in the gay community and around the world, would call simply to make my life a little easier. She didn't have to do that. Her act of kindness touched me.

Rosie also told me, "Now when somebody else comes out, you have a responsibility to reach out to them."

Before I came out, I used to speak occasionally at schools. Kids would tell me I was their role model. When Rosie called, that was the first time I felt like one of those little kids with her as my role model.

In Los Angeles, I had the chance to meet another role model who had reached out to me without knowing it. Howard was a friend of David Kopay, the gay former NFL player whose book had inspired me and given me hope to pursue someone if he came my way. If I hadn't read *The David Kopay Story,* Mitchell would have been just another man who passed through the night. I was so excited to meet David that I wanted to cry as soon as we pulled up to his Hollywood home. Along with my mom and God, David was one of the reasons I was still alive.

He opened the door, and we hugged right away. I was crying. He was crying. He felt a solidarity meeting another gay man who had played in the NFL. I felt the affirmation of meeting someone who had meant so much to me.

We finally made it inside. His house was modest but impeccably decorated. I admired the beautiful photos, including one of him and Vince Lombardi, who had been his coach with the Washington Redskins. Later, we walked to dinner at a nearby restaurant. The whole time, we talked about our lives, the NFL, and about the type of role model I would need to be. We spent a wonderful evening together.

I returned to Minnesota. The day before the *Real Sports* segment was to air, Mitchell and I flew to New York. Howard had booked me for a live interview with Diane Sawyer on *Good Morning America* the following morning. Despite the call from Rosie O'Donnell and my evening with David Kopay, I was still worried how people would respond to Mitchell and me. There was still time to pull the plug on the show.

Mitchell helped remind me of the reasons we had decided to go ahead with the interview. The two of us watched the segment that night in our hotel room. We both cried. Afterward, I looked at him and said, "We're out."

We knew there was no turning back. We were out. Never in my wildest dreams did I think it would feel so wonderful. Being the big crybaby I am, I started to cry again.

We called Michele and Mitchell, who were back home with Shelly and Dan. Talking to our children reminded me that they were the reason for the moment.

The next morning, we walked across the street to the ABC studios for *Good Morning America*. I felt different. That morning was the first time that Mitchell and I had woken up without having to worry about slipping up. People knew we were gay. We could hold hands outside of our room. We didn't have to lie.

I was nervous, though, doing a live interview on national television. They showed clips of our children from the HBO segment. Seeing Michele and Mitchell, my eyes teared up. The *Good Morning* camera panned to me. I knew I had to tell a joke or else the waterfall would start.

Diane Sawyer asked, "How do you feel?"

"A huge burden has been lifted off my back," I said. "I feel light as a feather, but when I stepped on the scale this morning, I still weighed three hundred and thirty pounds."

Everybody laughed. I could relax.

I had stepped into a different world. One I should have been in since I was a little kid. One that all kids should be allowed to live in, whether gay or straight. And one that all kids who tell their parents they are gay should be able to live in. I had stepped into the free world.

After the show, we walked outside. Mitchell said, "Look, look!" There, we saw scrolling across the news ticker in Times Square: "Gay NFL football player Esera Tuaolo comes out." We took a picture.

People on the street had just watched us on television and recognized us. They stopped to say, "Congratulations," and, "Those children are beautiful."

On our way to a restaurant for breakfast, a sidewalk vendor spotted us. "Good for you. I so happy for you," he said in broken English. "Here, please, take T-shirt." He gave me more for our children. I thought, *This is incredible. You never get anything for free in New York City.*

He held out another T-shirt. "Here. For your, uh, um—" He didn't know what word to use. Lover? Husband?

"For my partner?" I said.

"Yeah, yeah," he said. "For your partner."

"He's right here." I introduced Mitchell.

"Good job," the vendor said. "Good job."

Billy Bean called. He had told his story of being a gay baseball player in his book, *Going the Other Way.* He offered his support and told me to call if I had any questions on how to handle the response from people. We instantly became good friends.

I went on a wild media ride. Connie Chung had me on her television show. Robert Lipsyte, who had written about David Kopay almost twenty-five years earlier, wrote a beautiful piece about my story in the *New York Times.* Luke Cyphers wrote a wonderful article in *ESPN The Magazine.* Newspaper reporters from all over wanted to talk to me. I did hundreds of radio interviews.

Gay, lesbian, bisexual, and transgender (GLBT) organizations reached out to embrace me and my family. One of the first was GLAAD (Gay & Lesbian Alliance Against Defamation), a media watchdog for the gay community similar to the Jewish anti-defamation league. Cathy Renna, GLAAD's news media director, told me if anyone lashed out at us, they would be on top of it. PFLAG (Parents, Family, and Friends of Lesbians and Gays), an advocacy and support organization, and HRC (Human Rights Campaign), which lobbies for equal rights for the GLBT community, were also quick to reach out to us. This family we had never met stepped forward to welcome us.

Once back in Minnesota, I was a little nervous how people would respond. I had lived in the closet for thirty-four years. To be out was a whole new life. I didn't know what it would be like to go back to the gym or the supermarket.

At first, I expected somebody would drive by and yell, "Faggot!" or, "Queer!" but that never happened. Instead, people went out of their way to thank me for my courage. Some said my coming out had made it easier for them. People were generally so supportive that Mitchell and I joked that we should have done this earlier. I had wasted so much energy on my fear.

Of course, not everybody reacted positively and supportively. I heard rumors that HBO paid me for the interview. For the record, that's not true. I did not sell my story. I would not accept any money. It wasn't about money, anyway; it was about happiness. That's what motivated me. Some people accused me of coming out on *Real Sports* for the publicity. There are people who need to find a negative twist in everything. They can't let others do something just to be happy.

I did not think I would receive a negative email from a family member. Those in my family who didn't agree with my life kept to themselves and did not contact me. But one of my cousins, who is a lesbian, lashed out at me in an email she copied to several national GLBT organizations. She was upset that I was getting so much attention for coming out when she had done a lot of work herself to improve the lives of gay and lesbian people. The difference was that I had played in the NFL, a gay man in the manly man's world. I tried to talk to her, but our phone conversation erupted into a screaming match. The gay organizations she had contacted stood by me.

Only about .5 percent of the response from the gay community was negative. Mostly it was saying, "What's the big deal about him? He's a football player? So what? I go through the same struggles." I recognize that everybody's coming-out story is basically the same. It's just that playing in the NFL magnified my situation. We go through the same pain in the closet, feeling the isolation, anxiety, and depression. We all fear losing our family and friends. We also experience the same release and freedom in coming out. I read that Martina Navratilova, the tennis player who was brave enough to come out twenty years ago, said she had never met anyone that wanted to go back into the closet. I haven't either.

I received emails through my website (www.bigE98.com) from Christians quoting scripture that condemned homosexuality—a lot of Leviticus. I replied, quoting other Bible passages about God's love. I didn't hear back. The emails weren't hateful like the comments I read about me on other websites where people called me names and declared I was going to Hell. I left myself out there with my website, but those people never contacted me directly.

Some people called me a hypocrite for being gay and calling myself a Christian. These were people who I had introduced to Jesus after they had gone through a hard time. I had invited them to church and let the Holy Spirit take over. They felt I had somehow let them down, as though my sexual orientation canceled my faith. Those emails hurt the most. I had helped those people find a better life, done something good for them, and they turned on me.

I came out during the football season. The reaction from football players was mixed. Some told the media they wouldn't have a problem with a gay teammate. Others, who didn't know me, said they would be uncomfortable in the locker room and showers with a gay man. Former teammates like the Packers' Sterling Sharpe and the Vikings' Cris Carter said they figured players would take out a gay teammate in practice. I understood the NFL thug mentality, but these were guys who knew me and had played with me. I always tried to support the players on my team, on the field and off of it. I've never talked bad about anyone in the NFL.

Running back Garrison Hearst said, "I don't want any faggots on my team." Hearing that didn't change the sympathy I had felt for him when he broke his ankle, but it did make me wish I were still playing so I could hit him on the field.

Don Davey, my teammate with Green Bay and Jacksonville, called right away to let me know we were still buddies. Jeff Novak, another Jacksonville teammate, also called to say he was happy for me. Greg Blache, my defensive line coach for the Packers, told me in an email that he was proud of my courage and delighted I was finally happy. Derek, my buddy from the Vikings who had that memorable moment with me sledding one Christmas night, emailed a note of support. I haven't heard more from him since. Brett Favre's brother sent me an email saying, "Our family still loves you." I did not hear from Brett directly, but that's okay. I understand that people need to process things in their own way. Homosexuality is so taboo that some people are afraid to touch it.

I played with hundreds of guys. Only a handful called or emailed me. I didn't lose sleep over that. I didn't come out to rekindle friendships. My focus was on my children and family.

I had to make some phone calls before the HBO segment aired. My brother Afa, who had watched me play in the Super Bowl in

Miami, wondered why I wanted to come out on national television, but ultimately he and his wife supported me. I also called Iris and Randy Butler, my Oregon family. Telling them was almost like telling my mom because they were my surrogate parents. I feared their rejection and didn't want to lose them. I think it was harder for Iris to accept because of her deep Christian faith. We talked about scripture and my understanding of various passages. She said I put a face to homosexuality, which helped her because she loved me like one of her own children. I was encouraged to hear that.

I had told my buddy Sai I was gay after I had come out to my mom and sisters. "So?" he said. "You don't think I'm going to love my brother?" He was great.

I never heard from Olivia and Mike, my California family who had also watched me play in the Super Bowl. I hadn't kept in touch and maybe that upset them. If they had known my struggle as a gay man in the NFL, I think they would have understood why I hadn't called. Sometimes it was easier for me to avoid people rather than lie to them.

Overall, most people I knew responded favorably to me. I had treated people with respect. I think that paid off. When you treat people with kindness, they cannot say anything negative about you. They can only avoid you, the way some of my extended family members did.

I was amazed at the response to my coming out. In addition to all of the media attention, my web site had a hundred thousand hits a month. I received hundreds of emails a day from all over the world. Everything was coming at us a hundred miles per hour.

Mitchell and I needed time to absorb it all. We had to adjust to our new life of being a gay family in the public eye.

The biggest adjustment I had to make was as a role model to gay and lesbian youth. They emailed me from all over, telling me their stories and thanking me for making it easier for them. That was humbling. I remember reading through those emails shortly after I had come out. It was weird to think of myself as a role model. Maybe I had been as an NFL player in a small way, but to hear I was a role model as a gay man was something I didn't understand at first. I didn't embrace that role. I was still adjusting to our new life.

Meeting Judy Shepard changed that. She was the mother of Matthew Shepard, the gay University of Wyoming student who was tied to a fence and beaten to death in 1998. I met Judy at the Gay Ski Week in Aspen, where I had been invited to sing and she was the keynote speaker. Her life inspired me. She was a mom who could have stayed home, but what happened to her son catapulted her into doing something to change the world. She told me that every individual can make a difference by speaking up. Hearing Judy speak and talking to her afterward instilled in me a missing ingredient. I wanted people to feel the same impact or motivation when I told my story as they did when Judy told hers.

There are not a lot of role models for the gay community. Gay kids can't identify with Michael Jordan or Barry Bonds the way they can with a professional athlete who is gay. It's great to know that my story might inspire someone else the way David Kopay's story inspired me.

I received invitations to speak at fundraisers, conventions, and colleges. I did not see myself as a public speaker. I could sing in front of thousands, but I didn't know if I was ready to speak until I met Judy Shepard. I gave my first speech at Indiana University to a group of over two hundred people in 2003. I was nervous as hell, wondering what I would say. At first, I tried to speak with statistics, but that wasn't natural for me. I think people at that first speech got something out of the simple fact that I was there, speaking up, breaking the silence and stereotypes. Now, I just tell my story. I speak from my heart. It's so much easier and so much more effective. People can tell what I have to say is genuine, not something slick.

The first thing I say is that I am not here to change you or convert you. I am here to educate you on some of the issues and inequalities we face as a gay community. It's incredible to have the opportunity to speak around the country. I've spoken at tons of colleges, from the University of Hawaii to Penn State, and at all sorts of other events, from the Out and Equal conference for *Fortune* 500 companies to Motorola events.

Two years ago, the GLBT group at Oregon State University invited me to speak. I was very emotional, returning to a place where I had been closeted. It was wonderful to be able to walk the halls of the field house and stand before my old locker stall as an openly gay man. There was a big crowd for my speech, including a lot of the football players. Steven Jackson, a running back who played at OSU and now plays with the St. Louis Rams, told a reporter afterward that hearing my speech would make him think twice before taking part in the negative gay banter of NFL locker rooms.

My life had come full circle. Back when I was a freshman at OSU, Iris and Randy Butler had invited me to a Bible camp in Seattle. One night that week, the guest speaker was a preacher famous for making prophecies. She spoke to a group of about four hundred of us in a circus tent. She called me up on stage, where she started prophesying over my life. I was embarrassed to be singled out and thrown into the spotlight. "You will reach people, younger people that Billy Graham and the Pope can't reach," she said.

Her message was, "Get ready. God is going to use you to reach people." I was rolling my eyes. *How can you put this huge responsibility on me?* I thought. *I'm just a freshman.*

I went on my merry way, but one day after I came out, when I was in a peaceful place, I remembered what she had said. Seeing how many young people email me, telling me of the impact I've had on their lives, I realize what that preacher meant. That gives me goose bumps. I've found the purpose in my life: to live and speak my truth.

The hate that some supposedly Christian leaders preach is turning away a lot of our younger generation. I feel it's my job to help bring young people back to the church. I can teach them about the Bible and God's love.

I received a sweet call from a young man I had met when I was a football player at Oregon State and he was in eighth grade. Brian (not his real name) was a hardcore rocker in the church youth group who didn't fit in with the others. One night, a group of football players took the youth group kids to a midnight movie. When I stopped by Brian's house to pick him up, I urged him to come along with us even though he didn't want to go. He told me after I came out that he had intended to kill himself that night. He had already written a goodbye note. "Thanks to you," he said, "I now have a family with three beautiful children." You never know when you're going to touch someone with an act of kindness that can change a life.

I've always felt God had a hand over my life, even through the times when I felt alone. It's such a powerful thing to feel loved in an unconditional way, the way I know my mom loves me. She didn't turn her back when I told her I was gay. Neither did God.

God has never turned his back on me—or anyone. He loves us too much.

Mitchell and I wanted to raise our children in a Christian environment where we could worship as a family and they could attend Sunday school to learn more about God's love. Before we came out, we shopped around and found a Lutheran church in Minneapolis that welcomed us. We sat down with the pastor and several heterosexual couples who wanted to join. He accepted us without question. The members of the parish have been kind and accepting. The pastor's preaching is positive and uplifting. I leave church feeling good about myself. That's the experience of church I want my children to have.

My first big public singing gig after coming out occurred before an unexpected audience. The organizers of the NCAA's Frozen Four invited me to sing the national anthem at the Xcel Energy Center in Saint Paul in April 2003. I was not sure how hockey fans would receive me.

I was really nervous. I was in a show at the Ordway Theatre, next door to the hockey arena, and I had to dart over to sing, then hurry back for the show. It had been four years since the Pro Bowl, which was the last time I had sung the national anthem. I didn't have Calvin there to prep me at a karaoke bar, so I tucked a cheat sheet with the words on it in my palm. I was afraid I would screw up. I did not want to have to suffer the boos of the crowd.

The sound system was incredible in the new arena. I didn't have to look at my cheat sheet. I nailed the national anthem. People cheered loudly. Their applause warmed me.

People are starting to know me as a singer. They now say, "He was an okay football player for a singer." But it wasn't always that way. They used to think my singing was a gimmick, a football player who wanted to sing or act. That was until they heard me sing or saw me on stage.

Rosie O'Donnell invited me and my family on the first "R Family" cruise in 2004. When Rosie introduced me at the variety show on the ship, I could hear mumbles in the crowd. People doubted that I could sing. They knew me as a football player. After I performed, friends in the audience told me they heard people praise my ability. I've had to break stereotypes even in the gay community.

Some people expect me to be different now that I'm out, to talk in a higher voice or act like a woman. That's just not me. I grew up in a straight way. Even now that I'm out, I'm too straight for the gay community, but I'm too gay for the straight community. Some friends feel they have to act like a girl once they're out. Their voice goes up an octave—from a bass to a soprano. I never felt the need to be a Nellie. My perception of being gay is me. I just want to be myself. Coming out has given me the freedom to do that.

The guys I lift weights with or play basketball with realize I don't walk or act differently than I did before I came out. They bump against me on the courts, same as before. I don't have an attitude of "Don't touch me." Neither do they. We're not flirting, we're playing ball. They see me breaking stereotypes. I give them another image of how a gay guy looks and acts.

Singing and acting continue to bring me satisfaction. I'm recording a full-length solo CD that I hope to release in 2006. I'm also working on a one-man play about my life that incorporates song.

The "R Family" cruise is a wonderful thing. Started by Rosie's partner Kelli O'Donnell and Gregg Kaminsky, it is for GLBT families and friends. Everybody is welcome. The cruise attracts a lot of families as well as gay couples interested in a romantic cruise where they can hold hands on deck or kiss under the moonlight. The cruise gives kids from gay families the chance to meet. They learn that they are not alone (there are an estimated eight million children with gay parents in the United States), and they are able to talk about issues they have in common.

This summer, I'll be an ambassador to the seventh quadrennial Gay Games Sports and Cultural Festival in Chicago along with David Kopay, Melissa Etheridge, Billy Bean, and Billie Jean King. I've served as the grand marshal in gay pride parades in Atlanta, Chicago, Raleigh, and San Diego. I used to run from those parades. Now I run to them. I run to the opportunity to educate people because I am proud of who I am.

HBO's *Real Sports* aired a follow-up segment on me in January 2005. Bernie Goldberg asked me if I wished I had come out while I was still playing in the NFL. No player in any of the major leagues—the NFL, NBA, MLB, or NHL—has dared to come out while still playing. It would be especially difficult to come out in the NFL, which is one of the only places where people think a gay man cannot exist or survive. In baseball, yeah, maybe people could see a baseball player being gay. But football? Never.

To stand up in that macho-crazed environment and say, "I'm gay," would be seen as an admission that you didn't have the testosterone to play in the NFL. It would certainly be admitting that you didn't have a place in its culture. That's what kept me in the closet during my years in the NFL.

When Bernie asked me that question, I said, "Yes." Knowing what I know now and having received the support that I have from the gay community and the general public, I wish I had come out while I was still playing. I think it could have made an impact on the level of Jackie Robinson breaking the color barrier. It would have helped the game of football and society at large. But, living in the fear that I was, it's hard for me to imagine myself doing that.

Frankly, it's hard for me to imagine any NFL player coming out while guys like Sterling Sharpe are saying his teammates would take out a gay man in practice and guys like Garrison Hearst are saying they don't want any "faggots" on their teams. It will take a tremendous amount of courage for that first gay player to come out.

The league needs to develop a more tolerant environment. That will start with educating the owners, management, and players. The NFL needs to humanize the professional gay athlete. Take away the negative stereotypes and create a more positive image of the gay athlete—one closer to the truth. It should include us in its diversity-training program. I want protection for gay players. The league can make the NFL a safe place by putting out a strong message that it won't tolerate discrimination because of gender, race, or sexual orientation. Education is half the battle. The other half requires each individual to process the information to the point where they realize discrimination based on sexual orientation is wrong. We are taking steps forward with awareness and tolerance. I think I will see an openly gay NFL player in my lifetime.

People ask me, Who else in the NFL is gay? They figure I must have noticed others like me. I didn't. Other than my OSU teammate who kissed me and Derek, the Viking who almost did, I have not been aware of other gay players. I'm sure there are gay men playing in the NFL, it's just that I didn't know who they were. My gaydar was not fine-tuned. I was too scared about my secret being discovered to pick up any signs from others.

Now that I'm out and retired, I want the rights of any other married football player. I want the NFL to treat Mitchell as my spouse and pass my benefits to him when I die. Right now, that wouldn't happen. The league discriminates against Mitchell and me because of our sexual orientation. That's not right. I want NFL officials to see us as a family and not dismiss us as a gay couple.

I do credit the NFL for bringing me in as part of its diversity-training program in 2004. I was able to tell my story to league employees and request that GLBT issues be added to its training program. I told them that there are over a thousand things that become binding and guaranteed when a heterosexual couple marries. Things like visiting rights in the hospital, making important decisions for one's spouse if they become incapacitated, social security and pension benefits for the survivor, being able to make funeral preparations, custody of the children if one parent passes away, and so on. Those are all rights that Mitchell and I as a gay couple do not have. We're not asking for special rights. We want equality. My talk was well received. The simple fact that the NFL invited me and acknowledged my presence was progress.

I want these things ultimately for my children, so that they don't suffer from discrimination. Speaking of them, how can I not tell you about them? They're growing fast. They turned five in November. They're big, like me. By four, they were wearing size seven clothes. Michele has beautiful, long, black hair that stretches to her waist. The older Mitchell gets, the more people say he looks like me.

Each one is developing a distinct personality. Michele is definitely the strong-willed leader. If she wants a piece of candy opened, she'll give it to Mitchell, who is sweet and polite, and tell him to ask Big Daddy or Little Daddy to open it. Michele loves the water. As a two-year-old, she was swimming without a life vest, going underwater while her brother dangled his feet in the pool. They have a great bond. They want to go everywhere together. At night, they ask to kiss the other goodnight before they'll go to bed. They're lucky to be good friends.

———

Sometimes, I watch film of myself and think, *Damn, I played well.* I wish I could have done that more regularly. I glimpsed my potential but didn't achieve it. Maybe it's easier for someone whose football career ends in high school to leave behind what might have been. It hurts a little more to have reached the NFL but not to have rung that bell.

I always downplayed my career. Now, I'm starting to recognize what an accomplishment it was. A lot of people can say they played in the NFL, but not many of them played as starters, especially not as rookies. I recognize now that was an accomplishment. I didn't just stick around nine years in the NFL; I played. All of those trophies and awards I won are starting to come out of their boxes. My son and daughter need to see them.

Maybe every father wonders what he could have been. I played against and alongside some great players. The difference between me and Henry Thomas or John Randle was that I was fighting my demons. That held me back. I used to dread every day. I would think, "God, I hope I don't fuck up today."

Now I have dreams for my son and daughter. I hope I can create a world for them, whether they are gay or not, where they can reach their full potential, no matter who they love. My goal now in life is to educate people to make that possible. I want my children to live in a better world because of me.

# ACKNOWLEDGMENTS

I WOULD LIKE TO FIRST thank God for the many blessings he has given us all.

To Mama, thank you for teaching me to respect others by treating them as human beings. For teaching me to be humble by being a servant and for your great hugs and smile that only a mother could give. I love you, Mom.

I would like to thank my husband, Mitchell, and our children Mitchell Jr. and Michele for giving me the support, strength, and inspiration to do this book.

You all are my life, my world, and my soul. Big Daddy loves you.

To Shelly and Dan (Mom and Dad), thank you for being there for Mitchell and me during some of the roughest times in our lives. Your love, support, and wisdom have been greatly appreciated. We love you both.

To Jill Willis, for rekindling the flame with Sourcebooks so I could write about my life, you are truly a great friend. Thank you for everything, and I love you.

To Howard Bragman, for all your help during the coming-out process and orchestrating a beautiful game plan to not only represent me and my family but also the GLBT community, showing the world a positive gay life. Howard, you rock!

A special thanks with Aloha goes out to Sourcebooks for helping me tell my story, for realizing the positive impact that this book will have on people's lives. You just don't know what you have done, thank you!

Special thanks goes out to Hillel Black, my editor, for believing in my story and finding me the best cowriter. We were like two peas in the pod. Thank you, my friend, and God bless you and your entire family.

Thanks to Steve Senk, sports info director at OSU, and Adam Woullard, Green Bay Packers media relations, for supplying information and answering questions. Thanks also to Deb Orenstein for tending to the legal issues.

Many thanks to Aunt Pat Lyon and Shelly Engelsma for their helpful comments after reading an earlier draft of this book. Your comments and corrections were very helpful. Love you both.

To Jack Law, a good friend and GLBT leader on the island of Oahu, thank you for giving me David Kopay's book during one of my darkest times. Just in the nick of time!

David Kopay, I thank God for bringing you into my life. Reading your book gave me hope and possibilities, and it gave me my family. Your book saved my life, and I pray that *Alone in the Trenches* will inspire people like yours did me. Also, meeting you in person and being able to hug you was one of the highlights in my life. I love you, man!

To the GLBT community and supporters, thank you for all your love and support and thank you for embracing my family when we stepped out into our truth—you all made the path a lot easier.

To my brother Billy Bean, your friendship, story, and everything about you inspires me. Thank you for being there for us when we discovered the new world. Let us both live as free men— love you, Bro! Oh! And thanks for introducing me to one of my new best friends, the Lady of New York, Bari Mattes. Also I can't forget, big hugs and kisses to your husband Efraín Veiga.

To Rosie O'Donell, from the first time you called me out of the blue and I thought a friend was playing a joke on me to when I finally met you in person, wow! You need to know that your phone call to me meant the world and came at the right time. Even though I was like a starstruck groupie who couldn't speak at the time, I understood what you said. Now that we are out and proud, it is our duty to reach out to others and let them know that they are loved and not alone.

To a new friend, brother, and writing companion, John Rosengren. Thank you for making this experience a wonderful one and for helping me through some tough decisions during our journey together. I'm not going to lie. It was hard to open doors that have been closed for a long time. Thank you for being patient and understanding. But most of all, thank you for believing in my story and writing something that I pray will inspire and help people. God continue to bless you and your entire beautiful family.